P9-CQJ-972

Notation used†

i	return measured as a simple interest rate
i^*	effective return when a simple interest rate is compounded
y	yield to maturity on a quote sheet
y^*	*true* yield to maturity
r	repo or reverse repo rate
r^*	break-even level of r
r_t	term repo rate
r_e	reinvestment rate
d	rate of discount
d^*	break-even level of d
d_b	equivalent bond yield
c	coupon rate
n	number of times compounding occurs during a year
N	number of remaining coupons
t	time measured in days
t_{is}	days from issue (or last coupon) to settlement
t_{im}	days from issue to maturity
t_{sm}	days from settlement to maturity
t_{sc}	days from settlement to next coupon
t_{ss}	days from settlement to settlement (e.g., on a transaction on which beginning and end dates fall between issue and maturity dates or between coupon dates)
a_i	accrued interest
P	dollar price‡
F	face value
D	dollar amount of discount on a discount security
B	basis (number of days in the coupon period)
v_{01}	value of an 01 (i.e., a basis point)
v_{32}	yield value of $1/32$

interest rate symbols all denote rates written in *decimal* form

† In a few situations where an equation is useful for figuring the outcome of more than one type or side of a transaction, subscripts 1 and 2 are affixed to key variables describing the security traded or financed. When this is done, subscript 1 denotes values, such as price, that apply on the day the transaction is initiated; subscript 2 denotes values that apply on the day the transaction is terminated.

‡ Includes accrued interest in the case of CDs, otherwise does not. In formulas for interest-bearing securities, P is always taken to be the price per $1 of face value.

Equivalent simple interest on a 360-day basis

Formula used: $\quad i = \dfrac{360d}{360 - dt_{sm}}$

Discount rate	30 days	60 days	90 days	180 days	270 days	360 days
5	5.02	5.04	5.06	5.13	5.20	5.26
1/8	5.15	5.17	5.19	5.26	5.33	5.40
1/4	5.27	5.30	5.32	5.39	5.47	5.54
3/8	5.40	5.42	5.45	5.52	5.60	5.68
1/2	5.53	5.55	5.58	5.66	5.74	5.82
5/8	5.65	5.68	5.71	5.79	5.87	5.96
3/4	5.78	5.81	5.83	5.92	6.01	6.10
7/8	5.90	5.93	5.96	6.05	6.15	6.24
6	6.03	6.06	6.09	6.19	6.28	6.38
1/8	6.16	6.19	6.22	6.32	6.42	6.52
1/4	6.28	6.32	6.35	6.45	6.56	6.67
3/8	6.41	6.44	6.48	6.58	6.70	6.81
1/2	6.54	6.57	6.61	6.72	6.83	6.95
5/8	6.66	6.70	6.74	6.85	6.97	7.10
3/4	6.79	6.83	6.87	6.99	7.11	7.24
7/8	6.91	6.95	7.00	7.12	7.25	7.38
7	7.04	7.08	7.12	7.25	7.39	7.53
1/8	7.17	7.21	7.25	7.39	7.53	7.67
1/4	7.29	7.34	7.38	7.52	7.67	7.70
3/8	7.42	7.47	7.51	7.66	7.81	7.96
1/2	7.55	7.59	7.64	7.79	7.95	8.11
5/8	7.67	7.72	7.77	7.93	8.09	8.25
3/4	7.80	7.85	7.90	8.06	8.23	8.40
7/8	7.93	7.98	8.03	8.20	8.37	8.55
8	8.05	8.11	8.16	8.33	8.51	8.70
1/8	8.18	8.24	8.29	8.47	8.65	8.84
1/4	8.31	8.37	8.42	8.60	8.79	8.99
3/8	8.43	8.49	8.55	8.74	8.94	9.14
1/2	8.56	8.62	8.68	8.88	9.08	9.29
5/8	8.69	8.75	8.82	9.01	9.22	9.44
3/4	8.81	8.88	8.95	9.15	9.36	9.59
7/8	8.94	9.01	9.08	9.29	9.51	9.74
9	9.07	9.14	9.21	9.42	9.65	9.89
1/8	9.19	9.27	9.34	9.56	9.80	10.04
1/4	9.32	9.39	9.47	9.70	9.94	10.19
3/8	9.45	9.52	9.60	9.84	10.08	10.34
1/2	9.58	9.65	9.73	9.97	10.23	10.50
5/8	9.70	9.78	9.86	10.11	10.37	10.65
3/4	9.83	9.91	9.99	10.25	10.52	10.80
7/8	9.96	10.04	10.12	10.39	10.66	10.96
10	10.08	10.17	10.26	10.53	10.81	11.11
1/8	10.21	10.30	10.39	10.66	10.96	11.27
1/4	10.34	10.43	10.52	10.80	11.10	11.42
3/8	10.46	10.56	10.65	10.94	11.25	11.58
1/2	10.59	10.69	10.78	11.08	11.40	11.73
5/8	10.72	10.82	10.91	11.19	11.54	11.89
3/4	10.85	10.95	11.05	11.36	11.69	12.04
7/8	10.97	11.08	11.18	11.50	11.84	12.20
11	11.10	11.21	11.31	11.64	11.99	12.36
1/8	11.23	11.34	11.44	11.78	12.14	12.52
1/4	11.36	11.46	11.58	11.92	12.29	12.68
3/8	11.48	11.59	11.71	12.06	12.44	12.83
1/2	11.61	11.72	11.84	12.20	12.59	12.99
5/8	11.74	11.88	11.97	12.34	12.74	13.15
3/4	11.87	11.98	12.11	12.48	12.89	13.31
7/8	11.99	12.11	12.24	12.62	13.04	13.48

Discount rate	30 days	60 days	90 days	180 days	270 days	360 days
12	12.12	12.24	12.37	12.77	13.19	13.64
1/8	12.25	12.38	12.50	12.91	13.34	13.80
1/4	12.38	12.51	12.64	13.05	13.49	13.96
3/8	12.50	12.64	12.77	13.19	13.64	14.12
1/2	12.63	12.77	12.90	13.33	13.79	14.29
5/8	12.76	12.90	13.04	13.48	13.95	14.45
3/4	12.89	13.03	13.17	13.62	14.10	14.61
7/8	13.01	13.16	13.30	13.76	14.25	14.78
13	13.14	13.29	13.44	13.90	14.40	14.94
1/8	13.27	13.42	13.57	14.05	14.56	15.11
1/4	13.40	13.54	13.70	14.19	14.71	15.27
3/8	13.53	13.68	13.84	14.33	14.87	15.44
1/2	13.65	13.81	13.97	14.48	15.02	15.61
5/8	13.78	13.94	14.11	14.62	15.18	15.77
3/4	13.91	14.07	14.24	14.77	15.33	15.94
7/8	14.04	14.20	14.37	14.91	15.49	16.11
14	14.17	14.33	14.51	15.05	15.64	16.28
1/8	14.29	14.47	14.64	15.20	15.80	16.45
1/4	14.42	14.60	14.78	15.34	15.96	16.62
3/8	14.55	14.73	14.91	15.49	16.11	16.79
1/2	14.68	14.86	15.05	15.63	16.27	16.96
5/8	14.81	14.99	15.18	15.78	16.43	17.13
3/4	14.93	15.12	15.31	15.92	16.58	17.30
7/8	15.06	15.25	15.45	16.07	16.74	17.47
15	15.19	15.38	15.58	16.22	16.90	17.65
1/8	15.32	15.52	15.72	16.36	17.06	17.82
1/4	15.45	15.65	15.85	16.51	17.22	17.99
3/8	15.57	15.78	15.99	16.66	17.38	18.17
1/2	15.70	15.91	16.12	16.80	17.54	18.34
5/8	15.83	16.04	16.26	16.95	17.70	18.52
3/4	15.96	16.17	16.40	17.10	17.86	18.69
7/8	16.09	16.31	16.53	17.24	18.02	18.87
16	16.22	16.44	16.67	17.39	18.18	19.05
1/8	16.34	16.57	16.80	17.54	18.34	19.22
1/4	16.47	16.70	16.94	17.69	18.51	19.40
3/8	16.60	16.83	17.07	17.84	18.67	19.58
1/2	16.73	16.97	17.21	17.98	18.83	19.76
5/8	16.86	17.10	17.35	18.13	18.99	19.94
3/4	16.99	17.23	17.48	18.28	19.16	20.12
7/8	17.12	17.36	17.62	18.43	19.32	20.30
17	17.24	17.50	17.75	18.58	19.48	20.48
1/8	17.37	17.63	17.89	18.73	19.65	20.66
1/4	17.50	17.76	18.03	18.88	19.81	20.85
3/8	17.63	17.89	18.16	19.03	19.98	21.03
1/2	17.76	18.03	18.30	19.18	20.14	21.21
5/8	17.89	18.16	18.44	19.33	20.31	21.40
3/4	18.02	18.29	18.57	19.48	20.48	21.58
7/8	18.15	18.42	18.71	19.63	20.64	21.77
18	18.27	18.56	18.85	19.78	20.81	21.95
1/8	18.40	18.69	18.99	19.93	20.98	22.14
1/4	18.53	18.82	19.12	20.08	21.14	22.32
3/8	18.66	18.96	19.26	20.23	21.31	22.51
1/2	18.79	19.09	19.40	20.39	21.48	22.70
5/8	18.92	19.22	19.53	20.54	21.65	22.89
3/4	19.05	19.35	19.67	20.69	21.82	23.08
7/8	19.18	19.49	19.81	20.84	21.99	23.27
19	19.31	19.62	19.95	20.99	22.16	23.46
1/8	19.43	19.75	20.09	21.15	22.33	23.65
1/4	19.56	19.89	20.22	21.30	22.50	23.84
3/8	19.69	20.02	20.36	21.45	22.67	24.03
1/2	19.82	20.16	20.50	21.61	22.84	24.22
5/8	19.95	20.29	20.64	21.76	23.01	24.42
3/4	20.08	20.42	20.78	21.91	23.18	24.61
7/8	20.21	20.56	20.91	22.07	23.36	24.80
20	20.34	20.69	21.05	22.22	23.53	25.00

Money market calculations
Yields, break-evens, and arbitrage

MARCIA STIGUM

in collaboration with
John Mann

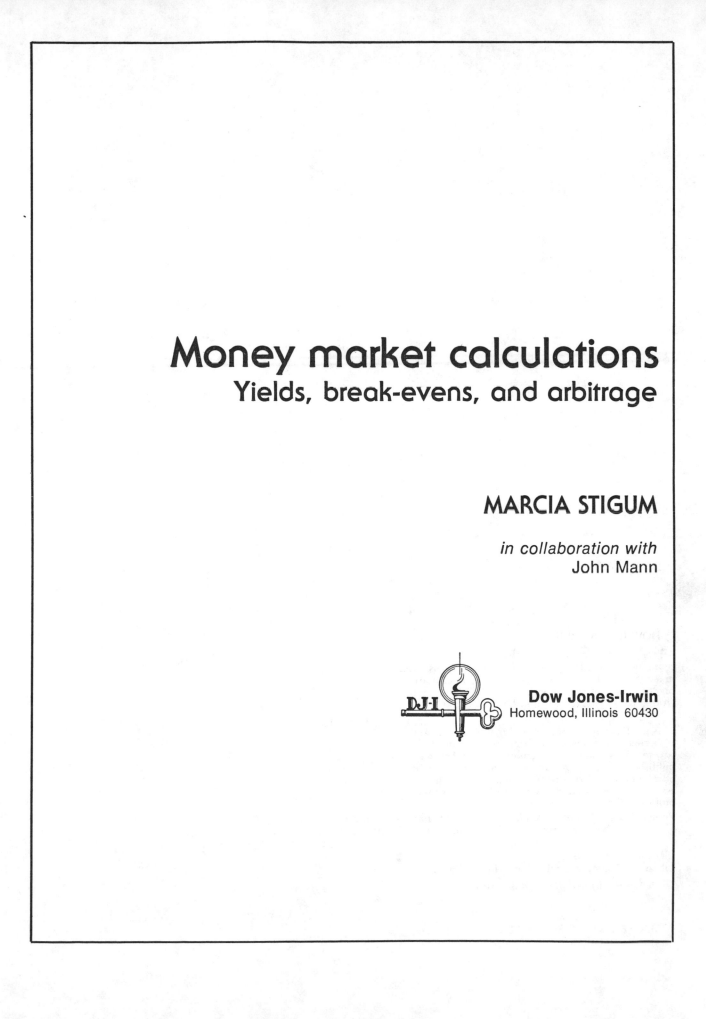

Dow Jones-Irwin
Homewood, Illinois 60430

© DOW JONES-IRWIN, 1981

All rights reserved. No part of this publication may be
reproduced, stored in a retrieval system, or transmitted,
in any form or by any means, electronic, mechanical,
photocopying, recording, or otherwise, without the prior
written permission of the publisher.

This publication is designed to provide accurate and
authoritative information in regard to the subject matter
covered. It is sold with the understanding that the
publisher is not engaged in rendering legal, accounting, or
other professional service. If legal advice or other expert
assistance is required, the services of a competent
professional person should be sought.
*From a Declaration of Principles jointly adopted by a Committee
of the American Bar Association and a Committee of Publishers.*

ISBN 0-87094-192-5
Library of Congress Catalog Card No. 80–66022

Printed in the United States of America

3 4 5 6 7 8 9 0 K 8 7 6 5 4 3 2

To my mother

*with regrets for the absence
of M. Poirot in search of a
culprit bearing a smoking gun*

Preface

This book describes and illustrates as simply and clearly as possible a wide range of important money market calculations: (1) standard formulas used by the industry to calculate numbers such as yield to maturity, security prices, and accrued interest,[1] (2) correct formulas for calculating these numbers when the industry formulas are wrong; (3) approximations used by traders to calculate, such numbers as a break-even figure on a trade; and (4) correct formulas for calculating such break-even figures when the trader's approximation is likely to produce a number far off the mark. The book also shows how yields on instruments that differ with respect to type and/or maturity can be put on a directly comparable basis—a calculation vital to the portfolio manager who is selecting investments or evaluating swaps.

The book should be extremely useful to dealers, portfolio managers, brokers, and all others whose work brings them in contact with the money market. Such people need to make money market calculations as part of their daily work; and, before publication of this book, there was no written source that provided a clear and comprehensive description of how such calculations can be made.

To add to the usefulness and clarity of this book, several features have been incorporated. All key notation used is reproduced in a table on the right-hand front endpaper; useful money market tables in abbreviated form are reproduced on the other endpapers. All key formulas have been presented, as developed, in a *box*, which emphasizes their importance. To facilitate reference to these formulas, they are listed by page in a table following the index.

In a previous book, *The Money Market: Myth, Reality, and Practice* (Homewood, Ill.: Dow Jones-Irwin, 1978), I presented a comprehensive picture of the U.S. money

---

[1] The source used for standard industry formulas is the Security Industry Association's *Standard Securities Calculation Methods* (New York, 1973). The scope of that book is limited. Also, because of the way it is written, it is a hard read—for most "street" people.

market and the Eurodollar market. This book is meant to complement and to be a companion to that volume.

The pronoun *he* is used frequently throughout this book. It is my opinion that *he* has for years been used to mean *person* and that any attempt to avoid this use of the term leads to nothing but bad and awkward English.

In writing this book I was particularly fortunate to have the help of John Mann, who time and again suggested to me what calculations were important and how they could be made, often by use of a quick approximation. I am also indebted to many others for their help, particularly John Friel, David Kurfess, John Murray, Nancy Shaw and Andrew Threadgold. Naturally, the author bears full responsibility for any remaining errors.

Marcia Stigum
New York, New York

Contents

List of boxes
giving key formulas

1

Introduction

For all participants—issuers, dealers, salespeople, and investors—the money market reduces to a *numbers game* when superficial characteristics of individual transactions are brushed aside. And as in any numbers game, those who earn most are those who best understand how to figure odds and make other simple but important calculations.

Thus, one would expect the majority of money market people to be not only comfortable with, but also handy at, calculating crucial figures such as the *true* yield to maturity on a short government or federal agency security, the break-even rate on a reverse to maturity, or the "tail" on a bill hung out on term repo. Most market participants, however, have an acute aversion to numbers and refuse te to generalize results if it requires the use of even elementary algebra.

The aversion of Wall Street, or "street," people to mathematical reasoning has several easily identifiable sources. First, teachers of mathematics seem to have induced in this group, as well as in others, a healthy case of *terror mathematicus*, the principal symptom of which is the conviction that algebra, not to mention calculus, is a mysterious, frightening, and difficult discipline that could not conceivably be applied by nonmathematicians to solve simple and important everyday problems.

A second source of the street's aversion to mathematical reasoning is the sloppy notation that people who write about money and bond market equations have chosen to use. A prime example is the following equation taken from the Security Industry Association's *Standard Securities Calculation Methods:*[1]

$$Y = \left[\frac{\left(\frac{RV}{100} + \frac{R}{M}\right) - \left(P + \left(\frac{A}{E} \times \frac{R}{M}\right)\right)}{P + \left(\frac{A}{E} \times \frac{R}{M}\right)} \right] \cdot \left[\frac{M \times E}{DSM}\right]$$

To anyone who knows a little mathematics, following the algebra involved in this equation is trivial. Figuring out the meaning of the equation requires some work, however; the problem is that the notation used is not mnemonic with the result that, no

---

[1] (New York, 1973), p. 32.

matter how many times one reads through the equation and the accompanying definitions of terms (omitted here), the equation continues to appear to be so much jibberish. What it in fact says is:

$$\left(\frac{\text{Value at maturity} - \text{Amount invested}}{\text{Amount invested}}\right) \times \left(\begin{array}{c}\text{An annualizing}\\\text{factor}\end{array}\right) = \left(\begin{array}{c}\text{Rate of return}\\\text{on investment}\end{array}\right)$$

This is a relationship children learn before they leave grade school!

There is no reason why money market participants should be victims of *terror mathematicus* or bad notation. Most of the relationships they need are simple enough once they are put in comprehensible form, which is precisely what this book—designed to be a handy desk reference—does.

This book begins with fundamentals in Part I. Knowledgeable readers may want to skip some of this part, but Chapter 3 should be read carefully by all, since the notation used throughout the book is introduced there. This notation is reproduced for convenient reference on the right-hand front endpaper.

In Parts II to V, the book develops important yield and price relationships for each type of instrument. It also gives examples of how these relationships can be used in practical and common situations to derive break-even and other key numbers. Chapter 5, the first on applications, also contains important comments on fundamentals and should be read carefully.

The money market is an innovative place and those who participate in it are constantly developing new instruments, approaches, and transactions. Consequently, no book could give an equation to cover every possible situation, and this book does not purport to do so. What it does offer the careful reader is a kit of simple analytic tools that he can use to solve particular problems as they arise.

As a final aid in calculations, the book contains key money market tables at the front and back. Those in abbreviated form are meant to provide the user with a quick way to determine the order of magnitude of a particular number: for example, roughly how many basis points one should add to get from a particular discount yield to the equivalent bond yield. This information would be useful to the salesperson or investor faced with a constantly changing screen of securities offerings.

One last note: Anyone desiring a complete description of the money market should read *The Money Market: Myth, Reality, and Practice* by Marcia Stigum (Homewood, Ill.: Dow Jones-Irwin, 1978). This book was written as a companion to and extension of that book.

Some fundamentals

part I

2

The instruments in brief

Here's a quick rundown of the major money market instruments. Don't look for subtleties; just enough is said to lay the groundwork for the chapters that follow.

DEALERS AND BROKERS

The markets for all money market instruments are made in part by brokers and dealers. *Brokers* bring buyers and sellers together for a commission. By definition, brokers never position securities. Their function is to provide a communications network that links market participants who are often numerous and geographically dispersed. Most brokering in the money market occurs between banks that are buying funds from or selling funds to each other and between dealers in money market instruments.

Dealers make markets in money market instruments by quoting bid and asked prices to each other, to issuers, and to investors. Dealers buy and sell for their own accounts, so assuming a position is an essential part of a dealer's operation.

U.S. TREASURY SECURITIES

To finance the U.S. national debt, the Treasury issues several types of securities. Some are nonnegotiable, for example, savings bonds sold to consumers and special issues sold to government trust funds. The bulk of the securities sold by the U.S. Treasury are, however, negotiable.

What form these securities take depends on their maturity. Those with a maturity at issue of a year or less are known as *Treasury bills,* or for short, *T bills* or just plain *bills.* T bills do not bear interest. An investor in bills earns a return because bills are issued at a discount from face value and redeemed by the Treasury at maturity for full face value. The amount of the discount at which investors buy bills and the length of time bills have to be held before they mature together imply some specific yield that the bill will return if held to maturity.

T bills are currently issued in 3-month, 6-month, and 1-year maturities. In issuing bills the Treasury does not set the amount of the discount. Instead the Federal Reserve auctions off each new bill issue to investors and dealers, with the bills going to those bidders offering the highest price, i.e., the lowest interest cost to the Treasury. By using the auction technique, the Treasury lets currently prevailing market conditions establish the yield at which each new bill issue is sold.

The Treasury also issues interest-bearing *notes*. These securities are issued at or very near face value and redeemed at face value. Notes have an *original maturity* (maturity at issue) of 1 to 10 years. Currently the Treasury issues 2- and 4-year notes on a regular cycle. Notes of other maturities are issued periodically depending on the Treasury's needs. Interest is paid on Treasury notes semiannually. Notes like bills are typically sold through auctions held by the Federal Reserve. In these auctions bidders bid yields, and the securities offered are sold to those dealers and investors who bid the lowest yields, that is, the lowest interest cost to the Treasury. Thus the coupon rate on new Treasury notes, like the yield on bills, is normally determined by the market. The only exceptions are occasional subscription and price auction issues on which the Treasury sets the coupon.

In addition to notes, the Treasury issues interest-bearing negotiable *bonds* that have a maturity at issue of 10 years or more. The only difference between Treasury notes and bonds is that bonds are issued in longer maturities. In recent years the volume of bonds offered by the Treasury has been small. The reason is that Congress has imposed a 4.25 percent ceiling on the rate the Treasury may pay on bonds. Since this rate has for years been far below prevailing market rates, the Treasury is able to sell bonds only to the extent that Congress authorizes it to issue bonds exempt from the ceiling, something that Congress does only sparingly. Currently Treasury bonds, like notes, are normally issued through yield auctions.

Banks, other financial institutions, insurance companies, pension funds, and corporations are all important investors in U.S. Treasury securities. So too are some foreign central banks and other foreign institutions. The market for government securities is largely a wholesale market and, especially at the short end of the market, multimillion-dollar transactions are common. However, when interest rates get extremely high, as they did in 1974 and again in 1978–80, individuals with small amounts to invest are drawn into the market.

Because of the high volume of Treasury debt outstanding, the market for bills and short-term government securities is the most active and most carefully watched sector of the money market. At the heart of this market stands a varied collection of *dealers* who make the market for *governments* (market jargon for government securities) by standing ready to buy and sell huge volumes of these securities. These dealers trade actively not only with investors, but also with each other. Most trades of the latter sort are carried out through brokers.

Governments offer investors several advantages. First, because they are constantly traded in the *secondary market* in large volume and at narrow spreads between the bid and asked prices, they are highly *liquid*. A second advantage is that governments are considered to be free from credit risk because it is inconceivable that the government would ever default on these securities short of destruction of the country. Third, interest income on governments is exempt from state taxation. Because of these advantages, governments normally trade at yields below those of other money market instruments. Municipal securities are an exception because they offer a still more attractive tax advantage.

Generally yields on governments are higher the longer their *current maturity*, that is, time currently left to run to maturity.[1] The reason, explained in Chapter 6, is that the

---

[1] A 5-year note has an *original maturity* at issue of 5 years. One year after issue it has a *current maturity* of 4 years.

longer the current maturity of a debt security, the more its price will fluctuate in response to changes in interest rates and therefore the greater the *price risk* to which it exposes the investor. There are times however, when the yield curve *inverts,* that is, yields on short-term securities rise above those on long-term securities. This, for example, was the case during much of 1979 and early 1980. The reason for an inverted yield curve is that market participants anticipate, correctly or incorrectly, that interest rates are going to fall. As a result borrowers choose to borrow short-term while investors seek out long-term securities; the result is that supply and demand force short-term rates above long-term rates.

FUTURES MARKETS

In talking about the market for governments, we have focused on the *cash market,* that is, the market in which existing securities are traded for same- or next-day delivery. In addition, there are markets in which Treasury bills, Treasury bonds, and other money market instruments are traded for *future* delivery. The futures contracts in Treasuries that are most actively traded are for 3-month bills with a face value of $1 million at maturity and for long bonds having a par value of $100,000.

Interest-rate futures markets offer institutions that know they are going to borrow or lend in the future a way to *hedge* that future position, that is, to lock in a reasonably fixed borrowing or lending rate. They also provide speculators with a way to bet money on interest-rate movements that is easier and cheaper than going short or long in cash securities.

Since being introduced in 1976, futures markets for financial instruments have grown at a generally unforseen and astonishing rate. In fact futures contracts for Treasury bills and bonds have been among the most successful contracts ever launched on commodities exchanges.

The newness and rapid growth of markets for financial futures has, not surprisingly, created situations in which the relationship between the rates on different futures contracts or between the rates on a futures contract and the corresponding cash instrument get, as the street would say "out of sync," that is out of synchronization or line. Thus yet another major class of traders in financial futures has been arbitrageurs who seek to establish positions from which they will profit when a reasonable relationship between the out-of-line rates is inevitably reestablished.

FEDERAL AGENCY SECURITIES

From time to time Congress becomes concerned about the volume of credit that is available to various sectors of the economy and the terms at which that credit is available. Its usual response is to set up a federal agency to provide credit to that sector. Thus, for example, there is the Federal Home Loan Bank System, which lends to the nation's savings and loan associations as well as regulates them; the Government National Mortgage Association, which funnels money into the mortgage market; the Banks for Cooperatives, which make seasonal and term loans to farm cooperatives; the Federal Land Banks, which give mortgages on farm properties; the Federal Intermediate Credit Banks, which provide short-term financing for producers of crops and livestock; and a host of other agencies.

Initially all the federal agencies financed their activities by selling their own securities in the open market. Today all except the largest borrow from the Treasury through an institution called the Federal Financing Bank. Those agencies still borrowing in the open market do so primarily by issuing notes and bonds. These securities (known in the market as *agencies*) bear interest, and they are issued and redeemed at face value. Instead of using the auction technique for issuing their securities, federal agencies look to the market to determine the best yield at which they can sell a new issue, put that yield on the issue, and then sell it through a syndicate of dealers. Some agencies also sell short-term discount paper that resembles commercial paper.

Normally agencies yield slightly more than Treasury securities of the same maturity. There are seveal reasons. Agency issues are smaller than Treasury issues and are therefore less liquid. Also, while all agency issues have *de facto* backing from the federal government (it's inconceivable that the government would let one of them default on its obligations), the securities of only a few agencies are explicitly backed by the full faith and credit of the U.S. government. Finally, interest income on some federal agency issues is not exempt from state taxation.

The agency market, while smaller than that for governments, has in recent years become an active and important sector of the money market. Agencies are traded by the same dealers who trade governments and in much the same way.

FEDERAL FUNDS

All banks that are members of the Federal Reserve System are required to keep reserves on deposit at their district Federal Reserve Bank. A commercial bank's reserve account is much like a consumer's checking account; the bank makes deposits into it and can transfer funds out of it. The main difference is that, whereas a consumer can run the balance in his checking account down to zero, each member bank is required to maintain some minimum average balance over the week in its reserve account. How large that minimum balance is depends on the size and composition of the bank's deposits over the previous 2 weeks.

Funds on deposit in a bank's reserve account are referred to as *Federal funds*, or *Fed funds*. Any deposits a bank receives add to its supply of Fed funds, while loans made and securities purchased by it reduce that supply. Thus the basic amount of money any bank can lend out and otherwise invest equals the amount of funds it has received from depositors minus the reserves it is required to maintain.

For some banks this supply of available funds roughly equals the amount they choose to invest in securities plus that demanded from them by borrowers. But for most banks it does not. Specifically, because the nation's largest corporations tend to concentrate their borrowing in big money market banks in New York and other financial centers, the loans and investments these banks have to fund exceed the deposits they receive. Many smaller banks, in contrast, receive more money from local depositors than they can lend locally or choose to invest otherwise. Because large banks have to meet their reserve requirements regardless of what loan demand they face and because excess reserves yield no return to smaller banks, it was natural for large banks to begin borrowing the excess funds held by smaller banks.

This borrowing is done in the *Federal funds market*. Most Fed funds loans are overnight transactions. One reason is that the amount of excess funds a given lending bank holds varies daily and unpredictably. Some transactions in Fed funds are made directly, others through New York brokers. Despite the fact that transactions of this sort are all loans, the lending of Fed funds is referred to as a *sale* and the borrowing of Fed funds as a *purchase*. While overnight transactions dominate the Fed funds market, there are also some lending and borrowing for longer periods. Fed funds traded for periods other than overnight are referred to as *term* Fed funds.

The rate of interest paid on overnight loans of Federal funds, which is called the *Fed funds rate,* is *the* main interest rate in the money market, and all other short-term rates key off it. The level of the Fed funds rate used to be closely pegged by the Fed. Starting in October 1979, however, the Fed, which still controls the general level of this rate, allowed it to fluctuate over a wider band.

EURODOLLARS

Many foreign banks will accept deposits of dollars and grant the depositor an account *denominated in dollars.* So too will the foreign branches of U.S. banks. The practice of accepting dollar-denominated deposits outside of the United States began in Europe, so such deposits came to be known as *Eurodollars.* The practice of accepting dollar-denominated deposits later spread to Hong Kong, Singapore, the Middle East, and other centers around the globe. Consequently today a *Eurodollar deposit is simply a deposit denominated in dollars in a bank outside the United States,* and the term *Eurodollar* has become a misnomer.

Most Eurodollar deposits are for large sums. They are made by corporations—foreign, multinational, and domestic; foreign central banks and other official institutions; U.S. domestic banks; and wealthy individuals. With the exception of call money,[2] all Euro deposits have a fixed term, which can range from overnight to 5 years. The bulk of Euro transactions are in the range of 6 months and under. Banks receiving Euro deposits use these dollars to make loans denominated in dollars to foreign and domestic corporations, foreign governments and government agencies, domestic U.S. banks, and other large borrowers.

Banks that participate in the Eurodollar market actively borrow and lend Euros among themselves just as domestic banks borrow and lend in the market for Fed funds. The major difference between the two markets is that in the market for Fed funds most transactions are on an overnight basis while in the Euromarket interbank placements (deposits) of funds for longer periods are common.

For a domestic U.S. bank with a reserve deficiency, borrowing Eurodollars is an alternative to purchasing Fed funds. Also, for a domestic bank with excess funds, a Euro *placement* (i.e., a deposit of dollars in the Euromarket) is an alternative to the sale of Fed funds. Consequently the rate on overnight Euros tends to track closely the Fed funds rate. It is also true that, as one goes out on the maturity scale, Euro rates continue to track U.S. rates, though not so closely as in the overnight market.

CERTIFICATES OF DEPOSIT

The maximum rate banks can pay on savings deposits and time deposits (a time deposit is a deposit with a fixed maturity) is set by the Fed through *Regulation Q.* Essentially what Reg Q does is to make it impossible for banks to compete with each other or with other savings institutions for small deposits by offering depositors higher interest rates. On large deposits, $100,000 or more, banks may currently pay any rate they choose so long as the deposit has a minimum maturity of 14 days.

There are many corporations and other large investors that have hundreds of thousands, even millions, of dollars they could invest in bank time deposits. Few do so,

---

[2] Call money is money deposited in an interest-bearing account that can be called (withdrawn) by the depositor on a day's notice.

however, because they lose liquidity by making a deposit with a fixed maturity. The lack of liquidity of time deposits and their consequent lack of appeal to investors led the banks to invent the *negotiable certificate of deposit,* or *CD* for short.

CDs are normally sold in $1 million units. They are issued at face value and typically pay interest at maturity. CDs can have any maturity longer than 14 days, and some 5- and even 7-year CDs have been sold (these pay interest semiannually). Most CDs, however, have an *original maturity* of 1 to 3 months.

The quantity of CDs that banks have outstanding depends largely on the strength of loan demand. When demand rises, banks issue more CDs to help fund the additional loans they are making. The rates banks offer on CDs depend on their maturity, how badly the banks want to write new CDs, and the general level of short-term interest rates.

The bulk of bank CDs are sold directly by banks to investors. Some, however, are issued through dealers, often for a small commission. These same dealers also make an active secondary market in CDs.

Yields on CDs exceed those on bills of similar maturities by varying spreads. One reason for the bigger yield is that buying a bank CD exposes the investor to some credit risk—would he be paid off if the issuing bank failed? A second reason CDs yield more than bills is that they are less liquid.

Variable-rate CDs

Recently banks have introduced on a small scale a new type of negotiable CD, *variable-rate CDs.* The two most prevalent types are 6-month CDs with a 30-day *roll* (on each roll date, accrued interest is paid and a new coupon is set) and 1-year paper with a 3-month roll.

The coupon established on a variable-rate CD at issue and on subsequent roll dates is set at some amount (12.5 to 30 basis points depending on the name of the issuer and the maturity) above the average rate (as indicated by the *composite* rate published by the Fed) that banks are paying on new CDs with an original maturity equal to the length of the roll period.

Variable-rate CDs give the issuing bank the opportunity to make a rate play. To customers they offer some rate protection, but they also have the offsetting disadvantage of illiquidity because they trade at a concession to the market. During their last *leg* (roll period) variable-rate CDs trade like regular CDs of similar name and maturity.

Eurodollar CDs

A Eurodollar time deposit, like a domestic time deposit, is an illiquid asset. Since some investors in Eurodollars wanted liquidity, banks that accepted such deposits in London began to issue Eurodollar CDs. A *Eurodollar CD* resembles a domestic CD except that instead of being the liability of a domestic bank, it is the liability of the London branch of a domestic bank or of a British bank or of some other foreign bank with a branch in London.

Many of the Eurodollar CDs issued in London are purchased by other banks operating in the Euromarket. A large proportion of the remainder are sold to U.S. corporations and other domestic institutional investors. Many Euro CDs are issued through dealers and brokers who also maintain secondary markets in these securities.

The Euro CD market is younger and smaller than the market for domestic CDs, but it has grown rapidly since its inception. For the investor, a key advantage of buying Euro

CDs is that they offer a higher return than domestic CDs. The offsetting disadvantages are that they are less liquid and expose the investor to some extra risk because they are issued outside of the United States.

The most recent development in the "Eurodollar" CD market is that some large banks have begun offering such CDs through their Caribbean branches. Note a CD issued, for example in Nassau, is technically a Euro CD because the deposit is held in a bank branch outside the U.S.

Yankee CDs

Foreign banks issue dollar-denominated CDs not only in the Euro market but also in the domestic market through branches established there. CDs of the latter sort are frequently referred to as *Yankee CDs;* the name is taken from Yankee bonds, which are bonds issued in the domestic market by foreign borrowers.

Yankee, as opposed to domestic, CDs expose the investor to the extra (if only in perception) risk of a foreign name, and they are also less liquid than domestic CDs. Consequently Yankees trade at yields close to those on Euro CDs. The major buyers of Yankee CDs are corporations that are yield buyers and fund to dates.

COMMERCIAL PAPER

While some cash-rich industrial firms participate in the bond and money markets only as lenders, many more must at times borrow to finance either current operations or expenditures on plant and equipment. One source of short-term funds available to a corporation is bank loans. Large firms with good credit ratings have, however, an alternative source of funds that is cheaper, namely, the sale of commercial paper.

Commercial paper is an unsecured promissory note issued for a specific amount and maturing on a specific day. All commercial paper is negotiable, but most paper sold to investors is held by them to maturity. Commercial paper is issued not only by industrial and manufacturing firms but also by finance companies. Finance companies normally sell their paper directly to investors. Industrial firms, in contrast, typically issue their paper through dealers.

The maximum maturity for which commercial paper may be sold is 270 days, since paper with a longer maturity must be registered with the Securities and Exchange Commission (SEC), a time-consuming and costly procedure. In practice, very little 270-day paper is sold. Most paper sold is in the range of 30 days and under.

Since commercial paper has such short maturities, the issuer rarely will have sufficient funds coming in before the paper matures to pay off his borrowing. Instead he expects to *roll* his paper, that is, sell new paper to obtain funds to pay off the maturing paper. Naturally the possibility exists that some sudden change in market conditions, such as when the Penn Central went "belly up" (bankrupt), might make it difficult or impossible for him to sell paper for some time. To guard against this risk, commercial paper issuers back all or a large proportion of their outstanding paper with lines of credit from banks.

The rate offered on commercial paper depends on its maturity, on how much the issuer wants to borrow, on the general level of money market rates, and on the credit rating of the issuer. Almost all commercial paper is rated with respect to credit risk by one or more of several rating services: Moody's, Standard & Poor's, and Fitch. While only top-grade credits can get ratings good enough to sell paper these days, there is still a slight risk that an issuer might go bankrupt. Because of this, yields on commercial paper are higher than those on Treasury obligations of similar maturity.

BANKERS' ACCEPTANCES

Bankers' acceptances (BAs) are an unknown instrument outside the confines of the money market. Moreover, explaining them isn't easy because they arise in a variety of ways out of a variety of transactions. The best approach is to use an example.

Suppose a U.S. importer wants to buy shoes in Brazil and pay for them 4 months later, after he has had time to sell them in the United States. One approach would be for the importer to borrow from his bank; however, short-term rates may be lower in the open market. If they are, and if the importer is too small to go into the open market on his own, then he can go the bankers' acceptance route.

In that case he has his bank write a letter of credit for the amount of the sale and then sends this letter to the Brazilian exporter. Upon export of the shoes, the Brazilian firm, using this letter of credit, draws a time draft on the importer's U.S. bank and discounts this draft at its local bank, thereby obtaining immediate payment for its goods. The Brazilian bank in turn sends the time draft to the importer's U.S. bank, which then stamps "accepted" on the draft (that is, the bank guarantees payment on the draft and thereby creates an *acceptance*). Once this is done, the draft becomes an irrevocable primary obligation of the accepting bank. At this point, if the Brazilian bank did not want cash immediately, the U.S. bank would return the draft to that bank, which would hold it as an investment and then present it to the U.S. bank for payment at maturity. If, on the other hand, the Brazilian bank wanted cash immediately, the U.S. bank would pay it and then either hold the acceptance itself or sell it to an investor. Whoever ended up holding the acceptance, it would be the importer's responsibility to provide its U.S. bank with sufficient funds to pay off the acceptance at maturity. If the importer should fail to do so, his bank would still be responsible for making payment at maturity.

Our example illustrates how an acceptance can arise out of a U.S. import transaction. Acceptances also arise in connection with U.S. export sales, trade between third countries (e.g., Japanese imports of oil from the Middle East), the domestic shipment of goods, and domestic or foreign storage of readily marketable staples. Currently most BAs arise out of foreign trade; the latter may be in manufactured goods but more typically it is in bulk commodities, such as cocoa, cotton, coffee, or crude oil, to name a few. Because of the complex nature of acceptance operations, only large banks that have well-staffed foreign departments act as accepting banks.

Bankers' acceptances closely resemble commercial paper in form. They are short-term, non-interest-bearing notes sold at a discount and redeemed by the accepting bank at maturity for full face value. The major difference is that payment on commercial paper is guaranteed by only the issuing company. In contrast, bankers' acceptances, in addition to carrying the issuer's pledge to pay, are backed by the underlying goods being financed and also carry the guarantee of the accepting bank. Consequently bankers' acceptances are less risky than commercial paper, and thus sell at slightly lower yields.

The big banks through which bankers' acceptances are originated generally keep some portion of the acceptances they create as investments. The rest are sold to investors through dealers or directly by the bank itself. Major investors in BAs are other banks, foreign central banks, corporations, and other domestic and foreign institutional investors. BAs have liquidity because dealers in these securities make an active secondary market in them.

REPURCHASES AND REVERSES

A variety of bank and nonbank dealers act as market makers in governments, agencies, CDs, and BAs. Because dealers by definition buy and sell for their own accounts, active dealers will inevitably end up holding some securities. They will, moreover, buy and hold substantial positions if they believe that interest rates are likely to fall and that the value of these securities is therefore likely to rise. Speculation and risk taking are an inherent and important part of being a dealer.

While dealers have large amounts of capital, the positions they take are often several hundred times that amount. As a result, dealers have to borrow to finance their positions. Dealers, using the securities they own as collateral, can and do borrow from banks at the dealer loan rate. For the bulk of their financing, however, they resort to a cheaper alternative, entering into *repurchase (RP or repo for short) agreements* with investors.

Much of the RP financing done by dealers is on an overnight basis. It works as follows. The dealer finds a corporation or other investor who has funds to invest overnight. He sells this investor, say, $10 million of securities for roughly $10 million, which is paid in Federal funds to his bank by the investor's bank against delivery of the securities sold. At the same time, the dealer agrees to repurchase these securities the next day at a slightly higher price. Thus the buyer of the securities is in effect making the dealer a one-day loan secured by the obligations sold to him. The difference between the purchase and sale prices on the RP transaction is the interest the investor earns on his loan. Alternatively, the purchase and sale prices in an RP transaction may be identical; in that case the dealer pays the investor some explicit rate of interest.

Often a dealer will take a speculative position that he intends to hold for some time. In that case he might do an RP for 30 days or longer. Such agreements are known as *term RPs*.

From the point of view of investors, overnight loans in the RP market offer several attractive features. First, by rolling overnight RPs, investors can keep surplus funds invested without losing liquidity or incurring a price risk. Second, because RP transactions are secured by top-quality paper, investors expose themselves to little or no credit risk.

The overnight RP rate generally is less than the Fed funds rate. The reason is that the many nonbank investors who have funds to invest overnight or very short term and who do not want to incur any price risk have nowhere to go but the RP market, because they cannot (with the exception of S&Ls) participate directly in the Fed funds market. Also, lending money through an RP transaction is safer than selling Fed funds because a sale of Fed funds is an unsecured loan.

On term as opposed to overnight RP transactions, investors still have the advantage of their loans being secured but they do lose some liquidity. To compensate for that, the rate on an RP transaction is generally higher the longer the term for which funds are lent.

Banks that make dealer loans fund them by buying Fed funds, and the lending rate they charge—which is adjusted daily—is the prevailing Fed funds rate plus a one-eighth to one-quarter markup. Because the overnight RP rate is lower than the Fed funds rate, dealers can finance their positions more cheaply by doing RP than by borrowing from the banks.

A dealer who is bullish on the market will position large amounts of securities. If he's bearish, he will *short* the market, that is, sell securities he does not own. Since the dealer has to deliver any securities he sells whether he owns them or not, a dealer who shorts has to borrow securities one way or another. The most common technique today for borrowing securities is to do what is called a *reverse RP*, or simply a *reverse*. To obtain securities through a reverse, a dealer finds an investor holding the required securities; he then buys these securities from the investor under an agreement that he will resell these same securities to the investor at a fixed price on some future date. In this transaction the dealer, besides obtaining securities, is extending a loan to the investor for which he is paid some rate of interest.

An RP and a reverse are identical transactions. What a given transaction is called depends on who initiates it: typically if a dealer hunting money does, it's an RP; if a dealer hunting securities does, it's a reverse.

A final note: The Fed uses reverses and RPs with dealers in government securities to make adjustments in bank reserves.

MUNICIPAL NOTES

Debt securities issued by state and local governments and their agencies are referred to as *municipal securities*. Such securities can be divided into two broad categories: bonds issued to finance capital projects and short-term notes sold in anticipation of the receipt of other funds, such as taxes or proceeds from a bond issue.

Municipal notes, which are an important money market instrument, are issued with maturities ranging from a month to a year or more. They bear interest, and minimum denominations are highly variable, ranging anywhere from $5,000 to $5 million.

Most muni notes are general obligation securities; that is, payment of principal and interest is secured by the issuer's pledge of its full faith, credit, and taxing power. This sounds impressive but, as the spectacle of New York City tottering on the brink of bankruptcy brought home to all, it is possible that a municipality might default on its securities. Thus the investor who buys muni notes assumes a credit risk. To aid investors in evaluating this risk, publicly offered muni notes are rated by Moody's. The one exception is project notes, which are issued by local housing authorities to finance federally sponsored programs, and which are backed by the full faith and credit of the federal government.

The major attraction of municipal notes to an investor is that interest income on them is exempt from federal taxation and usually also from any income taxes levied within the state where they are issued. The value of this tax exemption is greater the higher the investor's tax bracket, and the muni market thus attracts only highly taxed investors—commercial banks, cash-rich corporations, and wealthy individuals.

Large muni note issues are sold to investors by dealers who obtain the securities either through negotiation with the issuer or through competitive bidding. These same dealers also make a secondary market in muni notes.

The yield a municipality must pay to issue notes depends on its credit rating, the length of time for which it borrows, and the general level of short-term rates. Normally a good credit can borrow at a rate well below the yield on T bills of equivalent maturity. The reason for this is the value to the investor of the tax exemption on the municipal security. A corporation that has its profits taxed at a 50 percent marginal rate would, for example, receive approximately the same after-tax return from a muni note yielding 5 percent that it would from a T bill yielding 10 percent.[3] For a corporation subject to high *state* income taxes, the difference between the rate offered on a municipal note issued in the firm's state of domicile and the bill rate that would give the firm the same after-tax return would be substantially larger.

---

[3] We say "approximately" because most muni notes are sold on an *interest-bearing* basis while bills are quoted on a *discount* rate so that the rates at which the two securities are offered are rarely directly comparable.

3

Concepts of interest and notation

One of the first and most distressing lessons a money market neophyte learns is that yields on different money market instruments are rarely quoted on the same basis and are therefore rarely directly comparable. The principal reasons are:

1. Some instruments are sold on a discount basis; others bear interest.
2. Yields on some instruments are quoted on the basis of a 365-day year; yields on others are quoted on the basis of a 360-day year.
3. Interest is accrued on different instruments in different ways.
4. Different instruments offer different opportunities for compounding the return earned.
5. A security may mature on a nonbusiness day with the result that the holding period is longer than the period during which the securities are assumed to be held in the yield calculation.

These issues, as they apply to individual securities, will be discussed in later chapters. Before we broach that broad topic, however, it is vital to introduce several measures of the rate of interest earned and to show (1) why they are not comparable and (2) how they can be made comparable. This is accomplished in the first part of this chapter. In the second part we turn to an equally vital issue: developing a notation that is both economical and mnenomic (easy to remember).

CONCEPTS OF INTEREST

Simple interest

Consider an investor who lends $1,000 for 1 year and who receives at the end of that year the $1,000 of principal plus $80 of interest. On a *simple interest basis (no compounding)*, the rate of return he earns is calculated as follows:

$$\frac{\left(\begin{array}{c}\text{Principal invested plus interest}\\\text{paid at the end of 1 year}\end{array}\right) - \left(\begin{array}{c}\text{Principal}\\\text{invested}\end{array}\right)}{\text{Principal invested}} = \left(\begin{array}{c}\text{Annual return}\\\text{as a simple}\\\text{interest rate}\end{array}\right)$$

Plugging the numbers in our example into this equation, we get

$$\frac{\$1,080 - \$1,000}{\$1,000} = 0.08 = 8\%$$

That is, our investor earns an annual simple interest rate of 8 percent.

Annualizing simple interest. Suppose now that the borrower in our example needs $1,000 for only half a year and that he offers the investor $40 of interest for this period. If our investor were able to make the same deal (invest $1,000 and earn $40) during the second half of the year, he would earn $80 of interest over the whole year, so the simple interest rate on an annual basis that he is being offered is 8 percent.

We can annualize the rate of return earned on any investment that pays interest at maturity and is outstanding for less than a year as follows: We substitute the actual interest paid into the preceding expression for calculating the return on a 1-year security; we then divide the resulting expression by the fraction of the year for which the security is outstanding. Doing so gives us:

$$\left[\frac{\left(\substack{\text{Principal invested plus} \\ \text{interest paid at maturity}} \right) - \left(\substack{\text{Principal} \\ \text{invested}} \right)}{\text{Principal invested}} \right] \div \left(\substack{\text{Fraction of the year} \\ \text{the investment is} \\ \text{outstanding}} \right) = \left(\substack{\text{Annualized return} \\ \text{as a simple} \\ \text{interest rate}} \right)$$

Inserting the numbers in our second example into this equation, we get

$$\frac{\$1,040 - \$1,000}{\$1,000} \div \frac{1}{2} = 0.08 = 8\%$$

That is, over *half* the year our investor earns, as we concluded, an annualized rate of 8 percent.

To simplify our example we used a half-year loan. Obviously no such thing exists in real life because half a year is 182.5 days, and money market investments never are outstanding for half a day nor do they pay a return on a half-day basis. Therefore, to be precise, *the annualizing factor should be stated in terms of days.*

Let

$$t = \text{days the investment is outstanding}$$

then for a security on which t is less than 365,

$$\left[\frac{\left(\substack{\text{Principal plus interest} \\ \text{paid at maturity}} \right) - \left(\substack{\text{Principal} \\ \text{invested}} \right)}{\text{Principal invested}} \right] \div \frac{t}{365} = \left(\substack{\text{Annualized return} \\ \text{as a simple} \\ \text{interest rate}} \right)$$

Compound interest

The next wrinkle to which we turn is the *compounding* of interest. Suppose now that our investor places $1,000 in a savings-account-type security that pays interest semiannually and permits the *reinvestment* of interest. Assuming that the rate offered is again 8 percent, our investor will receive $40 of interest at the end of the first half year:

$$0.08(\$1,000)(\tfrac{1}{2}) = \$40$$

If, moreover, that $40 is added to the principal invested, he will receive $41.60 of interest at the end of the second half year:

$$0.08(\$1,040)(\tfrac{1}{2}) = \$41.60$$

Since

$$\$40 + \$41.60 = \$81.60$$

semiannual compounding clearly raises the *effective* return the investor receives from 8.00 percent to 8.16 percent.

Let

n = times during the year compounding occurs
i = nominal rate of interest paid
i^* = effective rate paid with compounding

As Table 3–1 shows, the amount by which compounding raises the effective return earned depends on how high the nominal rate offered is and on how often compounding occurs. Thus we need a general formula to calculate the effective rate of interest when compounding is possible. It is:[1]

$$i^* = \left(1 + \frac{i}{n}\right)^n - 1$$

Converting a simple interest rate to the equivalent effective rate when compounding occurs†

$$i^* = \left(1 + \frac{i}{n}\right)^n - 1$$

† A formula for calculating an annualized compound rate of return when the investment period is less than 1 year is developed on pages 37–39.

Table 3–1
The effect of compounding a simple interest rate on the effective return earned

i, simple interest rate, %	n, times during year compounding occurs	i*, effective return with compounding, %	i* − i, %
4.00	2	4.04	0.04
4.00	4	4.06	0.06
4.00	Daily	4.08	0.08
—	—	—	—
8.00	2	8.16	0.16
8.00	4	8.24	0.24
8.00	Daily	8.33	0.33
—	—	—	—
12.00	2	12.36	0.36
12.00	4	12.55	0.55
12.00	Daily	12.75	0.75

---

[1] In the appendix to this chapter, we show how this general result can be suggested by simple induction.

For reasons discussed in later chapters, compounding must be taken into account to put different rates on a comparable basis. Therefore the formula for i^* is crucial and should be *committed to memory* by the reader. This formula, like all key formulas in the book, has been displayed in a *box* for emphasis and easy reference.

With daily compounding, as occurs on some savings accounts, n equals 365. With daily compounding on money market transactions, such as overnight sales of Fed funds or repo money, n equals the number of business days in the year, a number in excess of 250. Raising any number to a power is impossibly time-consuming unless one has a calculator programmed to do it. If yours is not, buy one programmed to calculate y^x or better still the *Basis Point Calculator* to be marketed in 1981.

Rate of discount

Many money market securities, bills, BAs, and commercial paper, are sold on a discount basis. They do not pay interest; instead they are sold at a discount from face value and redeemed at maturity for face value. The investor in a discount security earns a return because he receives more for the security at maturity than he paid for it at issue or purchase.

The rate of discount earned on discount paper always understates the rate of return earned on a simple interest basis. To see this, let's work an example. Suppose an investor buys $1 million of 6-month Treasury bills at an 8 percent rate of discount. The discount he receives at purchase will be *roughly:* $\frac{1}{2} \times 0.08 \times \$1$ million. We say roughly for the following reasons:

1. The 6-month bill normally matures in precisely 26 weeks, or 182 days.
2. On *all* discount securities the discount is figured as if the year had 360 days.

Thus the discount at which our investor buys $1 million of bills is calculated as follows:

$$\left(\begin{array}{c}\text{Discount at 8\% on}\\ \text{\$1 million of 6-month bills}\end{array}\right) = \$1,000,000\,(0.08)\,\frac{182}{360} = \$40,444.44$$

Subtracting this number from $1 million, we find that the investor must put up $959,555.56 to purchase his bills:

$$\$1,000,000 - \$40,444.44 = \$959,555.56$$

If we now insert the face value of the bills, the price paid for them, and the days they are outstanding into a variation of the formula on page 16.

$$\left[\frac{\left(\begin{array}{c}\text{Face value}\\ \text{at maturity}\end{array}\right) - \left(\begin{array}{c}\text{Principal}\\ \text{invested}\end{array}\right)}{\text{Principal invested}}\right] \div \frac{t}{365} = \left(\begin{array}{c}\text{Annualized return}\\ \text{as a simple}\\ \text{interest rate}\end{array}\right)$$

we find that the simple interest rate earned by the investor is

$$\frac{\$1,000,000 - \$959,555.56}{\$959,555.56} \div \frac{182}{365} = 8.45\%$$

which is substantially *more* than the quoted rate of discount.

Converting a rate from a 360-day to a 365-day basis. We will delve deeper into the mathematics of discount securities in the next two chapters. There is, however, one important point that should be made here. We could have annualized the rate of return earned by the investor on the basis of a 360-day year. That would have given us a rate comparable to the rate paid on term repo, since the repo rate is quoted on a 360-day basis. Had we done so, we would have obtained

$$\frac{\$1,000,000 - \$959,555.56}{\$959,555.56} \div \frac{182}{360} = 8.34\%$$

Once that step was taken, we could then have converted the annualized rate on a 360-day basis to a rate on a 365-day basis by dividing it by the appropriate analyzing factor, 360/365, as shown here:

$$0.0834 \div \frac{360}{365} = 8.45\%$$

The conversion of a rate quoted on a 360-day basis to one on a 365-day basis is something that anyone who works with money market numbers must do constantly. *The easiest way to make the calculation is to think not of dividing by 360/365, but of multiplying by 365/360.* The reason is that one can always remember the proper operation by reasoning as follows:

It is worth *more* to the investor to get his return in 360 days than in 365. Therefore if one converts a rate from a 360-day basis to a 365-day basis, the figure for return earned must get *bigger.* If that is so, then the proper term by which to multiply the 360-day rate must be 365/360 (which is *greater* than 1) rather than 360/365 (which is *less* than 1).

This is hardly a profound observation but for people who have trouble memorizing formulas, tricks of this sort will save time and money.

In some instances, to get comparable rates one needs to go from a 360-day rate to a 365-day rate. In this respect a handy magic number to remember is:

$$\frac{365}{360} = 1.013889$$

which rounds to 1.014. This number tells you that converting a 360-day rate at a 10 percent level of interest to a 365-day basis will raise that rate from 10 percent to

$$0.10(1.014) = 10.14\%$$

that is, by 14 basis points.[2] On a tight transaction, 14 ignored basis points can turn an apparently profitable deal into a losing one. A final important point: In annualizing any dollar return earned on an investment over *less than one year,* it is easier to remember to *multiply* by 365/t than to *divide* by t/365. The reason is that multiplying by 365 obviously *raises* the rate of return earned which is precisely what intuition suggests is required. It is for this reason that the formulas in the box on page 20 are written as they are.

In a leap year, such as 1980, the magic number, 1.013889, becomes

$$\frac{366}{360} = 1.016667$$

NOTATION

All the publications that have been widely circulated in the dealer community and that deal tangentially or primarily with money and bond market calculations make frequent use of multiletter symbols, such as *DSM* and *RV*, to denote individual variables. This practice can be faulted on several counts.

First, a mathematical purist, as opposed to a computer programmer, would regard

---

[2] A *basis point,* also called an *01* by the street, is $^1/_{100}$ of 1 percent.

**Calculating return earned on a simple interest basis
(i.e., opportunity for compounding ignored)**

Let

$$i = \text{return on a simple interest basis}$$
$$t = \text{days investment is outstanding}$$

Then

Case I: The instrument bears interest; i calculated on a 365-day-year basis:

$$i = \left[\frac{\left(\substack{\text{Principal plus interest} \\ \text{paid at maturity}} \right) - \left(\substack{\text{Principal} \\ \text{invested}} \right)}{\text{Principal invested}} \right] \frac{365}{t}$$

Case II: The investment is a discount security; i calculated on a 365-day-year basis:

$$i = \left[\frac{\left(\substack{\text{Face value at} \\ \text{maturity}} \right) - \left(\substack{\text{Principal} \\ \text{invested}} \right)}{\text{Principal invested}} \right] \frac{365}{t}$$

Case III: Converting from one basis to another:
Let

$$i_{365} = i \text{ on a 365-day-year basis}$$

$$i_{360} = i \text{ on a 360-day-year basis}$$

Then

$$i_{360} = i_{365} \left(\frac{360}{365} \right) = 0.986 i_{365}$$

$$i_{365} = i_{360} \left(\frac{365}{360} \right) = 1.014 i_{360}$$

---

such notation as sloppy and awkward. Since the subset of all money market participants who are mathematical purists probably has zero members, this objection seems of minor importance. Mathematical purists have, however, a good reason for insisting that all variables in a relationship be represented by a single letter. When this practice is followed, one letter next to another means that the first variable is *multiplied* by the second. Use of this convention permits one to reduce an expression such as

$$i \times I$$

to the more economical and more easily manipulated form

$$iI$$

an expression that appears in the appendix to this chapter.

A second and more serious problem with using expressions such as *DSM* to denote a single variable is that this practice eats up obvious letter combinations at a voracious pace so that the practitioner is soon reduced to adopting nonmnenomic symbols. The equation on page 1 is a case in point. In it, *DSM* stands for days from settlement to maturity, while *E* stands for days in the coupon period. The reader may well be able to remember that *DSM* stands for days from settlement to maturity because it is mnemonic, but how is he to remember that *E* stands for what is normally called the basis? In this equation, as in others of its genre, the reader's major difficulty in figuring out what the equation says is not in following the algebra but in remembering what all the symbols mean. If, like the author, he forgets what the first denotes while he is committing to memory the meaning of the sixth, he will never get it straight.

Fortunately there is an easy way around this difficulty—the use of subscripts and asterisks. It is not clear why money market writers never use subscripts. Probably they believe subscripts look "too mathematical" and are therefore likely to frighten or confuse lay readers.

Subscripts are simple

Actually there is nothing mathematical about subscripts. They denote names, not operations. To illustrate, let's take a simple example. Suppose we want to represent in symbols the Hanson family, composed of Helen, Peter, and Marcia. The computer programmer would undoubtedly denote Helen Hanson as HH, Peter Hanson as PH, and Marcia Hanson as MH. The mathematician, on the other hand, would observe that the important identifying characteristic of the group is that they are all Hansons, and, to identify the individuals in the group, he would use subscripts as follows: H_h for Helen Hanson, H_p for Peter Hanson, and H_m for Marcia Hanson. *Moral:* If you understand how surnames and given names are used, you understand all you need to know about subscripts.

With that introduction, let us turn to Table 3–2, which presents the major notation used throughout the book. Note there are six interest rates that we will have frequent occasion to use:

$$i = \text{simple interest rate}$$
$$y = \text{yield to maturity}$$
$$r = \text{repo or reverse repo rate}$$
$$r_e = \text{reinvestment rate}$$
$$d = \text{rate of discount on discount securities}$$
$$c = \text{coupon rate}$$

Note also that all these symbols are mnemonic.

The symbol *t* is used to denote *time* measured in days, again a mnemonic choice. If several time periods are used in a single relationship, individual periods are represented by *t* with subscripts also mnemonically chosen, e.g.,

$$t_{sm} = \text{days from settlement to maturity}$$

Many of the problems we will tackle in later chapters involve solving for *true* yields to maturity or for *break-even* yields or prices. In every case, these variables are affixed with an asterisk; for example, r^* is used in a later chapter to denote a dealer's break-even rate on a reverse to maturity.

The symbols in Table 3–2 are about all the notation we will need. In special situations where an additional symbol is needed or a symbol's meaning is slightly changed, this will be clearly indicated when the equation is given. Otherwise, we will consistently use the notation presented in Table 3–2. For easy reference this table is repeated on the right-hand front endpaper.

Table 3–2
Notation used†

i	return measured as a simple interest rate
i^*	effective return when a simple interest rate is compounded
y	yield to maturity on a quote sheet
y^*	*true* yield to maturity
r	repo or reverse repo rate
r^*	break-even level of r
r_t	term repo rate
r_e	reinvestment rate
d	rate of discount
d^*	break-even level of d
d_b	equivalent bond yield
c	coupon rate

interest rate symbols all denote rates written in *decimal* form

n	number of times compounding occurs during a year
N	number of remaining coupons
t	time measured in days
t_{is}	days from issue (or last coupon) to settlement
t_{im}	days from issue to maturity
t_{sm}	days from settlement to maturity
t_{sc}	days from settlement to next coupon
t_{ss}	days from settlement to settlement (e.g., on a transaction on which beginning and end dates fall between issue and maturity dates or between coupon dates)
a_i	accrued interest
P	dollar price‡
F	face value
D	dollar amount of discount on a discount security
B	basis (number of days in the coupon period)
v_{01}	value of an 01 (i.e., a basis point)
v_{32}	yield value of $1/32$

† In a few situations where an equation is useful for figuring the outcome of more than one type or side of a transaction, subscripts 1 and 2 are affixed to key variables describing the security traded or financed. When this is done, subscript 1 denotes values, such as price, that apply on the day the transaction is initiated; subscript 2 denotes values that apply on the day the transaction is terminated.

‡ Includes accrued interest in the case of CDs, otherwise does not. In formulas for interest-bearing securities, P is always taken to be the price per $1 of face value.

Parentheses and brackets

For the nonmathematical reader a few words should be said about parentheses and brackets. An expression such as

$$a(b + x)$$

simply means that a is multiplied by the sum of the two numbers, b and x, inside the parentheses.

If two expressions in parentheses are placed next to each other, that means that the one is multiplied by the other; for example,

$$(a - y)(b + x)$$

means that the difference between a and y is multiplied by the sum of b and x.

Sometimes a multiterm expression such as

$$\left[\frac{ay + b(x + c)}{b} \right]$$

is placed in brackets when it is to be multiplied or otherwise operated on by another term. Brackets, like parentheses, indicate that whatever is inside them forms a single term in the equation. In an algebraic expression there is no difference in use or meaning between parentheses and brackets. It is simply a matter of style to substitute brackets for oversized parentheses when an expression gets to a certain size or when parentheses are used within the expression.

With our notation in hand, we now turn to discount securities.

APPENDIX

The general formula

$$i^* = \left(i + \frac{i}{n} \right)^n - 1$$

can be suggested by induction as follows. Let

$$I = \text{amount (principal) invested}$$
$$i = \text{nominal rate of interest paid}$$

With semiannual compounding, the amount the investor will have at the end of a year equals principal *plus* the interest paid at the end of the first half-year *plus* the interest (including interest on interest) paid at the end of the second half-year. In symbols, this amount can be represented as follows:

$$I + \frac{i}{2} \, I + \frac{i}{2} \left(I + \frac{i}{2} \, I \right)$$

which reduces to

$$I \left(1 + \frac{i}{2} \right)^2$$

With compounding three times a year, the amount the investor will have at the end of the year equals principal plus three interest payments. This amount represented in symbols is:

$$I + \frac{i}{3} \, I + \frac{i}{3} \left(I + \frac{i}{3} \, I \right) + \frac{i}{3} \left[I + \frac{i}{3} \, I + \frac{i}{3} \left(I + \frac{i}{3} \, I \right) \right]$$

which reduces to

$$I \left(1 + \frac{i}{3}\right)^3$$

As the emerging pattern correctly suggests, with compounding n times a year, the amount the investor will have at the end of a year is

$$I \left(1 + \frac{i}{n}\right)^n$$

Thus the effective rate, i^*, he will earn over the year when compounding is taken into account is

$$i^* = \left[I \frac{\left(1 + \frac{i}{n}\right)^n - I}{I} \right]$$

which reduces to

$$i^* = \left(1 + \frac{i}{n}\right)^n - 1$$

the formula given on page 17.

Discount securities

part II

Basic calculations

In this chapter we develop the basic formulas for calculating the amount of the discount, the price, and the yield on discount securities. We also show how the rate at which a discount security is quoted can be converted to a bond equivalent yield. In Chapter 5 we will illustrate various ways in which these calculations—all important and fundamental—can be used by imaginative traders and investors.

CALCULATING DISCOUNT AND PRICE WITH RATE GIVEN

Assume that an investor who participates in an auction of new Treasury year *bills* picks up $1 million of them at 8 percent. What this means is that the Treasury sells the investor $1 million of bills that mature in 1 year at a price approximately but not precisely 8 percent below their face value. The "approximately but not precisely" qualifier reflects, as suggested in Chapter 3, two factors. First, the year bill is outstanding not for a year but for 364 days.[1] Second, the Treasury calculates the discount as if a year has only 360 days. So the fraction of the year for which the security is outstanding is 364/360, and the true discount is:

$$\begin{pmatrix} \text{Discount of \$1 million of} \\ \text{year bills issued at 8 percent} \end{pmatrix} = \$1,000,000 \, (0.08) \frac{364}{360} = \$80,888.89$$

The price the investor pays for his bills equals *the face value minus the discount*, i.e.,

$$\begin{pmatrix} \text{Price paid for \$1 million of} \\ \text{year bills bought at 8 percent} \end{pmatrix} = \$1,000,000 - \$80.888.89 = \$919,111.11$$

Generalizing from this example, we can construct formulas for calculating both the discount from face value and the price at which T bills will sell, depending on their current maturity and the discount at which they are quoted. These formulas are given in the box on page 28.

---

[1] From November 1979 to November 1980, the original maturity of the year bill was shortened to 359 days. The Treasury's purpose was to change the cycle of the year bill so that a later 6-month bill and a still later 3-month bill would be reopenings of an old year bill.

Calculating dollar discount and price on discount securities with rate of discount given

Let

D = discount from face value in dollars
F = face value in dollars
d = rate of discount (decimal)
t_{sm} = days from settlement to maturity
P = price in dollars

Then

$$D = dF \frac{t_{sm}}{360}$$

and

$$P = F - D = F \left(1 - \frac{dt_{sm}}{360}\right)$$

Numerical examples. We can illustrate use of the formulas in the above box as follows. Let

$$d = 0.08$$
$$t_{sm} = 11$$
$$F = \$225,000$$

Then

$$D = 0.08(\$225,000)\frac{11}{360}$$

$$= \$550$$

Alternatively reversing the calculation, let the givens be

$$d = 0.08$$
$$t_{sm} = 11$$
$$D = \$550$$

Then

$$P = \$225,000 \left[1 - \frac{0.08(11)}{360}\right]$$

$$= \$224,450$$

CALCULATING RATE OF DISCOUNT WITH DOLLAR DISCOUNT OR PRICE GIVEN

Using these formulas, it is easy to obtain expressions for d when the value of either D or P are given. Let's start with D *given*. We know that

$$D = dF \frac{t_{sm}}{360}$$

Solving this equation for d, we obtain d as the following function of D:

$$d = \frac{D}{F}\,\frac{360}{t_{sm}}$$

If *P is given,* we recall that

$$D = F - P$$

and substitute this expression for D into the equation

$$d = \frac{D}{F}\,\frac{360}{t_{sm}}$$

which yields

$$d = \left(\frac{F - P}{F}\right)\frac{360}{t_{sm}}$$

an expression that reduces to

$$d = \left(1 - \frac{P}{F}\right)\frac{360}{t_{sm}}$$

**Calculating the rate of discount on discount securities
with dollar discount or price given**

Let

D = discount from face value in dollars
F = face value in dollars
d = rate of discount (decimal)
t_{sm} = days from settlement to maturity
P = price in dollars

Then

Case I: Discount in dollars given:

$$d = \frac{D}{F}\,\frac{360}{t_{sm}}$$

Case II: Price in dollars given:

$$d = \left(1 - \frac{P}{F}\right)\frac{360}{t_{sm}}$$

Numerical examples. We can illustrate the formulas in the box above using the same numbers given in the examples above where we solved for D and P given d, t_{sm} and F. Let

$$t_{sm} = 11$$
$$D = \$550$$
$$F = \$225{,}000$$

Then

$$d = \frac{\$550}{\$225,000} \left(\frac{360}{11}\right)$$

$$= 8\%$$

If alternatively the calculation is made using the dollar value not for D but for P, which is \$224,450.00, then

$$d = \left(1 - \frac{\$224,450}{\$225,000}\right) \frac{360}{11}$$

$$= 8\%$$

VALUE OF AN 01

Table 4–1 reproduces Discount Corporation's T-bill quote sheet for Friday, April 6. Note the quotes are closing rates on Thursday, April 5, and the assumed settlement is regular settlement on Monday, April 9. Two columns in this table are of special interest: the one headed "Value of .01 Per M" and the other, "Coupon Yield Equivalent."

Let's start with the *value of an 01*. Bills, like all discount securities, are normally quoted in terms of bid and asked *percentage* yields to *two decimal places*. For that reason, the basic unit in which fluctuations in a bill's price are measured is *1/100 of 1 percentage point*—a unit that the street refers to as *a basis point* or *an 01*. Note 100 basis points equal 1 percent.

Naturally investors and dealers in bills would like to know how much the price of a given bill would fluctuate if its yield changes by an 01. This calculation is easily made, since an 01 is simply a small value of d. To illustrate, let's find the value of an 01 and \$1 million of the bill in Table 4–1 that matures on 7/26/79. To do so, we substitute $d = 0.0001$ and $t_{sm} = 108$ into the equation

$$D = dF \left(\frac{t_{sm}}{360}\right)$$

Table 4–1
Bill quotes from a dealer's quote sheet for use on April 6, 1979

DISCOUNT CORPORATION OF NEW YORK

58 Pine Street, New York, N.Y. 10005
Telephone 212-248-8900 • WUI Telex 620863 Discorp • WU Telex 125675 Discorp - NYK

QUOTATIONS FOR
U.S. TREASURY SECURITIES
Closing   APR. 5, 1979
Ylds. for Dely. APR. 9, 1979

U. S. TREASURY BILLS[1]

Issue	Days to Mat.	Rate of Discount Bid	Asked	Chge.	Coupon Yield Equiv.	Value of .01 Per M	Amount of Issue ($ millions)	Issue	Days to Mat.	Rate of Discount Bid	Asked	Chge.	Coupon Yield Equiv.	Value of .01 Per M	Amount of Issue ($ millions)
4/12/79	3	9.85	9.75	--	9.89	.83	6201	8/02/79	115	9.49	9.45	--	9.88	31.94	3000
4/19/79	10	9.85	9.75	--	9.91	2.78	14200	8/09/79	122	9.52	9.48 + .03	9.93	33.89	3000
4/26/79	17	9.85	9.75	--	9.93	4.72	12205	8/16/79	129	9.50	9.46 + .01	9.93	35.83	2900
5/01/79	22	9.55	9.45 + .05	9.64	6.11	3022	8/21/79	134	9.48	9.44 - .02	9.92	37.22	3539
5/03/79	24	9.50	9.40	--	9.59	6.67	6300	8/23/79	136	9.50	9.46	--	9.95	37.78	3001
5/10/79	31	9.60	9.50 - .05	9.71	8.61	6207	8/30/79	143	9.48	9.44 - .02	9.94	39.72	3001
5/17/79	38	9.65	9.55	--	9.78	10.56	6200	9/06/79	150	9.45	9.41 - .01	9.93	41.67	3000
5/24/79	45	9.65	9.55	--	9.80	12.50	5900	9/13/79	157	9.46	9.42	--	9.96	43.61	3000
5/29/79	50	9.65	9.55	--	9.81	13.89	2477	9/18/79	162	9.44	9.40 - .01	9.95	45.00	3348
5/31/79	52	9.65	9.55	--	9.82	14.44	5900	9/20/79	164	9.45	9.41	--	9.97	45.56	3001
6/07/79	59	9.65	9.55 + .05	9.84	16.39	5800	9/27/79	171	9.43	9.39 - .02	9.96	47.50	3000
6/14/79	66	9.65	9.55 + .05	9.86	18.33	5900	10/04/79 ##	178	9.40	9.36 - .01	9.95	49.44	3003
6/21/79	73	9.65	9.55	--	9.87	20.28	5800	10/16/79	190	9.39	9.35 - .02	9.95	52.78	3469
6/26/79	78	9.65	9.55	--	9.89	21.67	2781	11/13/79	218	9.38	9.34	--	9.96	60.56	3893
6/28/79	80	9.50	9.40	--	9.73	22.22	5900	12/11/79	246	9.34	9.30 - .02	9.94	68.33	4023
7/05/79 ##	87	9.50	9.46 - .01	9.82	24.17	5900	1/08/80	274	9.29	9.25 - .02	9.92	76.11	3698
7/12/79	94	9.54	9.50 - .01	9.88	26.11	2900	2/05/80	302	9.28	9.24 - .02	9.96	83.89	3536
7/19/79	101	9.54	9.50 - .02	9.90	28.06	2900	3/04/80	330	9.18	9.14 - .02	9.90	91.67	3320
7/24/79	106	9.57	9.53 - .05	9.94	29.44	3377	4/01/80 ##	358	9.18	9.14	--	9.95	99.44	3343
7/26/79	108	9.56	9.52 + .02	9.94	30.00	3000								

to obtain

$$\text{Value of an 01} = \$1,000,000(0.0001)\frac{108}{360}$$

$$= \$30$$

which is the number given on the quote sheet in Table 4–1.

Value of an 01, i.e., a basis point, on a discount security

Let

v_{01} = Value of an 01 per \$1 million of face value on a discount security

Then

$$v_{01} = 0.0001(1,000,000)\frac{t_{sm}}{360}$$

which reduces to

$$v_{01} = \$0.277778t_{sm}$$

A useful number to remember is that on a 90-day bill, with a \$1 million face value

$$v_{01} = \$0.277778(90)$$
$$= \$25$$

For handy reference a table giving the values of an 01 per \$1 million for securities that mature from 1 to 365 days hence is reproduced on the back endpapers.

EQUIVALENT SIMPLE INTEREST YIELD

As noted in Chapter 3, the rate at which a discount security is offered understates the *simple interest* rate that the investor in such a security would earn. Moreover, as the figures in Table 4–2 show, *the discrepancy between the two rates is greater the higher the rate of discount and the longer the time to maturity.*

Table 4–2
Comparisons at different rates and maturities between rates of discount and the equivalent *simple interest* rates on a 365-day-year basis

Rate of discount (%)	Equivalent simple interest (%)		
	30-day maturity	182-day maturity	364-day maturity
4	4.07	4.14	4.23
6	6.11	6.27	6.48
8	8.17	8.45	8.82
10	10.22	10.68	11.27
12	12.29	12.95	13.84
14	14.36	15.28	16.53
16	16.44	17.65	19.35

Obviously investors in and issuers of discount securities need a formula to convert discount rates to simple interest rates. With a few manipulations this formula can easily be obtained. Let

$$i = \text{rate of simple interest}$$

Referring to the formula on page 18, we observe that on a discount security the simple interest yield is given by

$$i = \frac{F - P}{P} \div \frac{t_{sm}}{365}$$

If we now substitute for P the expression $F - D$ and simplify, we get

$$i = \left(\frac{D}{F - D}\right) \frac{365}{t_{sm}}$$

Next we recall that

$$D = dF \frac{t_{sm}}{360}$$

and substitute this expression for D into the preceding formula. Doing so yields

$$i = \left[\frac{dF \dfrac{t_{sm}}{360}}{F - dF \dfrac{t_{sm}}{360}}\right] \frac{365}{t_{sm}}$$

which reduces to

$$i = \frac{365d}{360 - dt_{sm}}$$

Converting a discount rate to the equivalent simple interest rate, 365-day-year basis

Let

d = rate of discount (decimal)
i = equivalent simple interest rate (decimal)
t_{sm} = days from settlement to maturity

Then

$$i = \frac{365d}{360 - dt_{sm}}$$

Numerical example

To illustrate the use of this formula, let us return to the bill example given on pages 18–19; using $d = 0.08$ and $t_{sm} = 182$. Plugging these numbers into our equation for i, we get

$$i = \frac{365(0.08)}{360 - (0.08)(182)}$$
$$= 8.45\%$$

which is exactly the simple interest rate we demonstrated the investor was earning (pages 18 and 19).

EQUIVALENT BOND YIELD

Next we turn to what is called *coupon yield equivalent* or *equivalent bond yield*. This topic calls for a short preface.

In the secondary market bids for and offerings of coupon securities are quoted not in terms of yields (as in the case of discount securities) but in terms of dollar prices. On a coupon quote sheet, however, there is always a number for each security stating what its *yield to maturity* would be if it were purchased at the quoted *asked* or *offered* price.

For present purposes the important thing to note is that, if a bond with an 8 percent coupon were to sell at *par* (i.e., at a price equal to its face value), its yield to maturity on the quote sheet would be given as 8 percent. However, since coupon securities typically pay interest semiannually, the actual yield to the investor in that security would be something more than 8 percent when possibilities for compounding were taken into account. Specifically, using the formula developed in Chapter 3,

$$i^* = \left(1 + \frac{i}{n}\right)^n - 1$$

we find that with $i = 0.08$ and $n = 2$ because there are two coupon-periods,

$$i^* = \left(1 + \frac{0.08}{2}\right)^2 - 1 = 8.16\%$$

The lesson is clear. The yield to maturity figure on a quote sheet for coupon securities *understates* the effective yield to maturity because it ignores the fact that interest is paid *semiannually;* that is, whatever the investor does with coupon interest, it is worth something to him to get semiannual interest payments rather than a single year-end interest payment.

In converting the yield on a discount security to an add-on interest rate, various approaches are possible. One is to convert to a simple interest rate as we did in Table 4–2. However, the street, in putting together quote sheets, takes, a slightly different tack. *It restates yields on discount securities on a basis that makes them comparable to the yield to maturity figures quoted on coupon securities;* hence the term *coupon yield equivalent* or *equivalent bond yield.*

Six months (182 days) or less to maturity

The street's decision to restate bill yields on a coupon yield equivalent basis creates a need to distinguish between discount securities that have 6 months or less to run and those that have more than 6 months to run. When a coupon security is on its last *leg*, i.e., when it will mature on the next coupon date and thus offers no opportunity for further compounding, its stated yield to maturity equals its yield on a simple interest basis. For this reason, *on discount securities with 6 months or less to run, bond equivalent yield is taken to be the simple interest rate offered by the instrument.* Let

$$d_b = \text{equivalent bond yield}$$

Then from the formula given on page 32 for i on a discount security, it follows that for such a security

$$d_b = \frac{365d}{360 - dt_{sm}}$$

More than 6 months (182 days) to maturity

As noted, when a coupon security has more than 6 months to run, yield to maturity on the quote sheet understates the true yield by ignoring the opportunity for compounding. To state the interest yield on a long discount security on a comparable basis, *the same understatement must be introduced* in the calculation of that yield.

The way this is done is logical but tricky. The problem is that the simple interest yield on, say, a 9-month discount security is *too high* to be comparable with the yield on a coupon security of the same maturity because the coupon will yield an interest payment before it matures, while the discount security will not. To adjust downward the simple interest rate yielded by a long discount security, we think of that rate as being the rate i' that the investor would earn if interest were paid to him at the 6-month mark *and* if interest were paid on that interest over the bill's remaining days to maturity.

In this case the amount, price P, that would yield an investor \$1 of face value at maturity is given by the expression

$$P + \frac{i'}{2} P + \frac{i'}{365} \left(t_{sm} - \frac{365}{2} \right) \left(1 + \frac{i'}{2} \right) P = 1$$

This expression for i', which we take to be d_b, can be written more simply as follows

$$P \left(1 + \frac{i'}{2} \right) \left[1 + \frac{i'}{2} \left(\frac{2t_{sm}}{365} - 1 \right) \right] = 1$$

Solving this expression for i', we get[2]

$$i' = d_b = \frac{ -\dfrac{2t_{sm}}{365} + 2\sqrt{ \left(\dfrac{t_{sm}}{365} \right)^2 - \left(\dfrac{2t_{sm}}{365} - 1 \right) \left(1 - \dfrac{1}{P} \right) } }{ \dfrac{2t_{sm}}{365} - 1 }$$

To illustrate, consider the bill in Table 4–1 that matures on 10/16/79. Its asked rate was 9.35 and it had 190 days to run. Inserting these numbers into the formula for i', we get

---

[2] The solution is done as follows. First the expression

$$P \left(1 + \frac{i'}{2} \right) \left[1 + \frac{i'}{2} \left(\frac{2t_{sm}}{365} - 1 \right) \right] = 1$$

is multiplied out, and the resulting equation is simplified to obtain

$$i'^2 \left(\frac{2t_{sm}}{365} - 1 \right) + i' \frac{4t_{sm}}{365} + 4 \left(1 - \frac{1}{P} \right) = 0$$

This is a standard quadratic equation of the form

$$ax^2 + bx + c = 0$$

The solution to such an equation is

$$x = \frac{-2b \pm \sqrt{b^2 - 4ac}}{2a}$$

Applying this formula to our quadratic equation in i' and simplifying terms, we get

$$i' = \frac{ -\dfrac{2t_{sm}}{365} + 2\sqrt{ \left(\dfrac{t_{sm}}{365} \right)^2 - \left(\dfrac{2t_{sm}}{365} - 1 \right) \left(1 - \dfrac{1}{P} \right) } }{ \dfrac{2t_{sm}}{365} - 1 }$$

$$i' = \frac{-\dfrac{2 \times 190}{365} + 2 \sqrt{\left(\dfrac{190}{365}\right)^2 - \left(\dfrac{2 \times 190}{365} - 1\right)\left(1 - \dfrac{1}{0.950653}\right)}}{\dfrac{2 \times 190}{365} - 1}$$

$$= 0.0995$$

that is, 9.95 percent, which is the number given on the quote sheet as the bill's coupon yield equivalent.

Solving for equivalent bond yield (coupon yield equivalent) on a discount security

Let

$$d = \text{rate of discount (decimal)}$$
$$d_b = \text{equivalent bond yield (decimal)}$$
$$t_{sm} = \text{days from settlement to maturity}$$

Case A: Security has 6 months (182 days) or less to run:

$$d_b = \frac{365d}{360 - dt_{sm}}$$

Case B: Security has more than 6 months (182 days) to run:

$$d_b = \frac{-\dfrac{2t_{sm}}{365} + 2 \sqrt{\left(\dfrac{t_{sm}}{365}\right)^2 - \left(\dfrac{2t_{sm}}{365} - 1\right)\left(1 - \dfrac{1}{P}\right)}}{\dfrac{2t_{sm}}{365} - 1}$$

5

More fundamentals and some applications

This chapter is one of the key chapters in the book because it covers *two* important topics that, from the point of view of exposition, are difficult to separate. One is the application of the formulas derived in Chapter 4 for *discount* securities. The second is certain fundamentals of money market calculations that are most easily explained if concrete illustrations are used; these fundamentals are basic to much of what is said not only here about *discount* securities but also later about *interest-bearing* securities.

COMPOUNDING REVISITED

First we turn to fundamentals: the importance and meaning of compound rates and the problem of comparing rates on a correct basis. Suppose, to illustrate our remarks, that the yield curve at the short end of the market is flat and that 30-day and 90-day bills both yield 9 percent on a discount basis. Using the formula

$$i = \frac{365d}{360 - dt_{sm}}$$

it is easy to calculate that this means that on a simple interest basis the 30-day bill will yield 9.19 percent and the 90-day bill, 9.34 percent. These numbers correspond, of course, to the figures that would be recorded on the quote sheet as the equivalent bond yields, d_b, at which these bills are offered.

Note that converting to a simple interest rate raises the yield on the 90-day bill 15 basis points above that on the 30-day bill—a result we would expect because, from the preceding formula for i, it is obvious that i will be higher the longer the time period, t_{sm}, over which a given rate of discount d is earned.

So far so good, but our comparison of the yields on the 30- and 90-day bills is not yet correct. The reason is that it fails to take into account a subtle but simple fact: namely, that the 30-day bill is worth something extra to the investor because he gets his money in 30 rather than 90 days. To see this, note that if our investor had the opportunity to invest in three consecutive 30-day bill issues, each offered at a 9 percent rate of discount, he would earn something more than a 9 percent rate of discount over the 90-day period because he would have the opportunity to reinvest earnings twice. In short, our old friend from Chapter 3, *compounding*, would come into play.

Compounding over 1 year

Earlier we derived a formula for calculating the effective return earned, when a simple interest rate, i, is compounded n times during the year. It is

$$i^* = \left(1 + \frac{i}{n}\right)^n - 1$$

Using this formula, we observe that if our investor were to roll the 30-day bill over *a whole year* at a 9 percent rate of discount, there would be 365/30 compounding periods, and he would earn a compound rate of

$$i^* = \left(1 + \frac{0.0919}{365/30}\right)^{365/30} - 1 = 9.588\%$$

If, alternatively, he were to roll the 90-day bill over *a whole year* at a 9 percent rate of discount, there would be 365/90 compounding periods, and he would earn a compound rate of

$$i^* = \left(1 + \frac{0.0934}{365/90}\right)^{365/90} - 1 = 9.674\%$$

Over a year compounding would reduce the yield advantage offered by the 90-day bill from 15 to 8.6 basis points (Table 5–1).

Table 5–1
Yield comparison on different bases (%)

	d Rate d discount	$i = d_b$ Equivalent bond yield	i^*, Effective return with compounding Investment period is 90 days	Investment period is 365 days
30-day bill...........	9.00	9.19	9.260	9.588
90-day bill...........	9.00	9.34	9.340	9.674
Difference in yield	0.00	0.15	0.080	0.086

Compounding over less than 1 year

Assume now that our portfolio manager's investment period is *less than 1 year*, specifically, that it is 90 days because he must make a tax payment 90 days hence. If he invests in the 30-day bill, over the 90-day period he will be able to reinvest not 365/30 or 12.17 times, but only three times, and the i^* rate calculated above is therefore too high.

When *the investment period is known to be less than 1 year*, to convert a simple interest rate to the correct annual effective return, one must first calculate the compound rate of return earned over the investment period and then annualize that rate. Let

n = compounding periods *during 1 year*
n' = compounding periods *during the investment period*
t = days in the investment period

Then if t is less than 365,

$$i^* = \left[\left(1 + \frac{i}{n}\right)^{n'} - 1\right]\frac{365}{t}$$

Using this formula, we conclude that rolling a 9 percent, 30-day bill over a 90-day investment period would yield a compound rate of

$$i^* = \left[\left(1 + \frac{0.0919}{365/30}\right)^3 - 1\right]\frac{365}{90}$$

$$= 9.26\%$$

Note that when properly compounded rates are compared, the difference over a 90-day investment period between the yields at which the 30- and 90-day bills are offered is reduced from 15 to 8 basis points (Table 5–1). Note also that this difference is slightly less than the one that would prevail if the portfolio manager's investment period were a full year.

As our remarks suggest, the difference between a simple interest rate and the corresponding effective rate increases the more times compounding occurs; this difference thus grows as the investment period lengthens. A dramatic illustration of this point, which is easy to overlook but obvious once noted, is given by the figures in Table 5–2.

Calculating an effective return, i^*, when the investment period is *less than 1 year*

Let

i = simple interest rate paid
i^* = effective return with compounding
n = compounding periods *during one year*
n' = compounding periods *during the investment period*
t = days in the investment period

Then

$$i^* = \left[\left(1 + \frac{i}{n}\right)^{n'} - 1\right]\frac{365}{t}$$

The example we have just presented correctly suggests a crucial point: *Since it is always worth something to the investor to get yield dollars sooner than later, comparisons between the yields on securities of differing maturity should always be made on the basis of the appropriate effective rates (values of i^*) at which they are offered when opportunities for compounding are taken into account; also in making such comparisons, the length of the investment period should be taken into account if it is known to be less than 1 year.*[1]

---

[1] Among money market traders who appreciate the importance of compounding, it is always common practice to compare different rates on the basis of the effective rates that would be obtained if compounding occurred *over a full year*. Note that our formula for calculating i^* over a period of less than 1 year,

Table 5–2
Effective return earned when an 8% rate is compounded daily over investment periods of varying lengths

Investment period (days)	Effective return (%)
1	8.0000
30	8.0255
60	8.0519
90	8.0785
182	8.1608
365*	8.3278

* An institutional investor, even if he rolls overnight funds, cannot get compounding 364 times during a year because compounding occurs only on business days. A few investors take this into account in compounding overnight rates.

When compounding is possible, comparing rates on an effective basis is as important for *interest-bearing* as for *discount* securities—a point to which we will return in Part III. Here it suffices to note that yield to maturity figures given for coupon securities on a quote sheet all understate the effective rate offered over a year because they fail to reflect the fact that coupon interest is paid semiannually. In short, yield to maturity on a quote sheet is an i rate rather than the effective semiannually compounded i^* rate.

The Interpretation of i^*

An investor who calculates i^* on an investment that offers opportunities for compounding can never be sure that he will receive that rate. His estimate of the investment period may prove incorrect. Also and more important, the rate at which he reinvests may differ significantly from the rate at which he initially invests.

To illustrate, note that if the investor in our example chose to invest for 90 days by rolling the 30-day bill, he could be certain of earning a 9.26 percent rate on a compound basis only if he were certain (1) that his investment period would in fact be 90 days and (2) that he could reinvest on roll dates at a 9 percent rate of discount. Clearly certainty on at least the latter count would be hard, if not impossible, for him to come by.

In selecting securities, an investor seeks those that offer him the greatest *relative value*, which in street jargon means the securities that offer him the best available

$$i^* = \left[\left(1 + \frac{i}{n} \right)^{n'} - 1 \right] \frac{365}{t}$$

gives more accurate numbers when monies will be available for investment for a period substantially shorter than 365 days. Also in certain situations not to use our formula would be awkward. Consider, for example, a trader who wants to finance with *overnight* repo for 30 days a 90-day piece of paper. To put his financing cost on a basis comparable to the yield on the paper financed, he must either (1) use our formula to calculate his true financing rate with compounding or (2) less accurately and more awkwardly compound *both* rates over a full year. See, for example, Table 5–5 and the footnote to it on page 48.

combination of risk, liquidity, and return given his investment parameters. In comparing the returns offered by different securities, the logical first step for the investor is to compare these rates on a properly compounded basis assuming no change in either the general level of interest rates or the shape of the yield curve. Once that comparison is made, the investor can superimpose on it his own rate forecast. If, in a given situation, a short security offers him as much or more return when compounding is taken into account than a longer security does, and if in addition the investor anticipates that if rates change at all they will rise, his choice is easy. If, alternatively, he anticipates that rates might fall, his choice becomes more difficult. In either case the important thing to note about i^* is that it is a benchmark number that is used in the determination of a security's relative value; it is not a certain forecast of the return that the security will provide.

We have stressed that, in choosing among securities of differing maturities, the investor should compare the offered rates on a properly compounded basis because failing to do so would be to compare apples and oranges. To this we should add that in many situations it suffices to compare rates on a simple interest or discount basis because doing so in fact results in a comparison of apples and apples. For example, an investor who is swapping out of 60-day bills into 60-day BAs need not calculate either i or i^* values for the two securities to determine how large a yield pickup he is getting. Similarly, an investor who is considering buying a security and financing it with term repo to maturity need compare only the simple interest rates involved to determine whether the transaction would be profitable; he must, however, be careful, as noted below, to compare those rates on the same basis, namely a 365-day or a 360-day year.

FORMULAS, DOLLAR FLOWING, AND APPROXIMATIONS

So far we have concentrated on deriving formulas that permit us to derive precisely and interpret correctly various money market numbers. The ability to develop and manipulate simple algebraic expressions is important for any money market participant who wants to "know the numbers." Such formulas are, however, sometimes tricky to develop even for an experienced person. For this reason it is useful to *dollar flow* at least one example of every problem for which a new formula is worked out. Specifically, one starts by developing a formula for calculating some number on a given type of transaction, say, a break-even price or yield; next, one applies this formula to a particular numerical example of the transaction; finally, one calculates the dollars in and dollars out that would result if the transaction were actually carried out at the calculated number to test that the break-even number given by the formula is in fact a true break-even.

While precision is important to money market traders, so too is time. In a rapidly changing market, a trader will not be successful if his response time is 5 minutes because he must do two or three calculations to determine his proper action under prevailing market conditions. Recognizing this, traders have developed a number of *approximations* that permit them to make quick and quite accurate estimates of true numbers. Such approximations are useful, even vital, but the practitioner must know the fundamental equations because all approximations used by traders have a built-in *bias* that makes the individual transaction being evaluated look more or less favorable than it is. Thus, knowing (1) the direction of the bias and (2) how sensitive the approximation is to the length of the transaction and to the height of interest rates is crucial to market success. The first can be determined by knowing the fundamentals, the second by dollar flowing a few examples.

In cases where the bias becomes large or where it works against the trader, the way to make quick market judgments is to develop computer programs that will, when market quotes are inputed, produce a printout of vitally needed numbers that do not appear on the quote sheet. Production of such *visual aids* is particularly important because existing money and bond market calculators, which are all programmed identically and incorrectly, do not always give true yield to maturity figures. Also they are not wired nor can they be programmed to calculate instantaneously many numbers that money market people need. The forthcoming Basis Point Calculator promises to do this job.

Illustrations of approximations and the usefulness of visual aids are provided in the discussion of applications that follows.

FIGURING THE TAIL

One common calculation made by money market traders is to *figure a tail*. This calculation is sometimes done using a simple and quick *approximation*. In our discussion of tails, we will first illustrate the approximation with an example, then investigate the inherent bias in the approximation, and finally check our conclusion about the bias by dollar flowing our example. A better approximation plus a method for figuring the *true* tail are given in Table 5–5 and the accompanying footnote (p. 48). When interest rates are high, these should be used.

The approximation approach

Dealers and investors sometimes finance securities they position with term RP, for example, finance with 30-day RP a security with 3 months to run. Often, when they do so, they are creating a future security and betting that they can sell it at a profit. In judging the attractiveness of this bet, dealers always rely on an explicit prediction of where funds will trade and what yields spreads will prevail at the time the term RP comes off.

The easiest way to explain what is involved is with an example. Assume a dealer is operating in an environment in which the 90-day bill is trading at a rate ⅛ below the Fed funds rate. Assume also that Fed funds are trading at 4⅞, the 90-day bill at 4¾, and 30-day term RP at 4½.

If in this environment the dealer were to buy a 90-day bill and finance it with 30-day term RP, he would earn over the 30-day holding period a positive carry equal to approximately (because the two rates are not directly comparable):

$$4\tfrac{3}{4} - 4\tfrac{1}{2}$$

or a profit equal to ¼ over 30 days. He would also have created a *future* 60-day bill, namely, the unfinanced *tail* of the 90-day bill purchased.

If he thought, as dealers do, of the carry profit over the initial holding period as raising the yield at which he in effect buys the future security, then by purchasing the 90-day bill at 4¾ and RPing it for 30 days at 4½, he would have acquired a future 60-day bill at a yield of 4⅞.[2] The ¼ carry, which is earned for 30 days, adds only ⅛ to the yield at which the future security is effectively purchased because the latter has a maturity of 60 days, which is twice as long as the period over which positive carry is earned.

---

[2] Note that the *higher* the yield at which a discount security is purchased, the *lower* the purchase price. So buying the future security at 4⅞ is, from the dealer's point of view, better than buying it at 4¾.

Faced with this opportunity, the dealer would ask himself: How attractive is it to contract to buy a 60-day bill at 4⅞ for delivery 30 days hence? Note the dealer figures he would break even, clearing costs ignored, if he were able to sell that future bill at a rate of 4⅞. Thus, contracting to buy the future bill will be attractive if he believes he can sell the future bill at a rate lower than 4⅞.

The dealer's answer to the question he has posed might run as follows: Currently the yield curve is such that 60-day bills are trading ⅛ below the rate on 90-day bills. Therefore, if the 60-day bill were to trade at 4⅞ 1 month hence and if yield spreads did not change, that would imply that the 90-day bill was trading at 5 and Fed funds at 5⅛, that is, at a level ¼ above the present rate. I do not believe that the Fed will tighten or that yield spreads will change in an unfavorable way, therefore I will do the trade.

If the dealer were correct and the Fed did not tighten and yield spreads did not change, he would be able to sell 30 days hence the future 60-day bill he had created at 4⅝, which is the rate that would be the prevailing rate at that time on the 60-day bill, if his predictions with respect to yield and yields spread were correct.[3] In doing so, he would make, according to his calculation, a profit equal to ¼ (the purchase rate 4⅞ minus the sale rate 4⅝) on a 60-day security.

Of course, the dealer's predictions might prove to be too favorable. Note, however, he has some built-in margin of protection. Specifically, if he is able to sell his future bills at any rate above 4⅝ but still below 4⅞, he will, as his approximation tells him, make some profit, albeit less than he would if he sold at 4⅝. If, on the other hand, rates or rate spreads move so unfavorably that he ends up selling his future 60-day bill at a rate above 4⅞, he will incur a loss.

The approximation method used by dealers to figure the tail on a discount security can be stated as a simple formula;

$$\begin{pmatrix} \text{Effective yield} \\ \text{at which future} \\ \text{security is} \\ \text{purchased} \end{pmatrix} = \begin{pmatrix} \text{Yield at} \\ \text{which cash} \\ \text{security is} \\ \text{purchased} \end{pmatrix} + \begin{pmatrix} \dfrac{\dfrac{\text{Rate of profit}}{\text{on carry}} \times \dfrac{\text{Days}}{\text{carried}}}{\dfrac{\text{Days left to maturity}}{\text{at end of carry period}}} \end{pmatrix}$$

Applying this formula to our example, we get:

$$4\tfrac{3}{4} + \frac{\tfrac{1}{4} \times 30}{60} = 4\tfrac{3}{4} + \tfrac{1}{8} = 4\tfrac{7}{8}$$

The notation we developed in Chapter 3 makes it possible to restate the above formula more economically. To do so, all that is required is the introduction of an asterisk and several subscripts. See the box on page 43.

The nature of the approximation

For people accustomed to thinking in terms of dollars rather than yields, the dealer's method of approximating the tail is inherently confusing; such people have difficulty seeing how or why the method works. To minimize such confusion, we present in Table 5–3 the example we have just worked out on a step-by-step basis in terms of dollars.

The dealer's method of figuring the tail is an approximation because the two rates

---

[3] Recall the 60-day bill was assumed to be trading at a rate ⅛ below the rate on the 90-day bill, at 4¾ − ⅛ = 4⅝.

A formula for approximating the tail on a *discount* security financed with term repo*

Let

d = rate of discount at purchase (decimal)
$d*$ = approximate *break-even* sale rate
r_t = term repo rate
t_{is} = days from issue (or purchase) to settlement, which is taken to be the day the term repo comes off
t_{sm} = days from settlement to maturity

Then

$$d* = d + (d - r_t) \frac{t_{is}}{t_{sm}}$$

---

*For a more accurate approximation, see Table 5–5 and the accompanying footnote, page 48.

---

used in the calculation are not comparable; both are 360-day rates, but the bill rate, which is a discount rate, is understated relative to the term RP rate, which is an add-on rate.

To see the error this noncomparability introduces, note that in Table 5–3, in order to get to the result implied by the dealer's calculation, we had to figure the financing cost as if the bills were RPed for full face value. Had they been RPed at the lesser dollar figure paid for them, the financing cost:

$$0.045 \left(\frac{30}{360} \right) \$988,125 = \$3,705$$

would have been $45 less than the $3,750 figure shown in Table 5–3. The rate on the tail created by the dealer would have been slightly more than 4⅞.

The correct dollar figures for our example are summarized in Table 5–4, which dollar flows the transaction. Note that all inflows and outflows recorded are *dated*. The importance of dating is discussed on page 119.

Bias

Since the dealer's method of approximating a bill tail underestimates his true break-even sale rate, approximation will not cause the dealer to view the gamble he is considering as being more favorable than it is. Thus, estimation is justified.

This observation suggests an important point. If in this type of borrow-invest situation, the approximation understates the investment rate relative to the borrowing rate, the person who approximates is on safe ground. If it does the opposite, however, the trader must find a more accurate method of calculation or else dollar flow trades before he does them. Many traders forget this and end up locking in a loss when they think they are locking in a profit.

A final and important point about our example of figuring the tail is that the bias in the trader's method of approximating the tail is highly *sensitive to the level of interest rates*. Had we, for example, assumed that the 90-day bill was purchased at a rate of

Table 5–3
Figuring the tail: An example

Step 1: The dealer buys \$1 million of 90-day bills at 4¾ percent rate of discount.
$$\text{Discount at which bills are purchased} = \frac{dt_{sm}}{360}F = \frac{0.0475(90)}{360}\$1,000,000$$
$$= \$11,875$$

$$\text{Price at which bills are purchased} = F - D$$
$$= \$1,000,000 - \$11,875$$
$$= \$988,125$$
The dealer finances the bills purchased for 30 days at 4½ percent.
$$\text{Financing cost}^* = \frac{0.045(30)}{360}\$1,000,000$$
$$= \$3,750$$

Step 2: At the end of 30 days the dealer owns the bills at a net cost figure. Determine what yield this cost figure implies on the future 60-day bills created.
$$\text{Net cost of future 60-day bills} = \text{Purchase price} + \text{Financing cost}$$
$$= \$988,125 + \$3,750$$
$$= \$991,875$$

$$\text{Net discount at which future 60-day bills are owned} = F - \text{Net cost}$$
$$= \$1,000,000 - \$991,875$$
$$= \$8,125$$

$$\text{Rate at which future 60-day bills are purchased} = \frac{360D}{t_{sm}F}$$
$$= \frac{360(\$8,125)}{60(\$1,000,000)}$$
$$= 0.04875$$
$$= 4\tfrac{7}{8}\%$$

Step 3: Future 60-day bills created are sold at a 4⅝ percent discount rate. Calculate dollar profit.
$$\text{Discount at which bills are sold} = F\frac{dt_{sm}}{360}$$
$$= \$1,000,000\frac{0.04625(60)}{360}$$
$$= \$7,708$$

$$\text{Profit} = Net \text{ purchase discount} - \text{Discount at sale}$$
$$= \$8,125 - \$7,708$$
$$= \$417$$

Step 4: Figure the annualized yield on a discount basis that \$417 represents on a 60-day security.
$$d = \frac{360D}{t_{sm}F} = \frac{360(\$417)}{60(\$1,000,000)}$$
$$= 0.0025$$
$$= \tfrac{1}{4}\%$$

---

*Actually less than \$1 million has to be borrowed, so the dealer's approach to figuring the tail is only an approximation.

discount of 10 and RPed at 9.75, the trader's formula would estimate the rate on the tail as being 10.125 when in fact it would be 10.247. The trader's approximation would have underestimated by almost half the gain added by the term RP to the effective yield at which the tail is purchased.

This point is important. Our example was set in a period when the 90-day bill could be financed at a *positive* carry. Such financing was not possible in the high-interest-rate

Table 5–4
Dollar flowing the tail: An example

Dollars in		Dollars out	
Day 1:			
RP bills at 4½ percent	$ 988,125	$ 988,125	Buy bills at 4¾ percent
Day 30:			
Sell bills at break-even		988,125	Repay RP loan
rate of 4⅞ percent	991,875	3,705	Pay RP interest
Total dollars in	$1,980,000	$1,979,955	Total dollars out

(Total dollars in) − (Total dollars out) = $45

environment prevailing at the end of the 1970s. At that time a trader could hope to profit on a bill tail only if the *negative* slope of the yield curve created a high probability that he could sell the tail at a rate sufficiently below the purchase rate to more than cover his *negative* carry.

LOSING YOUR TAIL

A term RP to maturity

The importance of comparing money market rates on the same basis is hard to overemphasize. Here is a case in point, a situation in which traders who forget this rule unintentionally lock in losses—"lose their tails"—time and again.

To illustrate we set the stage as follows: The Treasury has put out a cash management bill that will mature in 40 days. The bill can be bought in the market at a discount of 9.76, and 40-day term repo money can be obtained at 9.90. A trader is considering whether to buy the bills and finance them to maturity. At first the transaction looks unattractive, *but* the trader realizes that the two rates are not comparable. So he looks at the equivalent bond yield on the bill, which is 10 percent. Now the transaction takes on some allure. It appears that, by buying the bill and putting it out on term RP to maturity, a profit margin of 10 basis points can be locked in over the length of the transaction.

A trader who reasons this way has forgotten an elementary but important point: The RP rate is quoted on a 360-day basis, whereas the equivalent bond yield on a bill is quoted on a 365-day basis. Therefore, to make the two rates comparable, he *must* convert the figure for equivalent bond yield to a 360-day basis as follows:

$$10\%(360/365) = 9.86\%$$

This simple calculation shows immediately that the proposed purchase and RP to maturity would result not in a profit but in a guaranteed loss of 4 basis points a day. On a $10 million transaction that would cost him around $11 a day plus transactions costs. Note that the size of the loss per day is not sensitive to the time for which the transaction is put on, but the longer it is outstanding, the greater the loss locked in will be.

Paying daily interest

Some people think that the major advantage of using term RP financing is the reduction in risk that locking up a certain borrowing rate affords the trader, but more is involved. A trader who does *overnight* RP or agrees to pay *daily interest* on a term RP is paying not a simple interest rate but a *daily* compounded one.

Using our formula for calculating effective return when compounding is done daily, we find that daily compounding increases a 9.90 percent rate over a 40-day period to[4]

$$\left[\left(1 + \frac{0.099}{360}\right)^{40} - 1\right] \frac{360}{40} = 9.95\%$$

Thus, if our trader had agreed to pay daily interest on his term RP or had happened to finance his bills *day to day* at 9.90 percent, he would have ended up *locking in a not a 4- but a 9-basis-point negative carry* on an apparently profitable transaction. At high interest rates the power of daily compounding is something no trader or investor can afford to forget.

Moral: If you receive or pay out interest on a daily basis, don't compare that rate with other nondaily rates before compounding it.

The increase in the RP rate—from 9.90 to 9.95—that occurred when we compounded it daily over a 40-day period may suggest to certain readers that some mathematical fiction has crept into the argument. Surely those traders who willingly agree to pay daily interest on term RP will feel that way. They are wrong, as a dollar-and-cents calculation of interest actually paid out in the two situations will show.

THE COST OF CAPITAL

In our example of figuring the tail, to keep things simple we assumed that the amount borrowed precisely equaled the purchase price of the bills financed. A more typical situation would be that the lender would demand some margin, *haircut* in street jargon, for protection against failure of the borrower; that is, he would value the bills as *collateral* (an RP is in essence a collateralized loan) at something less than market value.

In that case *the difference between the value of the bills purchased and the amount of the repo borrowing would have to be financed out of the dealer's capital.* Some cost should clearly be assigned to that capital. Otherwise the transaction would appear to be more profitable than it actually is, because if the capital were not used for that purpose, it could be used for another. In other words, the dealer who engages in a transaction that uses capital incurs some *opportunity cost.* There is no hard and fast rule as to how that cost should be measured, but for a dealer a good rule of thumb is to assign to its capital a cost equal to *at least* the prevailing dealer loan rate at its clearing bank. The reason is that dealers always finance some proportion of their total position at their bank, and a transaction that uses capital will require them to increase marginally their bank borrowing.

A dealer who takes haircuts on securities he RPs uses capital. In an equally obvious way, a dealer who pays daily interest on a repo that finances a security such as a bill that pays no return until it is sold or matures uses capital. Moreover, because he does, he is forced to increase his total borrowing, which costs money. That cost is not fully reflected even when the RP rate is compounded to allow for the daily payment of interest. The reason is that compounding the RP rate reflects the total dollars of interest that are paid out but *not* the fact that paying out dollars daily requires that the firm either use capital or borrow more dollars during the financing period.

---

[4] See pages 37–39. Assuming compounding over *a whole year*, i.e., using the formula

$$i^* = \left(1 - \frac{i}{n}\right)^n - 1$$

would yield too high a figure for the financing cost.

Why do traders so often ignore the effect of compounding when daily interest is paid? Savings institutions that pay it never do in their advertising. In some cases the answer is that the traders claim "they don't want to know about numbers," which means that they want to be free to gamble with someone else's money. In other cases the explanation is the way capital is assigned to traders in some dealerships. Not infrequently a trader in a dealership will be told that he has been assigned $X million of capital and that some percentage rate on that money will be charged against his profit and loss (P&L) account whether he uses the capital or not. That sort of arrangement may achieve some management goal such as holding down the profit and therefore the monetary reward attributed to the trader, but it also creates a perverse situation in which actions by the trader that cost the firm money are not reflected on his P&L.

For example, if a trader who is not using all the capital assigned to him wants to do a term RP and the lender casually asks for daily interest, the trader is likely to say yes even though his acquiescence costs the firm money. The reason is that the capital eaten up through the payment of daily interest is a *free good* to the trader because he is already paying for it. To the firm, however, that capital is anything but free. In fact, the opportunity cost of using it may be so high that a transaction that improves the trader's P&L may cost the firm money.

ANOTHER "TAIL" QUESTION

Earlier we asked: For a given bill that is going to be RPed for a fixed time at a known rate, what will the tail be? A second question traders of tails often ask is: If a given bill is repoed at a fixed spread between the bill and the repo rates, for how many days must the resulting positive carry be earned to add 1 basis point to the tail?

The answer can be dollar flowed but that is time-consuming. Fortunately, there is a quick method that gives a good approximation. To see why it works, note first that 1 basis point on a 90-day bill is worth 90 1-day basis points. Similarly 1 basis point on a year bill is worth 364 1-day basis points.

Now suppose that the year bill can be RPed at a positive spread of 90 basis points. This means that the repo adds to the yield on the tail approximately (the two rates are not comparable) 90 1-day basis points each day that it is on. Thus one can estimate that it will take 4 days for the repo to add 364 1-day basis points, i.e., 1 basis point, to the tail of

---

Method for calculating approximately how fast positive carry will increase the tail on a discount security financed with term repo*

Let

i = simple interest rate on 360-day basis yielded by the discount security being financed

r_t = term repo rate

t_{sm} = days from settlement to maturity

$$\begin{pmatrix} \text{Number of days required to} \\ \text{add 1 basis point to tail} \end{pmatrix} = \frac{t_{sm}}{100(i - r_t)}$$

* For a formula to calculate the true break-even rate on the sale of a bill tail, see the footnote to Table 5–5.

the year bill being financed. Obviously the more quickly the basis points build up on the tail, the more favorable buying the security and financing it will appear to a trader. (See the box on page 47.)

The calculation we have just outlined is an approximation. To make it as accurate as possible, the bill's yield should be calculated on a simple interest, 360-day basis before being compared with the repo rate. (See the boxes on pages 20 and 32.)

The accuracy of this technique is illustrated by the example in Table 5–5. Note that this technique is an improvement over the formula given on page 43 for figuring the tail on a discount security.

Table 5–5
Estimating the rate of tail pickup on a 10% year bill that is RPed†

Data

$$\text{Bill's current maturity} = 364 \text{ days}$$
$$d = 10.00$$
$$\text{Simple interest yield, 360-day basis} = i = 11.12$$
$$\text{Term repo rate} = r_t = 10.20$$
$$\text{Carry} = 100(i - r_t) = 92 \text{ basis points}$$

I. Approximate days needed to pickup one basis point

$$\text{Days needed to raise tail yield by 1 basis point} = \frac{364}{92} = 3.96 \text{ days}$$

True tail pickup produced by a 4-day RP = 0.93 basis points

II. Approximate yield pickup on a 30-day RP

$$\text{Anticipated yield pickup over 30 days} = \frac{30}{3.96} = 7.58 \text{ basis points}$$

True yield pickup produced by a 30-day RP = 7.47 basis points

---

† The true break-even rate of sale on the tail is figured as follows. Let

$$d^* = \text{break-even sale rate on the tail}$$
$$d_1 = \text{rate at which bill is purchased}$$
$$t_1 = \text{days to maturity at purchase}$$
$$t_2 = \text{days to maturity at sale}$$
$$r_t = \text{term repo rate}$$
$$t_1 - t_2 = \text{financing period}$$

Then, by setting dollars in equal to dollars out, it is easy to show that

$$d^* = \left[1 - \left(1 - \frac{d_1 t_1}{360}\right)\left(1 + r_t \frac{t_1 - t_2}{360}\right)\right] \frac{360}{t_2}$$

Using this formula, one calculates the *true* yield pick up on an RP as follows:

$$\text{true yield pickup} = d_1 - d^*$$

Visual aids

If the approximation method we have just outlined is applied to a bill with a current maturity of 6 months or less, calculating the bill's yield on a simple interest, 360-day basis is easy. One merely takes its equivalent bond yield and multiplies by 360/365.

If, however, the bill has a life of more than 6 months, the calculation has to be made by converting the discount rate directly to the appropriate simple interest rate. The formula for doing this:

$$\left(\begin{array}{c}\text{Simple interest rate yielded by a discount}\\ \text{security on a 360-day basis}\end{array}\right) = \frac{360d}{360 - dt_{sm}}$$

is not difficult, but in a rapidly moving market a trader or investor may not want to take the time to apply it.[5] The answer to this dilemma is *visual aids*.

Each morning a bill trader should get a sheet that displays the equivalent bond yield and the true simple interest rate on a 360-day basis that key long bill issues would yield at rates of discount identical with or near those at which these bills closed the preceding day. Another useful visual aid for a trader who is bidding in a bill auction or trading bills is sheets showing for 91-, 182- and 364-day bills the following: price, rate of discount, coupon equivalent yield, and true simple interest yield on a 360-day basis. Part of such a sheet is reproduced in Table 5–6 on page 50.

The major trick in creating visual aids is not programming the computer to produce the correct numbers but programming it to display those numbers in such a way that the trader can consult the sheet quickly and correctly.

SHORTING

A trader who anticipates an increase in rates and a decrease in bill prices may choose to short a particular issue. In order not to "fail," he must obtain bills to deliver to the buyer either by *borrowing* the securities or by doing a *reverse repo*, i.e., reversing in the needed securities.

The normal fee for borrowing securities is 50 basis points. Unless the period of the borrowing is fixed at the outset, borrowing securities exposes the trader to the danger that, just when interest rates are going up and the short is becoming profitable, the lender may decide to call back his securities either because he wants to sell them to get cash or because he thinks it is the correct moment to sell.

To avoid this difficulty and to cut costs, traders typically use reverses to cover shorts. When a trader does a reverse, he is *borrowing securities* and *lending money*. The rate he gets on the money he lends will depend on prevailing rate relationships and in particular on whether the issue he shorts is one that many traders want to short. Typically the rate at which he lends will be no more than 50 basis points below the rate on the bill shorted: However, if the trader wants to short an issue that many traders want to short, he will be shopping for what the street calls a *special*, and the rate he gets on his loan may be particularly depressed by the demand of shorters for that issue.

Regardless of how a trader covers a bill short, he will typically experience a *negative carry*—either a fee of 50 basis points charged by the borrower or some spread between the bill rate and the lower reverse rate. In such an environment the trader can make money on his short only if market rates rise (bill prices fall) sufficiently so that the spread between the prices at which he buys and sells exceeds the cost to him of putting on and maintaining the short.

In effect a trader who shorts bills is creating a *negative* tail; for him to profit, the rate at which he can purchase that tail must increase over the period of the short. Thus he faces a break-even problem that is similar to but opposite in direction to that of a trader creating a "positive" tail.[6]

---

[5] To derive this equation, simply take the expression for i on page 32 and multiply it by 360/365 to change i to a 360-day-year basis. Doing so yields:

$$i = \left(\frac{365d}{360 - dt_{sm}}\right)\frac{360}{365} = \frac{360d}{360 - dt_{sm}}$$

[6] Note the investor who creates a tail by buying a security and RPing it wants rates to remain stable or fall over the repo period.

Table 5–6
Visual aid for a bill trader

```
BILLS MATURE IN 182 DAYS

PRICE              DISC              CPN YIELD          TRUE YIELD
```

PRICE	DISC	CPN YIELD	TRUE YIELD
93.428	13	14.108	13.914
93.426	13.004	14.112	13.919
93.424	13.007	14.116	13.923
93.422	13.011	14.121	13.927
93.42	13.015	14.126	13.932
93.418	13.019	14.13	13.936
93.416	13.023	14.135	13.941
93.414	13.027	14.139	13.945
93.412	13.031	14.144	13.95
93.41	13.035	14.149	13.955
93.408	13.039	14.153	13.959
93.406	13.043	14.158	13.964
93.404	13.047	14.162	13.968
93.402	13.051	14.167	13.973
93.4	13.055	14.172	13.978
93.398	13.059	14.176	13.982
93.396	13.063	14.181	13.987
93.394	13.067	14.185	13.991
93.392	13.071	14.19	13.996
93.39	13.075	14.195	14
93.388	13.079	14.199	14.005
93.386	13.083	14.204	14.01
93.384	13.087	14.208	14.014
93.382	13.091	14.213	14.019
93.38	13.095	14.218	14.023
93.378	13.098	14.222	14.027
93.376	13.102	14.227	14.031
93.374	13.106	14.231	14.036
93.372	13.11	14.236	14.041
93.37	13.114	14.241	14.045
93.368	13.118	14.245	14.05
93.366	13.122	14.25	14.054
93.364	13.126	14.254	14.059
93.362	13.13	14.259	14.064
93.36	13.134	14.264	14.068
93.358	13.138	14.268	14.073
93.356	13.142	14.273	14.077
93.354	13.146	14.277	14.082
93.352	13.15	14.282	14.086
93.35	13.154	14.287	14.091
93.348	13.158	14.291	14.096
93.346	13.162	14.296	14.1
93.344	13.166	14.3	14.105
93.342	13.17	14.305	14.109
93.34	13.174	14.31	14.114
93.338	13.178	14.314	14.119
93.336	13.182	14.319	14.123
93.334	13.186	14.323	14.128
93.332	13.189	14.328	14.131
93.33	13.193	14.333	14.136
93.328	13.197	14.337	14.14
93.326	13.201	14.342	14.145
93.324	13.205	14.346	14.15
93.322	13.209	14.351	14.154
93.32	13.213	14.356	14.159
93.054	13.739	14.97	14.765

Specifically the trader who is contemplating a short wants to know in how many days his negative carry on the short will increase by 1 basis point the rate at which he must repurchase the bill shorted in order for him to break even on his short. That number as well as his break-even on a short for a longer period can easily be estimated for bills by using the formula in the box on page 47.

A trader who shorts is borrowing money, and to borrow is simply to run a negative portfolio. Thus on reflection it is obvious rather than surprising that formulas for calculating break-evens on tails can also be used to calculate break-evens on shorts.

RIDING THE YIELD CURVE

Frequently an investor who does a break-even analysis will find an opportunity to make a favorable bet, that is, an investment on which the odds favor his making a tidy profit, that he might not have otherwise perceived. Here is an example: the break-even analysis of a common and often misunderstood investment strategy—*riding the yield curve.*

Assume that an investor has funds to invest for 3 months. The 6-month (180-day) bill is trading at 8.50 and the 3-month (90-day) bill is trading at 8.10 (Figure 5–1). The alternatives the investor is choosing between are: (1) to buy the 90-day bill and mature it and (2) to buy the 6-month bill and sell it 3 months hence. To assess the relative merits of these two strategies, the investor does a *break-even analysis.*

Figure 5–1
Yield curve in an example of riding the yield curve

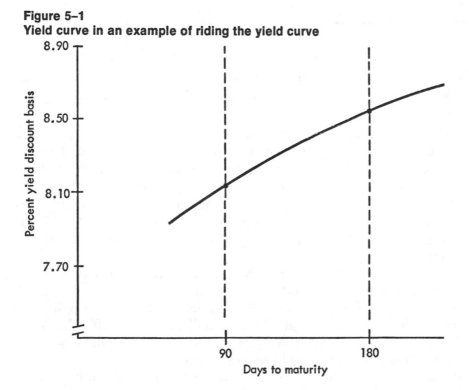

On $1 million of bills, a 90-day basis point is worth $25. If the investor bought the 6-month bill, he would earn 40 basis points more than if he bought the 3-month bill. Thus, he could sell out the 6-month bill after 3 months at a rate 40 basis points above the rate at which he bought it, that is, at 8.90 percent, and still earn as many *dollars* on his investment as he would have if he had bought and matured the 3-month bill (Table 5–7).

Table 5–7
Dollar calculations of return in example of riding the yield curve

I. Buy $1 million of 90-day bills at 8.10 percent and hold to maturity:

Discount at purchase	$20,250
—Discount at maturity	0
Return.	$20,250

II. Buy $1 million of 180-day bills at 8.50 percent and sell at break-even yield of 8.90 percent:

Discount at purchase	$42,500
—Discount at maturity	22,250
Return.	$20,250

III. Buy $1 million of 180-day bills at 8.50 percent and sell at 8.10 percent:

Discount at purchase	$42,500
—Discount at maturity	20,250
Return.	$22,250

Therefore the rate on the 3-month bill 3 months hence would have to rise above 8.90 percent before holding the 6-month bill for 3 months would pay out fewer dollars than buying and maturing the 3-month bill.

How likely is this? Note that because of the slope of the yield curve (a 40-basis-point drop between the 6-month and 3-month bill rates), the rate at which the 3-month bill trades 3 months hence would be 8.10 percent if no change occurred in interest rates, 80 basis points below the break-even rate of 8.90 percent. Thus the investor has 80 basis points of protection and the question he has to ask in making his choice is: How likely is it that the Fed will tighten in the next 3 months so sharply that the 3-month bill will rise 80 basis points? If his answer is that it is unlikely, then he would buy the 6-month bill and ride the yield curve.

Note that if the investor buys the 3-month bill and matures it, he will earn $20,250 on each $1 million of bills he buys (see Table 5–7). If, alternatively, he opts to ride the yield curve and does so successfully (i.e., buys the 6-month bill and is able, because the Fed does not in fact tighten, to sell out at 8.10), he will earn $22,250, which exceeds $20,250 by $2,000. This $2,000 equals the extra 80 90-day basis points he earns: 40 because the 6-month bill is bought at a 40-basis-point spread to the 3-month bill and 40 because he is able to sell it 3 months later at a rate 40 basis points below the rate at which he bought it.

Actually the investor riding the yield curve in our example has more protection than the break-even calculation used indicates. The reason is that, when he buys the 6-month bill, he invests fewer dollars than when he buys the 3-month bill. So on a *simple interest basis,* he would earn an annual return of 8.38 percent if he bought and matured the 3-month bill, whereas if he bought the 6-month bill at 8.10 and sold it at the break-even level of 8.90, he would earn an annual return of 8.40, which is slightly greater.

YIELD EARNED ON A BILL SOLD BEFORE MATURITY

Any trader who sells a bill before maturity will want to know what rate of return he has earned on his investment over the holding period. The formula for calculating this *holding period yield* on a simple interest, 365-day-year basis is easily derived.

To keep our notation simple, we will adopt here a convention also used in later chapters:

> When both prices and days to maturity on *two* separate dates before maturity are involved, we denote the variables referring to the first date with a subscript 1 and those referring to the second date with a subscript 2.

This is preferable to denoting one date as the buy date and the other as the sell date because frequently, as in the present case, the equation is equally useful for calculating the outcome of a reverse-type transaction.

Let

P_1 = dollar price at the beginning of the transaction
P_2 = dollar price at the end of the transaction
d_1 = rate of discount at the beginning of the transaction
d_2 = rate of discount at the end of the transaction
t_1 = days to maturity at the beginning of the transaction
t_2 = days to maturity at the end of the transaction

Then from the formula for simple interest on page 16, it follows that the return earned on a *purchase-sale* transaction in bills is given by

$$i = \left(\frac{P_2 - P_1}{P_1}\right)\frac{365}{t_1 - t_2}$$

which, if we substitute appropriate expressions for P_1 and P_2, reduces to

$$i = \left(\frac{1 - \dfrac{d_2 t_2}{360}}{1 - \dfrac{d_1 t_1}{360}} - 1\right)\frac{365}{t_1 - t_2}$$

If we want the return earned on a 360-day basis, we simply multiply this i value by 360/365.

Example.   Suppose an investor buys the 90-day bill at a 10.10 rate of discount, that is, at a bond equivalent yield of 10.51. Seven days later he sells the issue at the same 10.10 rate of discount. Over the 7-day holding period, he will have earned a simple interest rate on a 365-day basis of

$$i = \left(\frac{1 - \dfrac{0.101 \times 83}{360}}{1 - \dfrac{0.101 \times 90}{360}} - 1\right)\frac{365}{7} = 10.51\%$$

and on a 360-day basis of

$$10.51\% \left(\frac{360}{365}\right) = 10.36\%$$

The RP pitfall or opportunity

We have already pointed out one example of how a carry that looks *positive* can turn out to be *negative*. Here is a second and more subtle example; it also illustrates for an investor who can get away with it a method to generate a locked-in profit *plus* capital on an arbitrage in bills.

Suppose the 90-day bill is trading at 10, which implies a simple interest yield on a 360-day basis of *10.26*. Suppose also that 7-day RP money can be obtained at *10.10*. It would appear that by purchasing the 90-day bill and RPing it for 7 days, a positive carry of 16 basis points could be locked in.

Whether the carry is earned depends, however, on how the RP is done. Every RP is technically a sale and a repurchase, but RPs can be and are set up in different ways. Typically an RP is *priced flat*, which means on a discount security that the purchase and sale prices are identical and interest is paid on the amount "borrowed," i.e., the sale price, at the agreed-upon repo rate. An alternative, however, is for the borrower to sell the security at one rate and buy it back later at another rate with no payment of interest. Some investors prefer the latter approach because it allows them to show the RP on their books as a bona fide purchase and sale as opposed to a camouflaged collateralized loan.

Anyone who has not massaged the numbers might guess that in our example—$d = 10, r = 10.10$—it makes no difference which approach is used. The truth, however, is quite different. To understand, recall our discussion in the preceding section concerning how the return earned on a bill sold before maturity is determined. The formula we derived there obviously can be used to calculate the true interest rate paid by a dealer if he does an outright sale and repurchase of a bill as opposed to a flat-priced RP. The example we presented there shows that if our dealer, who is financing 10 percent 90-day bills for 7 days, agreed to do an outright sell and buy back RP at 10.10, as opposed to a flat-priced RP at 10.10, the true repo rate he would be paying would be 10.36 on a 360-day basis.[7] Thus, the dealer who does the latter type of repo would turn a locked-in positive carry of

$$10.26\% - 10.10\% = 16 \text{ basis points}$$

into a locked-in negative carry of

$$10.26\% - 10.36\% = -10 \text{ basis points}$$

For an investor who has wide parameters and understands the contrast on a discount security between the true RP rate paid when pricing is flat and that paid when the transaction is a strict sale and repurchase, there is an interesting arbitrage possibility. If in the above situation he (1) reversed in for 7 days at a 10.10 rate 90-day bills on a straight sale-repurchase basis, and (2) offset this transaction by repoing at 10.10 the same securities priced flat at 10.00, he could lock in a positive carry of 26 basis points *and* generate capital equal to $250 per $1 million, which is the difference between pricing $1 million of bills at a 10.00 rate of discount and pricing them at a 10.10 rate of discount, i.e.,

$$\$975,000 - \$974,750 = \$250$$

BILL PARITY OR THE IMPLIED FORWARD RATE

The observation is often made that the yield curve in the bill market displays implicitly investors' expectations with respect to future interest rates. To illustrate why, note that to earn a return of 9.90 over 6 months, an investor who buys a 3-month bill at 9.80 must—simple averaging suggests—be able to reinvest 3 months hence in a second 3-month bill at 10.00. Therefore if a 3-month bill is trading at 9.80 and the 6-month bill at 9.90, intuition suggests that investors must anticipate that the 3-month bill 3 months

---

[7] The example appears on page 53.

hence will trade at at least 10.00 because, if it did not, they would buy the 6-month bill in preference to two consecutive 3-month bills.

This observation raises the topic of *bill parity*. Specifically it leads us to ask: If an investor is choosing between a long bill and two consecutive short bills, what rate must he get on the second short bill to earn—when reinvestment of earnings on the first short bill is assumed—the same rate on the two short bills that he would earn on the long bill?

To derive a formula for this number, we start by picturing the choice visually in Figure 5–2. The investor is selecting between choice A—an investment in a single long bill, bill 1, and choice B—an investment in two consecutive shorts bills, bills 2 and 3.

Figure 5–2
The bill parity problem visualized

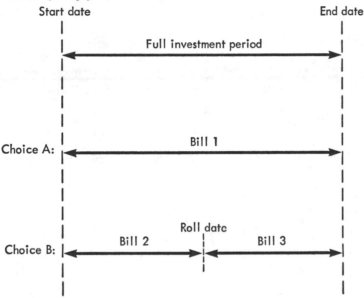

If we use subscript 1 to denote numbers associated with bill 1, subscript 2 to denote numbers associated with bill 2, and subscript 3 to denote numbers associated with bill 3, we can easily derive a formula for the break-even level for d_3. First, we observe that *if a principal amount I equal to 1 is invested in both bill 1 and bill 2*, then F_1 and F_2 (which are *not* equal) are derived as follows:

$$F_1 = 1 + D_1$$

$$= 1 + F_1 \frac{t_1 d_1}{360}$$

which reduces to

$$F_1 = \frac{1}{1 - \dfrac{t_1 d_1}{360}}$$

Similarly,

$$F_2 = \frac{1}{1 - \dfrac{t_2 d_2}{360}}$$

Let

$$d^* = \text{break-even (bill parity) rate on the second short bill, bill 3}$$

By definition,

$$d_3 = \frac{D_3}{F_3}\left(\frac{360}{t_1 - t_2}\right)$$

If

$$d_3 = d^*$$

that is, if the investor would earn as much investing $I = 1$ in choice B as he would investing $I = 1$ in choice A, then it is necessary that

$$D_3 = F_1 - F_2$$

and that

$$F_3 = F_1$$

But if this is so, then from the definition of d_3, it follows that $d_3 = d^*$ implies that

$$d^* = \left(\frac{F_1 - F_2}{F_1}\right)\frac{360}{t_1 - t_2}$$

If we now substitute into this equation for d^* the expressions obtained earlier for F_1 and F_2 and simplify, we get

$$d^* = \left(1 - \frac{1 - \frac{d_1 t_1}{360}}{1 - \frac{d_2 t_2}{360}}\right)\frac{360}{t_1 - t_2}$$

or alternatively

$$d^* = \left(1 - \frac{P_1}{P_2}\right)\frac{360}{t_1 - t_2}$$

Example. To illustrate, let's use the numbers in the example with which we began our discussion of bill parity, namely, for bill 1:

$$d_1 = 9.90 \quad \text{and} \quad t_1 = 180$$

and for bill 2:

$$d_2 = 9.80 \quad \text{and} \quad t_1 = 90$$

Inserting these numbers into our expression for d^*, we get

$$d^* = \left(1 - \frac{1 - \frac{0.099 \times 180}{360}}{1 - \frac{0.098 \times 90}{360}}\right)\left(\frac{360}{180 - 90}\right)$$

$$= 10.25\%$$

Calculating d^* shows us that the investor who is faced with the choice described at the beginning of this section must, when he rolls a short bill, get a higher rate parity between choices A and B, he must buy bill 3 not at a discount of 10.00 but at a discount of 10.25.

The 25-basis-point discrepancy between the break-even rate suggested by mathematical inspection and the rate indicated by more careful reasoning is simply explained. Our calculation of d^* requires in effect that the same rate i be earned on choices A and B. As noted earlier, the difference between a rate of discount d and the equivalent simple interest rate i is larger the bigger t is. In the case at hand, $t_1 = 2t_2$, a factor that outweighs the compounding permitted when choice B is selected.

The bill parity number, d^*, that we have just calculated is also often referred to, especially by academics, as an *implied forward rate*. This designation suggests that the behavior of investors is sufficiently rational so that the prevailing yield spread between a long bill and a short bill accurately reflects what yield investors anticipate will prevail in the *future* (specifically on the day the short bill matures) on a bill that covers the time gap between the short bill and the long bill. Note this is equivalent to saying that investors, given their rate anticipations, are indifferent between the short bill and the long bill.

CONCLUDING REMARKS

Throughout this chapter we have talked about bills, but the discussion applies equally well to other discount securities. The one exception is our remarks on shorting; commercial paper and BAs, because of their heterogeneity, cannot be shorted.

In Part III we turn to interest-bearing securities. Since we developed a number of general points in this chapter, it has been a preface to what follows, as were the chapters in Part I.

Interest-bearing securities

part III

6

Interest-bearing
securities: Mechanics

The stock-in-trade of the money market includes a wide range of *interest-bearing,* as opposed to discount, securities. Some have a short original maturity and pay interest only at maturity. Others have a long original maturity and pay interest periodically. Securities in the latter category typically pay interest every 6 months; their initial coupon period may, however, be irregular—shorter or longer than 6 months.

The rate of interest paid on an interest-bearing security, which is referred to as its *coupon,* is set at the time of issue to be in line with the prevailing yield in the secondary market on securities of the type and maturity of the new security being issued. Securities that pay periodic interest are often referred to as *coupon securities,* or simply *coupons.*

As a rule, interest-bearing securities are issued at a price equal or very close to their *par (face) value,* their coupon having been set at a level that permits this; at maturity such securities are redeemed at par.

PRICING

Pricing of interest-bearing securities is done in one of two ways. Unless CDs have an original maturity of more than 1 year, they pay interest at maturity. CDs are priced according to the *simple interest return* they offer the investor. Thus CD quotes look like bill or BA quotes, but the yield quoted on a CD is not comparable with the yield on a bill or BA because the former is a simple interest rate and the latter is a discount rate. Notes and bonds, which typically pay periodic interest, are quoted in terms of *dollar prices,* that is, in terms of a price of so many *dollars and 32nds* per $100 of face value.

Naturally, as interest rates change over time, this affects the prices at which interest-bearing securities trade. A rise in interest rates would, for example, decrease the attractiveness of outstanding low-coupon CDs, thereby causing a decrease in their value, which would be reflected in a rise in the yield at which they trade. A fall in rates would do the opposite.

Rising interest rates will also decrease the attractiveness and thereby lower the price of outstanding dollar-priced securities; and falling interest rates will do the

Table 6–1
Selected quotes: U.S. Treasury notes and bonds

DISCOUNT CORPORATION OF NEW YORK

58 Pine Street, New York, N.Y. 10005
Telephone 212-248-8900 • WUI Telex 620863 Discorp • WU Telex 125675 Discorp NYK

QUOTATIONS FOR U.S. TREASURY SECURITIES
Closing APR. 5, 1979
Ylds. for Dely. APR. 9, 1979

U.S. TREASURY NOTES AND BONDS (1)

Issue	Bid	Asked	Change from Prev Day	Yield to Maturity or Call(2)	Yield after Tax(3)	Taxable Coupon Equiv	Yield Value of 1/32	Current Markets	Amt of Issue ($millions) Total	Held Privately	1979 PRICE RANGE
N 5 7/8 4/30/79	99.22	99.24	--	9.95	5.37	9.95	.529	----------	1992	1828	99.22 98.19
N 7 7/8 5/15/79	99.23	99.25	--	9.79	5.29	9.79	.308	----------	2269	1740	99.24 99. 1
N 6 1/8 5/31/79	99.12	99.14	--	9.90	5.35	9.90	.218	----------	2087	1848	99.12 98. 8
N 6 1/8 6/30/79	99. 2	99. 4	--	9.91	5.35	9.91	.140	----------	2308	2019	99. 2 97.30
N 7 3/4 6/30/79	99.15	99.17	--	9.66	5.22	9.66	.138	----------	1782	1620	99.15 98.23
N 6 1/4 7/31/79	98.26	98.28	--	9.85	5.32	9.85	.103	----------	3180	3016	98.26 97.27
N 6 1/4 8/15/79	98.21	98.23	--	9.91	5.35	9.91	.091	----------	4559	2740	98.21 97.13
N 6 7/8 8/15/79	98.28	98.30	--	9.89	5.34	9.89	.091	----------	2989	2112	98.28 97.24
N 6 5/8 8/31/79	98.22	98.24	--	9.87	5.33	9.87	.083	----------	3481	3076	98.22 97.16
N 6 5/8 9/30/79	98.13	98.15	--	9.98	5.39	9.98	.069	----------	3861	3494	98.13 97. 6
N 8 1/2 9/30/79	99. 9	99.11	--	9.93	5.36	9.93	.069	----------	2081	1846	99. 9 98.24
N 7 1/4 1C/31/79	98.17	98.19	--	9.89	5.34	9.89	.060	----------	4334	4010	98.17 97. 8
N 6 1/4 11/15/79	97.26	97.28	--	9.97	5.38	9.97	.056	----------	3376	3112	97.26 96.14
N 6 5/8 11/15/79	98.	98. 4	--	9.90	5.35	9.90	.056	----------	1604	462	98. 96.27
N 7 11/15/79	98. 7	98.11	--	9.89	5.34	9.89	.056	----------	2241	1805	98. 7 97. 9
N 7 1/8 11/30/79	98. 7	98. 9	--	9.92	5.36	9.92	.052	----------	4791	4401	98. 7 97. 2
N 7 1/8 12/31/79	98.	98. 2	--	9.92	5.36	9.92	.046	----------	3920	3526	98. 96.26
N 7 1/2 12/31/79	98. 9	98.11	--	9.89	5.34	9.89	.046	----------	2006	1870	98. 9 97.11
N 7 1/2 1/31/80	98. 5	98. 7	--	9.81	5.30	9.81	.041	----------	3875	3505	98. 5 96.29
B 4 2/15/80	* 95.12	95.20	--	9.44	5.10	9.44	.040	----------	2494	1565	95.12 93.28
N 6 1/2 2/15/80	97.12	97.14	--	9.68	5.23	9.68	.040	----------	4608	3147	97.12 95.26
N 7 5/8 2/29/80	98. 2	98. 4	--	9.86	5.32	9.86	.038	----------	3820	3549	98. 4 96.26
N 7 1/2 3/31/80	97.26	97.28	--	9.83	5.31	9.83	.035	----------	6076	5374	97.26 96.16
N 7 3/4 4/30/80	98. 1	98. 3	--	9.68	5.57	10.32	.032	----------	3180	2736	98. 1 96.29
N 6 7/8 5/15/80	97. 3	97. 7	--	9.59	5.67	10.49	.031	----------	7265	1721	97. 3 95.13
N 8 5/31/80	98. 5	98. 7	--	9.67	5.52	10.22	.030	----------	3099	2922	98. 5 96.29
N 8 2/15/85	95.13	95.17	+ 2	9.00	5.04	9.33	.007	----------	4204	2749	96.16 94.10
B 3 1/4 5/15/85	* 78.24	79.	--	7.62	4.90	9.07	.007	----------	745	560	78.24 74.24
B 4 1/4 5/15/85-75*	81.20	81.28	--	8.07	5.05	9.34	.007	----------	1042	647	81.20 78.
## N 8 1/4 8/15/85	95.31	96. 3	+ 2	9.07	5.05	9.34	.007	----------	4836	3207	97. 4 95. 2
N 7 7/8 5/15/86	93.20	93.24	+ 4	9.09	5.13	9.49	.006	----------	5219	4158	94.14 92.18
N 8 8/15/86	94. 8	94.12	+ 2	9.06	5.08	9.41	.006	----------	9515	7506	95. 8 93. 8
B 6 1/8 11/15/86	85.	86.	--	8.68	5.15	9.53	.006	----------	1216	332	85. 83. 4
## N 9 2/15/87	99.19	99.21	+ 3	9.06	4.90	9.08	.006	----------	2250	2250	99.20 98.19
N 7 5/8 11/15/87	91.14	91.18	--	9.06	5.15	9.53	.006	----------	2387	1766	92.24 90.20
N 8 1/4 5/15/88	95.	95. 4	+ 2	9.05	5.03	9.31	.005	----------	4148	2465	96. 6 94.
## N 8 3/4 11/15/88	98. 2	98. 4	+ 4	9.04	4.93	9.13	.005	----------	3432	2501	99. 6 97.
B 3 1/2 2/15/90	* 78.	78.16	+16	6.26	3.88	7.18	.005	----------	2757	1864	78. 73.24
B 8 1/4 5/15/90	94.28	95. 4	--	8.95	4.96	9.18	.005	----------	1247	840	95.28 94. 8
B 4 1/4 8/15/92-87*	78.	78.16	--	6.71	4.07	7.53	.004	----------	2844	1716	78. 73.24
B 7 1/4 8/15/92	86.12	86.20	+ 4	8.99	5.17	9.57	.004	----------	1504	1411	87.16 85.20
B 4 2/15/93-88*	77.24	78.24	+16	6.33	3.84	7.10	.004	----------	180	127	77.24 73.24
B 6 3/4 2/15/93	83.	84.	--	8.77	5.10	9.44	.004	----------	627	418	84. 81.28
B 7 7/8 2/15/93	90.28	91.	+ 4	9.02	5.08	9.40	.004	----------	1500	1380	91.30 90.
B 7 1/2 8/15/93-88	87.	88.	--	9.00	5.13	9.50	.004	----------	1914	596	88.16 86.16
B 8 5/8 8/15/93	96.20	96.24	+ 4	9.03	4.95	9.16	.004	----------	1768	1701	97.28 95.18
B 8 5/8 11/15/93	96.18	96.22	+ 4	9.04	4.96	9.17	.004	----------	1504	1504	97.30 95.18
## B 9 2/15/94	99.22	99.24	+ 4	9.03	4.88	9.04	.004	----------	1502	1502	101. 4 98.21
B 4 1/8 5/15/94-89*	77.24	78.24	+ 8	6.33	3.82	7.06	.004	----------	1049	593	77.24 74. 6
B 3 2/15/95	* 77. 8	78. 8	+ 8	5.00	3.06	5.66	.003	----------	524	396	77. 8 72.24
B 7 5/15/98-93	83.	84.	--	8.74	5.03	9.32	.003	----------	692	364	84. 8 82.24
B 3 1/2 11/15/98	* 77.24	78. 8	+ 8	5.30	3.19	5.90	.003	----------	1942	1228	77.24 73.24
B 8 1/2 5/15/99-94	95. 4	95.12	--	9.00	4.95	9.16	.004	----------	2414	762	96.28 94.16
B 7 7/8 2/15/00-95	89.18	89.22	+ 2	8.98	5.05	9.34	.004	----------	2771	2190	90.30 88.16
B 8 3/8 8/15/00-95	93.30	94. 2	+ 2	9.00	4.97	9.20	.003	----------	4662	2599	95.12 92.28
B 8 8/15/01-96	90.12	90.20	--	8.98	5.03	9.30	.004	----------	1575	765	91.28 89.16
B 8 1/4 5/15/05-00	92.26	93. 2	--	8.94	4.95	9.17	.003	----------	4246	2068	94. 8 91.24
B 7 5/8 2/15/07-02	86.24	87.	--	8.89	5.03	9.31	.003	----------	4249	2692	88. 85.24
B 7 7/8 11/15/07-02	90.20	90.28	--	8.75	4.88	9.04	.003	----------	1495	1228	91.28 88.24
B 8 3/8 8/15/08-03	93.28	94.	+ 2	8.96	4.94	9.15	.003	----------	2101	1404	95. 8 92.24
## B 8 3/4 11/15/08-03	97.19	97.21	+ 3	8.98	4.89	9.05	.003	----------	4431	3753	99. 8 96.14

DENOTES MOST RECENT ISSUES.

(1) Interest on direct U.S. Treasury obligations is subject to all Federal taxes but is exempt under present laws from state and local taxation. For purposes of taxation, the difference between the price paid for Treasury bills and the amount received on sale or redemption of such bills is taxed as ordinary gain or loss.

(2) The calculations are to maturity date for issues selling below par and to earliest call date for issues selling above par.

(3) Yields after tax have been computed by using rates based upon the Tax Revenue Act of 1978. For ordinary income tax purposes we have used a rate of 46% and for long term capital gains purposes 28%.

*Redeemable at par under certain conditions in payment of Federal estate taxes.

opposite. Thus dollar-priced securities rarely trade for long after issue at par (i.e., at a dollar price of 100). They will trade at a discount, i.e., below 100, if yields in their sector of the market rise above the coupon they carry; and they will trade at a premium if the reverse occurs. This is seen in Table 6–1, which gives the prices at which selected U.S. Treasury notes and bonds closed on April 5, 1979.

The first column in Table 6–1 describes the issue quoted. For example, the first security quoted there is denoted

$$N\ 5\%\ 4/30/79$$

which means that it is a Treasury *note* bearing a 5⅞ coupon and maturing on 4/30/79. The last issue quoted

$$B\ 8\%\ 11/15/08\text{–}03$$

is a Treasury *bond* bearing an 8¾ coupon and maturing in 2008 but callable in 2003.

The second two columns in Table 6–1 show the bid and asked prices for the securities listed. Since the two numbers after the decimal point in these quotes refer to 32nds, the first bid price in column two, 99–22, means that the security in question was bid a dollar price per $100 of face value equal to

$$\$99^{22}/_{32} = \$99.687500$$

Actually, if an investor had sold the security at that bid price, he would have received something more per $100 of face value than the dollar price we just calculated to six decimal places. The reason is that, when a *dollar-priced*, interest-bearing security is sold, the buyer pays the quoted dollar price *plus* whatever interest has accrued on the security from its issue or last coupon date to the settlement date.

PRESENT VALUE

Present value is one of those concepts most people struggle to learn in school and promptly forget because they can think of nothing better to do with it. For money market people, however, present value is an important concept; in particular it is fundamental for interpreting the fifth column in Table 6–1, "Yield to Maturity or Call."

The concept

Suppose that someone offered to "sell" you $1 for delivery today. Obviously, the dollar offered would be worth exactly $1. A more interesting question is: What would $1 to be delivered 1 year from now be worth? As a moment's thought suggests, it would be worth whatever *principal* would have to be invested today in order that principal *plus* accrued interest equal $1 in 1 year.

Let

$$I = \text{principal invested}$$
$$i = \text{simple interest rate available on a 1-year investment}$$

Then by solving the expression

$$I + iI = \$1$$

for I, we can determine that the *present value* (PV), as it is called, of $1 to be received 1 year from now is given by

$$PV = \frac{\$1}{1 + i}$$

Note several things about present value. First, it is a *discounted* value of a future sum. Second, i is the rate at which this sum is discounted. Third, the higher i, the smaller is the present value of the future sum.

A security that pays interest at maturity

With this in mind, let's now turn to a key topic: how one determines the price of an interest-bearing security when it is offered at a specific yield.[1] We consider first a 1-year security that pays interest at maturity. Let

F = face value
P = price
c = coupon rate of interest
y = yield at which the security is offered

As our brief remarks suggest, the price of this security is its present value, that is, its value at maturity discounted at the yield y at which it is offered. In symbols,

$$P = \frac{F + cF}{1 + y}$$

$$= F \frac{1 + c}{1 + y}$$

To illustrate, consider a 1-year security with a face value of $1,000 and a 6 percent coupon. If it is offered at a 6 percent yield, its price will be *par*, as one would expect:

$$P = \$1,000 \frac{1 + 0.06}{1 + 0.06} = \$1,000$$

Alternatively, if it is offered at a lower yield, 4 percent, it will sell at a *premium:*

$$P = \$1,000 \frac{1 + 0.06}{1 + 0.04} = \$1,019.23$$

And if it is offered at a yield higher than its coupon, 8 percent, it will sell at a *discount:*

$$P = \$1,000 \frac{1 + 0.06}{1 + 0.08} = \$981.48$$

A security that pays interest semiannually

Notes and bonds that have a maturity at issue of 1 year or more pay interest *semiannually*. This means that the investor in such a security will, unless he buys it during its last coupon period, receive a *stream* of dollar flows—one or more coupon payments plus a final payment at maturity of face value plus coupon interest.

To determine the price of such a security when it is offered at some yield to maturity, y, one must appropriately discount all the anticipated dollar flows using the rate y. The *sum* of these discounted payments is the security's present value or price at the yield, y.

---

[1] Note our purpose here is to focus on *general* principles: how bond prices are determined and the proper interpretation of bond yields. In later chapters we turn to the application of these principles to *specific* securities that accrue interest in various ways and are issued in a world that has a 365-day year and months of varying lengths.

Just how this pricing procedure is carried out requires some explanation. As noted, the price of a 1-year security that pays interest *at maturity* is an amount P such that, if P were invested at a yield y for 1 year, P plus the interest earned at the yield y would equal at year's end the face value of the security plus coupon interest. In this situation there is *no* compounding of interest. If, however, we consider a 1-year note that pays interest *semiannually, compounding* comes into play because the first coupon payment can be reinvested for half a year before the security matures.

With semiannual payment of interest, the price of a note that has a current maturity of 1 year is an amount P such that, if P were invested at a yield y for 1 year with semiannual compounding, P plus the interest earned at the yield y would equal at the end of the year the sum of the dollar flows thrown off by the security plus the interest that could be earned by reinvesting the first coupon payment for half a year at the rate y; that is, P plus interest earned at the rate y would equal the security's first coupon payment plus interest on this payment for half a year at the rate y plus the value of the security at maturity.

We can express this equality succinctly in symbols. To do so, we note two things. First, the amount of coupon interest that will be received on each coupon date is

$$\frac{c}{2}F$$

Second, with semiannual compounding, the value of an amount P invested at a rate y will at the end of 1 year be

$$P\left(1 + \frac{y}{2}\right)^2$$

and the value of an amount $(c/2)F$ invested at a rate y for half a year will be

$$\frac{c}{2}F\left(1 + \frac{y}{2}\right)$$

Thus the price of a 1-year security that pays semiannual interest and is offered at a yield to maturity y must be P in the expression

$$P\left(1 + \frac{y}{2}\right)^2 = \frac{c}{2}F\left(1 + \frac{y}{2}\right) + \left(F + \frac{c}{2}F\right)$$

which, when solved for P, gives

$$P = \frac{\frac{c}{2}F}{1 + \frac{y}{2}} + \frac{F\left(1 + \frac{c}{2}\right)}{\left(1 + \frac{y}{2}\right)^2}$$

In examining this expression, note that the first coupon payment, $(c/2)F$, which will be received one coupon period hence, is discounted by the factor $[1 + (y/2)]$, while the value of the note at maturity, $F[1 + (c/2)]$, which will be received two coupon periods hence, is discounted by a factor $[1 + (y/2)]^2$.

The procedure we used to price a 1-year note can easily be extended to the pricing of securities with a current maturity of more than 1 year. As the reader who works out price formulas for long-term securities will quickly note, the general principle underlying the pricing of a security that pays semiannual interest is that each future dollar payment thrown off by it must be discounted by a factor

$$\left(1 + \frac{y}{2}\right)^n$$

where *n is the number of compounding (coupon) periods* hence that the payment will be received. Thus on a note with a current maturity of 2 years,[2]

$$P = \frac{\frac{c}{2}F}{1+\frac{y}{2}} + \frac{\frac{c}{2}F}{\left(1+\frac{y}{2}\right)^2} + \frac{\frac{c}{2}F}{\left(1+\frac{y}{2}\right)^3} + \frac{F\left(1+\frac{c}{2}\right)}{\left(1+\frac{y}{2}\right)^4}$$

To illustrate, consider a bond that has a current maturity of 2 years, has a face value of $1,000, and carries a coupon of 6 percent. As Table 6–2 shows, if this security were

Table 6–2
Present value is the price of a $1,000 note carrying a 6 percent coupon and maturing in 2 years

	Present value if yield to maturity is:		
Payment stream	*4 percent*	*6 percent*	*8 percent*
First coupon, $30	$\frac{30}{1+0.02} = \$\ 29.41$	$\frac{30}{1+0.03} = \$\ 29.13$	$\frac{30}{1+0.04} = \$\ 28.85$
Second coupon, $30	$\frac{30}{(1+0.02)^2} = 28.84$	$\frac{30}{(1+0.03)^2} = 28.28$	$\frac{30}{(1+0.04)^2} = 27.72$
Third coupon, $30	$\frac{30}{(1+0.02)^3} = 28.27$	$\frac{30}{(1+0.03)^3} = 27.45$	$\frac{30}{(1+0.04)^3} = 26.67$
Fourth coupon plus face value, $1,030	$\frac{1,030}{(1+0.02)^4} = 951.56$	$\frac{1,030}{(1+0.03)^4} = 915.14$	$\frac{1,030}{(1+0.04)^4} = 880.45$
Sum equal to present value equal to price	$1,038.08	$1,000.00	$963.69

priced to yield 6 percent, it would sell at par. If, alternatively, it were priced to yield less than 6 percent, it would sell at a premium; and if it were priced to yield more than 6 percent, it would sell at a discount.

The interpretation of yield to maturity

In the first example we presented, we showed that a 1-year security that had a face value of $1,000, carried a coupon of 6 percent, and paid interest at maturity would be priced at par if offered at 6 percent. As our second example suggests, a similar 1-year security that pays semiannual interest would also be priced at par if offered at a 6 percent yield.

The second security, however, would be worth more than the first to an investor because after 6 months he would get coupon interest, which he could reinvest. If, in particular, he could reinvest at the rate of 6 percent, over the full year on the second security he would earn a compound rate of return equal to

$$\left(1+\frac{0.06}{2}\right)^2 - 1 = 6.09\%$$

This observation points up something important: The way we calculated the price of a security that pays semiannual interest, that is, by using a compound rate of discount,

---

[2] For simplicity we limit our discussion here to the pricing of notes and bonds traded on a coupon date. For the calculation of accrued coupon interest, see Chapter 8. For a general pricing formula, see Chapter 9.

is the way this calculation is made by the street in pricing notes and bonds. Thus a note or bond with a yield to maturity on the quote sheet that was given as 6 percent would actually be priced, except during its last coupon period, to offer the investor a compound rate of 6.09 percent.

Yield to maturity figures given on a quote sheet such as the one in Table 6–2 are all simple, as opposed to compound rates, even when compounding would be possible because the security has more than 6 months to run. This not the first time we have made this observation. In our discussion of how equivalent bond yield d_b is calculated on bills, we noted that for bills with a current maturity of *more than* 6 months, d_b is not the simple interest rate offered by the bill; instead it is a number adjusted downward to make d_b comparable to the yield to maturity on a bond or note by reflecting the fact that long bills, unlike bonds and notes, offer *no* opportunity for compounding.[3]

The reinvestment rate

When we say that a note or bond is offered at a 6 percent yield to maturity, which is equivalent to a 6.09 percent rate when compounded semiannually, this in no way implies that the investor who buys the security will in fact earn a compounded rate of 6.09 over its life. As we took pains to explain (pages 16–18 and 64–65), the investor will earn that rate over any length of time only if strict conditions hold. In particular, an investor who bought a 1-year or a 2-year note at a 6 percent yield to maturity would earn a compound rate of 6.09 percent over the full life of the security only if he held the security to maturity *and* if he reinvested all coupon payments received before maturity at a 6 percent rate with semiannual compounding.

Expectations with respect to the *reinvestment rate* are important both for the manager of a liquidity portfolio and for the manager of a long-term bond portfolio. But the time horizons of the two differ. An expectation of falling interest rates might cause a manager of short-term money to extend maturities from 3 to 6 months. The manager of a bond portfolio in contrast might respond to such an expectation by switching from a current bond selling at par to a low-coupon bond selling at a discount. When a bond is selling at a deep discount, much of its yield to maturity comes in the form of price appreciation as opposed to coupon interest. For that reason a fall in the reinvestment rate will lower the actual yield to maturity earned on a deep discount bond by less than it would on a bond purchased at par.[4]

FLUCTUATIONS IN A COUPON SECURITY'S PRICE

When a new note or bond issue comes to market, the coupon rate on it is, with certain exceptions, set so that it equals the yield prevailing in the market on securities of comparable maturity and risk. This permits the new security to be sold at a price equal or very near to par. The price at which the security later trades in the secondary market will fluctuate in response to changes in interest rates.

Example

To illustrate, let's work an example. Suppose a new 6-year note with an 8 percent coupon is issued at par. Six months later the Fed tightens, and the yield on comparable

---

[3] See pages 34–35.

[4] For an in-depth discussion of the reinvestment rate and of techniques for managing a bond portfolio, see *Inside the Yield Book, New Tools for Bond Market Strategy* by Sidney Homer and Martin Leibowitz (Englewood Cliffs, N.J.: Prentice-Hall, 1972).

securities rises to 8.5 percent. Now what is this 8 percent security worth? Since the investor who pays a price equal to par for this "seasoned issue" is going to get only an 8 percent return, while 8.5 percent is available elsewhere, it is clear that the security must now sell at *less* than par.

When an investor buys a coupon security at a *discount* and holds it to maturity, he receives a two-part return: the promised interest payment *plus* a capital gain. The capital gain arises because the security that the investor bought at a price below par is redeemed at maturity for full face value. The investor who buys a coupon issue at a *premium* and holds it to maturity also receives a two-part return: interest payments due *plus* a capital *loss* equal to the premium paid.

For dollars invested in a coupon issue that sells at a discount or premium, it is possible to calculate the effective rate of return received, which is the rate that the investor earns on his dollars when both interest received *and* capital gains (or losses) are taken into account. It is the security's *yield to maturity.*

To get back to our example, once rates rise to 8.5 percent in the open market, the security with an 8 percent coupon has to be priced at a discount large enough so that its yield to maturity equals 8.5 percent. Figuring out how many dollars of discount this requires is a complicated calculation (see Chapter 8). Dealers used to use bond tables, but most have now switched to computers. Using either tool, one can determine that, with interest rates at 8.5 percent, a $1,000 note with an 8 percent coupon and a 3½-year current maturity has to sell at $985.13 (a discount of $14.87) in order to yield 8.5 percent to maturity.

Current maturity and price volatility

A capital gain of $14.87, which is what the investor in our discounted 8 percent note would realize if he held it to maturity, will raise effective yield more, the faster this gain is realized (the shorter the current maturity of the security). Conversely, this capital gain will raise effective yield less, the more slowly it is realized (the longer the current maturity of the security).[5]

But if this is so, then a one-half percentage point rise in the yield on comparable securities will cause a much larger fall in price for a security with a long current maturity than for one with a short current maturity. In other words, the discount required to raise a coupon security's yield to maturity by one-half percentage point is *greater*, the *longer* the security's maturity.

By reversing the argument presented above, it is easy to see that, if 6 months after the 6-year 8 percent note in our example were issued, the yield on comparable securities *fell* to 7.5 percent, the value of this note would be driven to a *premium*, i.e., it would sell at a price above par. Note also that a one-half percentage point *fall* in the yield on comparable securities would force an outstanding higher-coupon security to a *greater* premium, the *longer* its current maturity was.

As these observations suggest, when prevailing interest rates change, prices of long coupons will, unless there is an offsetting shift in the yield curve, respond more dramatically than prices of short coupons. Figure 6-1 shows this sharp contrast. It pictures for a $1,000 note carrying an 8 percent coupon, the relationship between *current* maturity and the discount that would prevail if the yield on comparable

---

[5] If you don't see this, just think—somewhat imprecisely— of the capital gain as a certain number of dollars of extra interest paid out in yearly installments to the investor as his security matures. Clearly the shorter the security's current maturity, the higher these extra annual interest installments will be, and consequently the higher the overall yield to the investor.

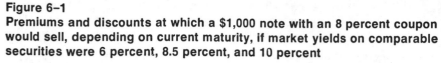

Figure 6–1
Premiums and discounts at which a $1,000 note with an 8 percent coupon
would sell, depending on current maturity, if market yields on comparable
securities were 6 percent, 8.5 percent, and 10 percent

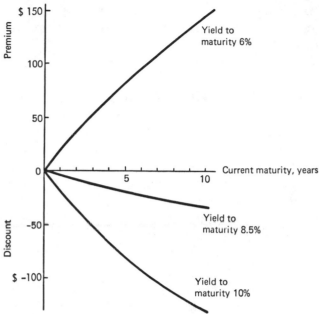

securities rose to 8.5 percent or to 10 percent. It also plots the premium to which a $1,000 note with an 8 percent coupon would, depending on its current maturity, be driven if the yield on comparable securities fell to 6 percent.

Coupon and price volatility

The price volatility of an issue depends not only on its current maturity but also on its coupon. Specifically, the *lower* the coupon, the *greater* is the percentage change in price that will occur when rates rise or fall. To illustrate, consider two notes with 4-year current maturities. Note A has an 8 percent coupon and note B a 6 percent coupon. Both are priced to yield 8 percent. Suppose now that interest rates on comparable securities rise to 10 percent. Note A will fall 6.46 percent in value, while note B will fall 6.64 percent in value. The reason for the greater percentage fall in the price of the low-coupon note B is that capital appreciation represents a greater proportion of promised income (capital appreciation plus coupon interest) on the low coupon than on the high coupon. Therefore, for the low-coupon note's yield to maturity to rise two percentage points, its price has to fall relatively more than that of the high-coupon note.

In falling markets, the investor who holds a low-coupon issue is at a disadvantage because it will fall faster in value than a high-coupon issue. In rising markets, precisely the opposite is true because a low-coupon, deeply discounted security will increase faster in price than a high-coupon security.

YIELD VALUE OF $1/32$

Bearing the above in mind, we turn to a final important column in the quote sheet in Table 6–1, the one labeled "Yield Value of $1/32$." The figures in this column record by how much the yield to maturity on individual issues would change if their *asked* price, which is the price from which yield to maturity is calculated, were to change by $1/32$.

An obvious use of this number is to track how yields to maturity on individual issues change during the trading day as the market moves up or down. To illustrate, consider the last issue quoted in the top part of Table 6–1, N 8 5/31/80. A price of 98– 7 was asked for this issue, which is equivalent to a yield to maturity of 9.67. The 0.030 figure given for the yield value of $1/32$ on this issue indicates that, if the price asked for this note had moved up to 98– 8 due to a fall in market rates or some other factor, its yield to maturity would have fallen to

$$9.67 - 0.030 = 9.64$$

A fall in the asked price would, in contrast, have raised yield to maturity on the issue.

As one looks down the "Yield Value of $1/32$" column, it is obvious that the numbers get smaller as the current maturity of the securities quoted increases. This is to be expected because a change in the price of a note or bond by $1/32$ will result in the investor receiving or losing an extra $1/32$ when the security matures and is paid off at par. Thus, the value of $1/32$ to an investor on a long note or bond is a discounted sum given (approximately except on coupon dates) by

$$\frac{1/32}{\left(1 + \frac{y}{2}\right)^n}$$

where n is the number of remaining coupon periods. Obviously, on a 20-year bond, a $1/32$ fall in price will result in a very small—when discounted—dollar gain to the investor and thus in the bond's yield to maturity. If, in contrast, the security is close to maturity, a $1/32$ fall in price will result in a significant discounted dollar gain to the bondholder and thus in the bond's yield to maturity.

Price volatility

The yield value of $1/32$ on an issue also tells something about its price volatility. The smaller it is, the more 32nds the issue's price will have to change for its yield to rise or fall by x basis points. In effect, the small yield values of $1/32$ on long issues tell an investor that holding such an issue exposes him to a considerable *price risk*—one not shared by an investor who holds a note or bond that will mature shortly.

While it is easy to spot in the figures given on the quote sheet for the yield value of $1/32$ the difference in price volatility between securities with long and short current maturities, it is difficult to spot the difference in price volatility between high- and low- coupon issues. The reason for this difficulty is that the impact of an issue's coupon on its price volatility is so small relative to the impact of its current maturity that the former would show up in a comparison of the yield values $1/32$ on two securities of similar current maturity only if the comparison were carried beyond the three decimal places shown on the quote sheet.

Certificates of deposit: Domestic and Euro

Interest-bearing securities have been created with the liberality of design that auto makers apply to producing cars. Some pay interest at maturity, others pay periodic interest; all accrue interest, but they do so in different ways on the basis of different day-count years. Therefore we cannot say more *in general* than we did in Chapter 6 about the mathematics of interest-bearing securities. Instead we must examine individual securities and the particular calculations that apply to them. We start in this chapter with CDs, a special breed of *interest-at-maturity* securities. Then in Chapter 8 we will turn to governments and agencies in their last coupon period, a second and different breed of the same genre.

YIELD GIVEN PRICE

Almost all CDs issued in the domestic market have a maturity at issue of less than 1 year and pay simple interest on a 360-day basis;[1] the rate of interest paid is the coupon rate, and interest is paid at maturity.

Convention I. To begin our discussion of CDs, we will derive formulas for determining yield given price and price given yield. In deriving formulas for CDs and all other interest-bearing securities, we will adopt the following *important convention: Price P is always taken to be price per $1 of face value.* The alternative and widely used convention of expressing price per $100 of face value (presumably because notes and bonds are priced this way) unnecessarily complicates price and yield equations by forcing one to include in them the factor of 100 again and again.

The virtue of working with price or value at maturity per $1 of face value can be seen in the simple expression we obtain for the value at maturity of a CD carrying a coupon, *c*. Let

$$t_{im} = \text{days from issue to maturity}$$
$$c = \text{coupon rate}$$

---

[1] The exceptions are variable-rate CDs and a few long-term issues that have been floated at various times.

Then

$$\text{Value at maturity per \$1 of face value} = 1 + c\,\frac{t_{im}}{360}$$

Using that expression, we can easily determine the value at maturity of a CD of any face value, F. Consider, for example, a CD with the following parameters:

$$c = 0.10$$
$$t_{im} = 90$$
$$F = \$1 \text{ million}$$

For this CD,

$$\text{Value at maturity per \$1 of face value} = 1 + 0.10\left(\frac{90}{360}\right) = 1.025$$

and

$$\text{Value at maturity per \$1 million of face value} = 1.025(\$1,000,000)$$
$$= \$1,025,000$$

Our example perhaps belabors the obvious, but we we are breaking with tradition as incorporated in the industry bible, *Standard Securities Calculations Methods*, and it seems appropriate to show that this iconclasm combined with our notation permits us to derive expressions that are shorter, simpler, and easier to manipulate than those presented in that book.

Convention II. In the case of CDs (but *not* other interest-bearing securities), we will also adopt a second important convention: Price P is always taken to be price per \$1 of face value, *with accrued interest, if any, included.* Because of the way yields are calculated and quoted on CDs, this convention greatly simplifies CD price and yield formulas. Also once a P value is calculated for a CD, separating that value into principal and accrued interest is trivial.

CDs are always quoted, at issue *and* in the secondary market, in terms of yield on a simple interest basis. Recalling the formula for simple interest on page 16, we can write a formula for the rate of return that a CD offered at a price P will yield to an investor. Let

$$y = \text{yield on the CD}$$
$$t_{sm} = \text{days from settlement to maturity}$$

Then

$$y = \left(\frac{\left(1 + c\,\frac{t_{im}}{360}\right) - P}{P}\right)\frac{360}{t_{sm}}$$

$$= \left(\frac{1 + c\,\frac{t_{im}}{360}}{P} - 1\right)\frac{360}{t_{sm}}$$

If a CD is bought on its issue date, then $P = 1$ and the expression reduces to

$$y = \left(\frac{1 + c\,\frac{t_{im}}{360}}{1} - 1\right)\frac{360}{t_{im}}$$

$$= c$$

as would be expected.

The fact that CDs pay interest on the basis of a 360-day year should not be forgotten when CD yields are compared with those on other interest-bearing securities, such as government notes and bonds, that pay interest on a 365-day basis. Our magic number (0.014) for the conversion from a 365- to a 360-day basis reminds us that the 10 percent level, getting a year's interest over 360 days is worth

$$0.014(0.10) = 0.0014$$

that is, 14 extra basis points.

PRICE GIVEN YIELD

Using the formula we have obtained for the yield on a CD, we can derive a formula for the price at which a CD will trade in the secondary market if it is offered at a yield y. To do so, we solve the expression

$$y = \left(\frac{1 + c\,\dfrac{t_{im}}{360}}{P} - 1 \right) \frac{360}{t_{sm}}$$

for P to get

$$P = \left(\frac{1 + c\,\dfrac{t_{im}}{360}}{1 + y\,\dfrac{t_{sm}}{360}} \right)$$

Example. Suppose that an investor buys at a yield of 9.50 a CD that carries a coupon of 10 and has an original maturity of 90 days and a current maturity of 60 days. The price, P, which includes accrued interest that he will pay per \$1 of face value is

$$P = \left(\frac{1 + 0.100\,\dfrac{90}{360}}{1 + 0.095\,\dfrac{60}{360}} \right) = 1.009024$$

Breaking out accrued interest

Separating the price P paid for a CD into principal and interest is easily done. Let

$$a_i = \text{accrued interest}$$
$$t_{is} = \text{days from issue to settlement}$$

On a CD accrued interest is given by the expression

$$a_i = c\,\frac{t_{is}}{360}$$

and

$$\text{Principal per \$1 of face value} = P - c\,\frac{t_{is}}{360}$$

Applying these formulas to the preceding example, we find that

$$a_i = 0.10\,\frac{30}{360} = 0.008333$$

and

$$\text{Principal} = 1.009024 - 0.008333$$
$$= 1.000691$$

Note that the CD in our example is selling at a premium. This is to be expected since it was traded at a yield *well below* its coupon.

Basic CD formulas

Let

c = coupon rate
y = yield at which the security is traded
P = price per \$1 of face value, accrued interest *included*
t_{im} = days from issue to maturity
t_{is} = days issue to settlement
t_{sm} = days from settlement to maturity
a_i = accrued interest

  I. Yield given price:

$$y = \left(\frac{1 + c\frac{t_{im}}{360}}{P} - 1 \right) \frac{360}{t_{sm}}$$

 II. Price given yield:

$$P = \left(\frac{1 + c\frac{t_{im}}{360}}{1 + y\frac{t_{sm}}{360}} \right)$$

III. To break P into accrued interest and principal, note

$$a_i = c\,\frac{t_{is}}{360}$$

and

$$\text{Principal} = P - a_i$$

FIGURING A CD TAIL

An approximation

Traders create tails on CDs just as they do on bills. Let

y^* = break-even sale rate on a CD tail
r_t = term repo rate

This break-even rate can be approximated for a new-issue CD financed with term repo by substituting c for d in the formula on page 43 to obtain

$$y^* = c + (c - r_t)\frac{t_{is}}{t_{sm}}$$

where s in the subscripts refers to the settlement day the term repo comes off and the CD is sold. On a secondary CD, one would substitute not c, but yield at purchase y, and t_{is} would be days from purchase to settlement at sale.

On discount securities the preceding approximation underestimates the true yield at which the trader "purchases" a tail, thereby affording the trader some extra protection. On CDs, the bias in the approximation works in the *opposite* direction. The yield on a CD and the rate on a term repo are both simple interest rates calculated on a 360-day basis. But if the term repo comes off before the CD matures, the two rates are not comparable because of an old friend, compounding. Proper compounding will raise the term repo rate by more than the CD rate and thereby narrow the spread in basis points between these two rates.

A precise formula

Since the bias in approximating the break-even yield on a CD tail works against the trader, a precise formula is needed for calculating the true break-even yield. To get it, we first dollar flow the transaction for a new-issue CD as in Table 7–1.

Table 7–1
Dollar flowing a CD tail created at issue
(flows are per \$1 of face value)

	Dollars in	*Dollars out*
Issue date	1	1
Settlement date	P	$1 + r_t \dfrac{t_{is}}{360}$

As Table 7–1 shows, dollars in equal dollars out on the issue date. Thus, the trader will break even on his tail if at settlement:

$$P = 1 + r_t \frac{t_{is}}{360}$$

Substituting the expression we derived earlier for P into this equation, we get

$$\left(\frac{1 + c \dfrac{t_{im}}{360}}{1 + y \dfrac{t_{sm}}{360}} \right) = 1 + r_t \frac{t_{is}}{360}$$

The y in this relationship is the break-even sale rate y^* we seek. Solving for it we get:

$$y^* = \left(\frac{1 + c \dfrac{t_{im}}{360}}{1 + r_t \dfrac{t_{is}}{360}} - 1 \right) \frac{360}{t_{sm}}$$

Example. Suppose that a 90-day CD carrying a 10 percent coupon is hung out on term repo at issue for 30 days at a 9 percent rate. According to the approximation formula on page 74, the break-even sale rate on the tail is 10.50 percent. Our precise formula for y^* shows that it is *less*. Specifically, inserting these numbers into our equation, we get

$$y^* = \left(\frac{1 + 0.10\,\dfrac{90}{360}}{1 + 0.09\,\dfrac{30}{360}} - 1 \right) \frac{360}{30} = 10.42\%$$

With minor modifications our equation for y^* can also be applied to figuring the tail on a secondary CD financed with term RP (Case B in the box on page 77). Here's an example: A 182-day CD is issued on 11/30/79 with a 13⅞ coupon. A trader buys this CD in the secondary market for settlement 19 days later on 12/19/79 at a yield of 14.25. He then finances the CD for 33 days (to January 21) with term repo at 14 percent. This gives him a break-even rate of sale on the tail of

$$y^* = \left(\frac{1 + 0.1425\,\dfrac{163}{360}}{1 + 0.1400\,\dfrac{33}{360}} - 1 \right) \frac{360}{130} = 14.132\%$$

A final caveat: In Chapter 5 we noted that paying daily interest on a term repo or doing daily RP turns the RP rate into a daily compounded rate. The same holds true of RPs done against CDs. The formulas we have derived to figure CD tails are based on the assumption that the RP is a *term* RP on which interest is paid at maturity. If daily interest is paid, r should be properly compounded before being inserted into the formula.

Visual aids again

Calculating the correct tail on a new-issue CD is not difficult but it takes time, more time than a trader may have. A simple way to obviate this problem is to program a computer to do a printout of the sort given in Table 7–2.

Table 7–2
A visual aid for a CD trader
(date: 2/7/79)

Days to maturity	Maturity date	Offered price	Tail after 30-day RP at 10.20	Projected bid in 30 days†	Price protection in basis points
30	3/9	10.55	10.92*	10.30	62
45	3/24	10.65	11.45	10.30	115
60	4/8	10.75	11.20	10.55	65
75	4/23	10.85	11.19	10.65	54
90	5/8	10.95	11.23	10.75	48
105	5/23	11.05	11.29	10.85	44
120	6/7	11.15	11.37	10.95	42
135	6/22	11.25	11.45	11.05	40
150	7/7	11.35	11.54	11.15	39
165	7/22	11.45	11.63	11.25	38
180	8/6	11.55	11.72	11.35	37

* RP for 15 days at 10.15.
† Figures in this column are based on the assumption that the general level of rates will not change; for example, the projected 60-day rate 30 days hence equals 10.75, the prevailing 60-day rate. Anticipated or possible changes in rate levels should be compared with the number of basis points of protection to evaluate risk in creating a tail.

Figuring the tail on a CD hung out on term repo

Let

y^* = break-even sale rate
c = coupon rate
r_t = term repo rate
t_{im} = days from issue to maturity
t_{is} = days from issue to settlement
t_{sm} = days from settlement to maturity

Case I: CD is RPed at issue:

$$y^* = \left(\frac{1 + c\dfrac{t_{im}}{360}}{1 + r_t\dfrac{t_{is}}{360}} - 1 \right) \frac{360}{t_{sm}}$$

Case II: A secondary CD is RPed: Let

y = yield at which security is purchased
t_1 = days from purchase to maturity
t_2 = days from purchase to sale

Then

$$y^* = \left(\frac{1 + y\dfrac{t_1}{360}}{1 + r_t\dfrac{t_2}{360}} - 1 \right) \frac{360}{t_1 - t_2}$$

Note that the first and third columns in Table 7–2 give the CD run the way traders and CD brokers quote it over the phone. The fourth column shows the true tail rate after a 30-day RP. The fifth column shows what the bid on that tail would be if the market did not move during the 30-day RP period, and the final column shows how many basis points of protection against an unfavorable movement in rates the trader has on any tails he creates.

A table in the format of Table 7–2 contains all the basic information the trader needs. To it he can easily add other information such as his view on how much paper the banks are likely to write during the next 30 days and where short-term rates in general are headed.

HOLDING PERIOD YIELD

Intuition, which seems to be invariably wrong in money market calculations, suggests that if an investor bought a CD at 10 percent and sold it before maturity at the same rate, he would earn 10 percent over the holding period. In fact, he would earn *less*. The reason is our old friend, compounding. It crops up because interest is not paid by the issuer on the CD until some period after the investor sells it; the CD is priced at sale, however, so that the buyer will earn the offered yield on an amount equal to the principal paid *plus* accrued interest.

A new-issue CD

Consider first a CD that is bought by an investor at issue and later sold before maturity. The rate of simple interest, i, earned by the investor over the holding period will be given by

$$i = \left(\frac{\text{Sales price} - \text{Purchase price}}{\text{Purchase price}}\right)\frac{360}{t_{is}}$$

where

$$t_{is} = \text{days from issue to settlement on the sale}$$

On a *new issue* the purchase price is 1, so the formula reduces to

$$i = \left(\frac{1 + c\,\dfrac{t_{im}}{360}}{1 + y\,\dfrac{t_{sm}}{360}} - 1\right)\frac{360}{t_{is}}$$

Calculating yield earned on a CD sold before maturity

Let

i = Simple interest return earned over the holding period

Case I: The CD is purchased at issue: Let

$$y = \text{sale rate}$$
$$c = \text{coupon rate}$$
$$t_{im} = \text{days from issue to maturity}$$
$$t_{is} = \text{days from issue to settlement}$$
$$t_{sm} = \text{days from settlement to maturity}$$

then

$$i = \left(\frac{1 + c\,\dfrac{t_{im}}{360}}{1 + y\,\dfrac{t_{sm}}{360}} - 1\right)\frac{360}{t_{is}}$$

Case II: The CD purchased in the secondary market: Let

$$y_1 = \text{purchase rate}$$
$$y_2 = \text{sale rate}$$
$$t_1 = \text{days from purchase to maturity}$$
$$t_2 = \text{days from sale to maturity}$$

then

$$i = \left(\frac{1 + y_1\,\dfrac{t_1}{360}}{1 + y_2\,\dfrac{t_2}{360}} - 1\right)\frac{360}{t_1 - t_2}$$

---

where y is the rate at which the CD is sold.[2]

Example. An investor buys a 90-day CD carrying a 10 percent coupon at issue and sells it 30 days later at a 10 percent yield. The return he earns is not 10 percent but a lower figure, 9.83 percent. The calculation is:

$$i = \left(\frac{1 + 0.10 \frac{90}{360}}{1 + 0.10 \frac{60}{360}} - 1 \right) \frac{360}{30} = 9.83\%$$

A secondary CD

The yield on a CD purchased in the secondary market and sold before maturity can be calculated using a similar but slightly more complex formula. See Case B in the box on page 78.

Sensitivity of return to sale rate and length of holding period

The figures in Table 7–3 show what return, i, an investor would earn if he sold a 6-month CD purchased at 9 percent after various holding periods and at various rates. Note first the column labeled 9 percent. It shows that if the investor resells his CD at the purchase rate, the return he earns will be higher the longer the holding period is, that is, the closer the sale date is to the date on which the CD matures and accrued interest is paid out.

Table 7–3
The rate of return, *i*, earned by an investor on a 9 percent, 6-month CD when sold at various rates after various holding periods
(all numbers are percents)

| Holding period (days) | Sale rate, y | | | | |
	11 percent	10 percent	9 percent	8 percent	7 percent
30.........	−0.96	3.84	8.67	13.55	18.46
60.........	4.82	6.77	8.74	10.71	12.70
90.........	6.81	7.80	8.80	9.80	10.81
120.........	7.86	8.36	8.87	9.38	9.88
150.........	8.59	8.73	8.93	9.14	9.35
179.........	8.99	8.99	9.00	9.00	9.01

If an investor sells a CD at a rate below the rate at which he bought it, he will receive a capital gain and earn over the holding period a return higher than the yield at which he bought the CD. As the columns labeled 8 percent and 7 percent show, this effect becomes smaller the longer the holding period is. If, conversely, the investor sells

---

[2] This can be proved, as can all the other equations in this chapter, by making appropriate substitutions—in this case for the sale price—and doing a few algebraic manipulations.

his CD at a rate *above* that at which he purchased it, the effect is the opposite and also decreases as the holding period is lengthened.

The reason that the impact of the sale rate on the return earned by the investor diminishes as the holding period increases is: The longer the holding period, the shorter is the time in which the buyer of the CD will earn the rate at which he buys the CD and therefore the smaller will be the impact of that rate on the principal amount he pays for the CD.

Compounding

We have noted that selling a CD before maturity tends to reduce the yield earned by the investor over the holding period. If the investor *fully* reinvests the proceeds (principal *plus* accrued interest) from the sale of the CD, this effect will be offset by the opportunity for compounding of interest earnings created by the sale and subsequent repurchase.

To illustrate, note that an investor who purchased at issue a 182-day CD at 9 percent and sold it 91 days later at 9 percent would earn a yield of 8.80 percent over that period. If he immediately fully reinvested the sale proceeds ($1.022750 per $1 of face value) in a 9 percent, 91-day CD, his total earnings over the 182-day investment period would be identical with what he would have earned if he had held the 182-day, 9 percent CD he originally bought to maturity.

The RP scam

CDs are normally RPed "par flat"; that is, the investor lends the dealer an amount equal to the par value of the CDs being financed rather than their full market value including accrued interest. This means that RPing a secondary CD uses a dealer's capital, and the older the paper, the more capital such financing uses. As noted in Chapter 5, capital has a cost, and when it is used, its cost should be taken into account in calculating both carry and tails. The high cost that dealers assign to capital is one reason they tend to bid low on "stale dated" paper.

Sometimes traders who are taking new paper into inventory can find lenders who are willing or prefer to do an RP on an outright sale-repurchase basis. The scam in this is that a trader can offer the naive investor what appears to be a high rate but actually finance at a cost below the repo rate.

Here's an example. Suppose a trader buys a 90-day CD at 10 percent. He could finance the CD with term repo for a week at 9.90. Instead he proposes to an investor that he sell the CD outright to the investor at 10.05 and buy it back from him a week later at 10.05. To the investor, who has not massaged the numbers, the 10.05 apparent yield looks attractive compared with the 9.90 repo rate, but in reality the investor who did this deal would get a return, *i,* of only 9.82 percent. To check this, use the formula we derived for the return earned on a CD sold before maturity.

Note that the kicker in an outright sale-repurchase transaction works in exactly the opposite direction on a CD transaction than it does on a bill transaction. Doing an outright sale-repurchase, as opposed to a flat-priced RP, makes the borrower's cost of money higher than the nominal borrowing rate in the case of a discount security but lower than the nominal borrowing rate in the case of a CD.

For the trader who realizes that it makes a difference how CDs are financed, an interesting *arbitrage* opportunity arises. By reversing in CDs flat and RPing them at even a slightly higher nominal rate on an outright sale-repurchase basis, he can lock in a profit margin *and* generate capital.

RIDING THE YIELD CURVE

An investor can ride the yield curve in CDs just as he can in bills. Before doing so, however, he should do a break-even analysis of the sort described in Chapter 5.

To illustrate, consider an investor who has 3-month money and is choosing between a 6-month CD yielding 9.00 and a 3-month CD yielding 8.80. The investor wonders: If he were to buy the 6-month CD and sell it 3 months hence, at what rate would he have to sell in order to earn at least the 3-month rate of 8.80?

Intuition suggests that, since the investor picks up 20 extra basis points over 3 months by buying the 6-month CD, he could sell that CD after 3 months at

$$9.00 + 0.20 = 9.20$$

and still earn 8.80 over the 3-month holding period. Intuition, however, grossly overestimates the true break-even rate. The reason is that the sale of a CD before maturity reduces the return earned by the investor for reasons already discussed.

To determine his true break-even rate, the investor needs a precise formula. We obtain it as follows. Let

i = rate of return offered by the short CD

y^* = investor's break-even yield on the sale of a longer CD

Next, recall our equation for the return earned by an investor when he buys a CD at issue and sells it a yield y before maturity:

$$i = \left(\frac{1 + c\,\dfrac{t_{im}}{360}}{1 + y\,\dfrac{t_{sm}}{360}} - 1 \right) \frac{360}{t_{is}}$$

If we interpret i in this equation to be the rate the investor can get on the short CD, then the y value in the equation is y^*, his break-even rate of sale on the long CD. Thus, solving the preceding equation for y ($= y^*$), we get:

$$y^* = \left(\frac{1 + c\,\dfrac{t_{im}}{360}}{1 + i\,\dfrac{t_{is}}{360}} - 1 \right) \frac{360}{t_{sm}}$$

If we now insert the numbers in our example into this formula, we obtain

$$y^* = \left(\frac{1 + 0.090\,\dfrac{180}{360}}{1 + 0.088\,\dfrac{90}{360}} - 1 \right) \frac{360}{90} = 9.00\%$$

This number tells us that, if our investor buys a 6-month CD at 9 percent and sells it 3 months later, he must sell it at a rate no higher than 9 percent in order to earn at least 8.80 over the 3-month holding period. Note the 8.80 figure corresponds to the number given in Table 7–3 for the yield earned on a 6-month CD purchased at 9 percent and sold 3 months later at 9 percent.

Figuring the break-even sale rate on a ride along the yield curve in CDs: The choice is between investing temporarily in the long CD and buying and holding the short CD to maturity

Let

y_L = yield (coupon on a new issue) at which the long CD can be bought

t_L = current maturity of the long CD

y_S = yield (coupon on a new issue) at which the short CD can be bought

t_S = current maturity of the short CD, which equals the length of the investment period

y^* = break-even yield on the sale of the long CD at the end of the investment period, i.e., at t_S

then

$$y^* = \left(\frac{1 + y_L \frac{t_L}{360}}{1 + y_S \frac{t_S}{360}} - 1 \right) \frac{360}{t_L - t_S}$$

CD PARITY

In Chapter 5 we derived a formula for bill parity. A similar formula can be derived for CDs. Suppose 1-month CDs are trading at 9 percent and 2-month CDs at 10 percent. An investor anticipates that CD rates will rise and wonders whether he would earn more purchasing a 2-month CD or two consecutive 1-month CDs. Answering this query requires a *break-even* calculation. Specifically, the investor needs to know how much he would have to earn on the second 1-month CD in order to earn a return of 10 percent over the full 2-month period.

Approximation suggests that, with 1-month CDs at 9 percent and 2-month CDs at 10 percent, the investor would have to be able to purchase 1 month hence a 1-month CD yielding 11 percent in order to break even on the purchase of a current 1-month CD at 9 percent. Actually the correct number is slightly lower.

Let

c_1 = coupon on the current long CD

c_2 = coupon on the current short CD

c_3 = coupon on the future CD covering the "gap" between the current long and short CDs

c^* = break-even coupon on this future CD

t_1 = days to maturity on the current long CD

t_2 = days to maturity on the current short CD

Assuming that an amount of principal equal to 1 is invested in both the long and the short CDs on day 1 and assuming reinvestment of interest, *the break-even rate purchase on the future CD, c^* is c_3 in the expression*

$$1 + c_1 \frac{t_1}{360} = 1 + c_2 \frac{t_2}{360} + c_3 \left(1 + c_2 \frac{t_2}{360} \right) \frac{t_1 - t_2}{360}$$

Solving this break-even expression for $c_3 (= c^*)$, we get

$$c^* = \frac{c_1 t_1 - c_2 t_2}{\left(1 + c_2 \dfrac{t_2}{360}\right)(t_1 - t_2)}$$

If we now plug the numbers in our example into this equation, we find that

$$c^* = \frac{0.10(60) - 0.09(30)}{\left(1 + 0.09 \dfrac{30}{360}\right) 30} = 10.92\%$$

The investor's break-even rate on the second CD is not 11 percent, but 10.92 percent. The approximation overestimates the break-even rate on the second 1-month CD because it fails to allow for the compounding that can occur if the investor purchases two consecutive 1-month CDs.

RESERVE REQUIREMENTS

Any investor in CDs should be aware that reserve requirements are imposed by the Fed on this form of bank borrowing. These requirements, which the Fed *often* changes as part of a move to ease or tighten credit, vary with the maturity of the CD at issue. They are generally lower the longer the period for which the CD is written.

A banker who funds via the CD route is interested not in the nominal rate he must pay for funds thus obtained, but in his *all-in cost*, which equals the coupon rate paid *plus* the cost of the idle reserve balance he must hold at the Fed. This all-in cost is easily calculated. Let

c = coupon on the CD
c' = all-in cost, i.e., c + Reserve cost
r_F = reserve ratio imposed by the Fed

then

$$c' = \frac{c}{1 - r_F}$$

The difference between the coupon rate on a CD and the all-in cost to the bank issuing it can be substantial. For example, if the coupon rate were 10 percent and the reserve ratio were 8 percent, then the all-in cost of the usable funds that a bank obtained by issuing a 10 percent CD would be 10.86 percent, that is, 86 basis points above its nominal borrowing rate.[3]

The reserve ratios imposed on bank time deposits are varied frequently by the Fed. Whatever their general level, reserve requirements are always lower for long-term deposits than for short-term deposits. To understand (1) the structure of CD rates—e.g., 3-month versus 6-month, Euro versus domestic—and (2) the appetite of banks for money in different maturity ranges, any investor in CDs should track reserve requirements on bank CDs and the impact of these requirements on the all-in cost of such money to banks.

---

[3] In September 1979 the Fed imposed reserve requirements of 8 percent on CDs with an initial maturity of 30–179 days and 4.5 percent on CDs with a an initial maturity of 180 days to 4 years. It also imposed an unusual extra 8 percent reserve requirement on a bank's borrowings in excess of its borrowings in a September 1979 base period. These are again being changed.

VARIABLE-RATE CDs

Variable-rate CDs were designed to appeal not to the ordinary investor but to money market funds. Such a fund will buy a 90-day variable-rate CD that pays interest monthly at, say ⅛ above the 30-day rate and get the selling dealer to give it a *put* on coupon dates. The latter technically gives the fund the right to sell the paper back to the dealer at par on the first and second interest dates. While it is understood that the put will never be exercised, it serves a purpose; namely, it permits the fund to treat what starts out as 90-day paper as 30-day paper for purposes of calculating the average maturity of its security holdings.

Variable-rate CDs are not attractive from the point of view of liquidity, but the extra return they offer because of compounding should not be neglected by the investor who holds to maturity. If 30-day CDs were offered at 9⅞ and a 3-month variable-rate CD were offered at an initial rate ⅛ above that, then with compounding, the true offered rate on the variable-rate CD would be

$$\left[\left(1 + \frac{0.10}{360/30}\right)^3 - 1\right] \frac{365}{90} = 12.22\%$$

It is this rate, which is 35 basis points above the 30-day rate, that the investor who holds until maturity should compare to the 90-day rate if he does not anticipate a fall in rates.

EURO AND INTERMEDIATE-TERM CDs

CDs, domestic and Euro, that have a maturity at issue of *more than 1 year* pay interest semiannually or, less typically, annually. Like other CDs that pay interest at maturity, CDs that pay periodic interest are priced in terms of yield.

The actual dollar price paid for such a CD equals the stream of future dollar flows it will throw off discounted back to the settlement day at the sale rate, i.e., the present value at the sale rate of these future dollar flows minus accrued interest as of settlement. This sounds simple, but on a CD that pays periodic interest, the calculation is complicated. On such a CD the amount of interest that the CD accrues for each coupon period is calculated as follows:

$$a_i = c \, \frac{B}{360}$$

where

B = basis, i.e., number of days in the coupon period

Table 7–4
Day periods needed to calculate the price of a CD that carries a 7.55 coupon, pays interest semiamiannually, was issued on 4/15/76, will mature on 10/15/77, and was traded for settlement on 4/19/76 at a rate of 7.50

Period	Dates	Number of days
Issue to first coupon	4/15/76 to 10/15/76	183
Settlement to first coupon	4/19/76 to 10/15/76	179
First to second coupon	10/15/76 to 4/15/77	182
Second to third coupon	4/15/77 to 10/15/77	183
Third coupon to fourth and maturity	10/15/77 to 4/14/78	181

Since $^{365}/_2 = 182.5$, consecutive bases are always unequal in length. The exact length of each coupon period is, moreover, taken into account not only in the calculation of interest accrued as of each coupon date, but also in the factors by which future sums to be received are discounted back to the settlement date. For that reason the present value (price) of an intermediate-term CD cannot be calculated using a simple general formula of the sort given for long bonds in Chapter 9. Instead an iterative process must be used.

To illustrate, consider a CD with a 7.55 coupon that was issued on 4/15/76, will mature on 10/15/77, and was traded for settlement on 4/19/76 at a rate of 7.50. To

Table 7–5
Calculating the price of the intermediate-term CD described in Table 7–4
(all dollar values are per $1 of face value)

Step 1: Discount maturity value back to third coupon date:

$$\left(\frac{1 + 0.0755 \frac{181}{360}}{1 + 0.0750 \frac{181}{360}} \right) = 1.00024225$$

Step 2: Discount sum obtained in Step 1 *plus* coupon interest due on third coupon date back to second coupon date:

$$\left(\frac{1.00024225 + 0.0755 \frac{183}{360}}{1 + 0.0750 \frac{183}{360}} \right) = 1.00047819$$

Step 3: Discount sum obtained in Step 2 *plus* coupon interest due on second coupon date back to first coupon date:

$$\left(\frac{1.00047819 + 0.0755 \frac{182}{360}}{1 + 0.0750 \frac{182}{360}} \right) = 1.00070426$$

Step 4: Discount sum obtained in Step 3 *plus* coupon interest due on first coupon date back to settlement date. This gives the value of the principal *plus* accrued interest per $1 of face value on the settlement date:

$$\left(\frac{1.000704 + 0.0755 \frac{183}{360}}{1 + 0.075 \frac{179}{360}} \right) = 1.00172735$$

Step 5: Calculate accrued interest on the settlement date:

$$0.0755 \frac{4}{360} = 0.00083889$$

Step 6: Subtract value obtained in Step 5 from value obtained in Step 4 to get the *principal* paid per $1 of face value:

$$1.00172735 + 0.00083889 = 1.00088846$$

Step 7: Multiply by $1,000,000 to find the dollar price of a CD with a face value of $1 million:

$$\$1,000,000(1.00088846) = \$1,000,888.46$$

calculate the price that an investor must pay for this security at settlement, we first calculate the number of days in the current and all future coupon periods and the number of days from settlement to the first coupon date (Table 7–4).

Next we discount the maturity value of the security back to its next to last coupon date (Step 1, Table 7–5). We then discount this discounted value (1.00024225) *plus* accrued interest on the next to last coupon date back to the preceding coupon date (Step 2, Table 7–5). This procedure is continued until the last period over which the security's value is discounted is the days from settlement to the next coupon (Step 4, Table 7–5). The value obtained in this step is the full amount the investor must pay per $1 of face value. Next accrued interest as of the settlement date is calculated and subtracted from this amount; this calculation gives the principal the investor must pay per $1 of face value (Steps 5 and 6 in Table 7–5). This amount can then be adjusted to reflect the security's face value (Step 7, Table 7–5).

Notes and bonds in their final coupon period

In this chapter we consider a second breed of *interest-at-maturity securities*— notes and bonds in their *last* (or in the case of short notes, *only*) coupon period. Securities of this type differ from CDs in the way they accrue interest; also, unlike CDs, they are quoted on the basis of dollar prices.

In our discussion we consider first short governments and then short agencies and municipal securities. Note that "short" is the jargon we use to denote a security in its last coupon period.

SHORT GOVERNMENTS

The Treasury issues notes and bonds with a minimum initial maturity of 2 years for notes and 10 years for bonds. Both pay interest *semiannually on the basis of a 365-day year.*

Accrued interest

The first coupon date on a government note or bond is determined at issue; the second is the same day of the month 6 months hence. Thus, if a security's first coupon date is May 15, its second will be November 15. This pattern continues throughout the life of the security. At each coupon date, an amount equal to half the coupon rate times the face value of the security, i.e., $c/2$ per \$1 of face value, is paid to the security holder.[1]

Interest on governments is accrued during each coupon period on an *actual day basis;* that is, a fixed sum of interest is accrued each day during the coupon period until an amount equal to $c/2$ per \$1 of face value is reached on the coupon date.

The number of days in a coupon period is referred to as its *basis,* and the amount of daily interest that accrues during any coupon period is calculated as follows: Let

B = basis, i.e., number of days in the coupon period
c = coupon rate

---

[1] For calculation of accrued interest when the first coupon period is irregular, see appendix to this chapter.

then

$$\left(\begin{array}{c}\text{Interest accrued per day}\\ \text{per \$1 of face value}\end{array}\right) = \frac{c}{2B}$$

The number of days between one day in a month and the same day 6 months later is never precisely half a year—182.5 days. Therefore, consecutive coupon periods are always unequal in length; one might be 181 days, the next 184 days. Since consecutive coupon periods always have different bases, *the interest that accrues per day on a government always differs by a small amount between consecutive coupon periods.*

Calculating accrued interest

When a government note or bond is traded, the buyer pays the dollar price quoted plus accrued interest as of the settlement date. The formula for calculating accrued interest on a government is as follows: Let

a_i = accured interest *per dollar* of face value
t_{is} = days from issue or last coupon to settlement

then

$$a_i = c\,\frac{t_{is}}{2B}$$

The only difficulty in making this calculation is determining t_{is} and B. One way to do that is to use a financial calculator programmed to calculate the number of days between two dates. A second alternative is to use a financial calendar. To illustrate the latter, let us assume that a specific security,

N 7⅛ 11/30/79

is traded for settlement on August 10 of its next to last coupon period. To find accrued interest on that date, we turn to the page in a financial calendar corresponding to the security's last coupon, May 31. There (Figure 8–1) we see by looking at the *lower* numbers for the appropriate dates that August 10 was 71 days after the last coupon and that the basis in the coupon period (i.e., the number of days to November 30) was 183. Thus, on August 10, accrued interest on the security was

$$a_i = 0.07125\,\frac{71}{2(183)}$$

$$= 0.013822$$

per \$1 of face value.

A financial calendar suffices for anyone who wants simply to determine a security's basis in the current coupon period or to calculate accrued interest as of a specific date. However, someone who programs a computer to make price, yield, and other bond calculations needs a general method for determining the number of days from one date to another. Simple algorithms for doing this are described in the Security Industry Association's book, *Standard Securities Calculation Methods* (New York, 1973). Note that because a security's yield to maturity will be distorted if it matures on a nonbusiness day, more complex algorithms than those described in this book are needed if the programmer's objective is to calculate true yield maturity as opposed to yield to maturity on the quote sheet. (More is said about the discrepancy between true and quoted yields later.)

Figure 8–1
A page from a financial Calendar

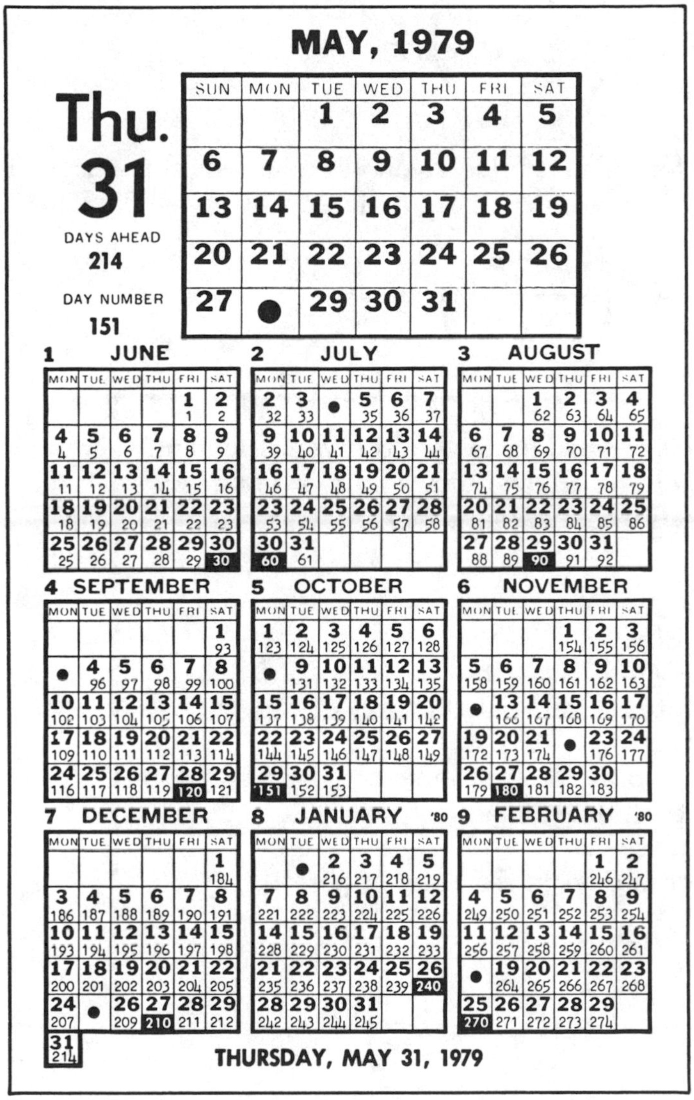

Yield given price

On governments in their last coupon period, yield to maturity is calculated as a simple interest rate. Let

y = yield to maturity on the quote sheet
t_{sm} = days from settlement to maturity
P = price *per $1* of face value, accrued interest *not* included
a_i = accrued interest per $1 of face value

Then the industry's formula for calculating yield, y, when price is given, can be written as follows:

$$y = \left(\frac{\left(1 + \frac{c}{2}\right) - (P + a_i)}{P + a_i} \right) \frac{2B}{t_{sm}}$$

which reduces to

$$y = \left(\frac{1 + \dfrac{c}{2}}{P + a_i} - 1 \right) \frac{2B}{t_{sm}}$$

Price given yield

If, alternatively, we want a formula for price given yield on a short government, we can obtain it simply by solving the preceding formula for P. Doing so gives us

$$P = \left(\frac{1 + \dfrac{c}{2}}{1 + y \dfrac{t_{sm}}{2B}} \right) - a_i$$

Industry formulas for calculating yield given price and price given yield on a government note or bond in *its final coupon period*

Let

y = yield to maturity
c = coupon rate
P = price per \$1 of face value, accrued interest *not* included
t_{is} = days from last coupon to settlement
t_{sm} = days from settlement to maturity
a_i = accrued interest
B = basis (number of days in the coupon period)

Case I: Yield given price:

$$y = \left(\frac{1 + \dfrac{c}{2}}{P + a_i} - 1 \right) \frac{2B}{t_{sm}}$$

where

$$a_i = c \, \frac{t_{is}}{2B}$$

Case II: Price given yield:

$$P = \left(\frac{1 + \dfrac{c}{2}}{1 + y \dfrac{t_{sm}}{2B}} \right) - a_i$$

True yield to maturity

Our formula for yield given price has the virtue of simplicity but the disadvantage that it *never* is correct because $2B$ (i.e., two times the number of days in the current coupon period) never equals 365. A second frequent source of error in the calculation of

y on a note or bond is that the security matures on a nonbusiness day, which means that the investor must wait 1 or more days after the security matures to receive principal and interest.

Let

$$y^* = \text{true yield to maturity}$$
$$t_{sm} = \text{days from settlement to maturity}$$
$$t_{ss} = \text{days from settlement to settlement (i.e., payout)}$$

Note, on a security that matures on a nonbusiness day, t_{ss} is greater than t_{sm}.

To obtain an expression for y^*, we must alter the industry's measure of y in two ways:

First, we multiply y by 365/2B to put y on a precise 365-day basis. *Second,* for securities that mature on a nonbusiness day, we multiply this value by t_{sm}/t_{ss} so that y is measured on the basis of the correct holding (investment) period.

Doing so gives us

$$y^* = y \left(\frac{365}{2B}\right) \frac{t_{sm}}{t_{ss}}$$

In this expression the final term, (t_{sm}/t_{ss}), reduces to 1 if the security matures on a business day, because in that case $t_{sm} = t_{ss}$.

Our formula for calculating y^* as a function of y on the quote sheet assumes that the security is actually traded at the *offered* price on the quote sheet. If the security is traded at some other price, y must be adjusted. Specifically, if the trade occurs at a higher price, then the y value on the quote sheet will be too high. To get the correct value, one must subtract from y a number of yield values of $1/32$ equal to the number of 32nds by which the trade price exceeds the offered price on the quote sheet. Conversely, if the trade occurs at a price below the offered price, yield values of $1/32$ will have to be added to y. When this adjustment is allowed for, the formula for y^* is the one shown in the box on page 92.

Example. To illustrate, we consider a security quoted in Table 6–1,

N 6⅛ 6/30/79

This security was offered for settlement on 4/9/79 at 99– 4, which implied a y value of 9.91; also the yield value of $1/32$ on the security was 0.140. Counting days, we find that the security's basis during the last coupon period was 181 days, that the security matured 82 days later on a Saturday, and that payment of principal and interest would thus be made 84 days hence on a Monday.

Using that information, let us first check the y value on the quote sheet. On the settlement date, which was 99 days after the last coupon date, accrued interest on this security *per $1 of face value* was

$$a_i = 0.06125 \frac{99}{2(181)} = 0.016751$$

Inserting this and other relevant numbers into the industry formula for yield, we obtain

$$y = \left(\frac{1 + 0.030625}{0.99\ ^{4}/_{32} + 0.016751} - 1\right) \frac{2(181)}{82}$$
$$= 0.0991 = 9.91\%$$

which corresponds to the yield figure given in Table 6–1.

Calculating true yield to maturity on a 365-day-year basis on a government note or bond during *its final coupon period*

Let

y = yield to maturity on the quote sheet
y^* = true yield to maturity
v_{32} = yield value of $1/32$
t_{sm} = days from settlement to maturity
t_{ss} = days from settlement to settlement (payout) on a security that matures on a nonbusiness day
B = basis, i.e., number of days in the coupon period

Case I: Security matures on a business day:†‡

$$y^* = (y \pm v_{32} \text{ as required}) \frac{365}{2B}$$

Case II: Security matures on a nonbusiness day:

$$y^* = (y \pm v_{32} \text{ as required}) \left(\frac{365}{2B}\right) \frac{t_{sm}}{t_{ss}}$$

---

† y is calculated on the basis of the offered price on the quote sheet. If a trade occurs at a higher price, y will be less; to calculate it, one subtracts an appropriate number of yield values of $1/32$ from y. On a trade that occurs at a lower price, values of v_{32} are added to y.

‡ Note y^* can be converted to a 360-day-year basis simply by replacing 365 in the above equations with 360.

Now using our formula for y^* and recalling that the security in question pays out 2 days *after* it matures, we find that its true yield to maturity at the offered price 99– 4, was:

$$y^* = 0.0991 \left(\frac{365}{2 \times 181}\right) \frac{82}{84} = 0.0975 = 9.75\%$$

In examining this equation, note two things. The fact that the basis was less than half a year caused the yield to maturity on the quote sheet to be too small. This effect, however, was swamped by the Saturday maturity, which, by lengthening the investment period 2 days, reduced true yield to maturity substantially below the quote sheet figure.

To illustrate the adjustment necessary if the trade is made away from the offered price, let's now assume that the security was traded at the bid side of the market, e.g., at 99– 2. That increases by 28 basis points true yield maturity, which is calculated as follows:

$$y^* = [0.0991 + 2(0.140)] \left(\frac{365}{2 \times 181}\right) \frac{82}{84} = 0.1003 = 10.03\%$$

Break-even rate on a reverse to maturity

Frequently an institution that holds a short government will find that by swapping out of that security into CDs, term Fed funds, or some other instrument, it can pick up 50 basis points or more. On a $1 million swap, a pickup of 50 basis point is worth approximately $2,500 if earned over 6 months, half as much if earned over 3 months. Thus, such swaps are attractive. Many institutions, however, cannot do such a swap on an outright basis if the security they want to sell is trading, because of a rise in interest rates, below the book value their accountant assigns to it.

Institutions in this situation have to resort to doing swaps indirectly. Instead of selling the maturing notes or bonds, they *reverse them out to maturity* to a dealer; that is, they borrow money against the securities. They then invest that money in a higher-yielding instrument, often one that matches in current maturity the security being reversed out. An institution that does this type of transaction is in effect arbitraging between the low term RP rate at which it can borrow on a collateralized basis and the higher rate at which it can invest.

For a dealer who is reversing in securities to maturity, there is some *reverse repo (i.e., lending) rate* at which the firm can just break even on the transaction. The calculation of this rate is easily made. The true yield to maturity on a short government is, as we have calculated it, a simple interest rate on a 365-day basis. The reverse rate is also a simple interest rate, but it is quoted on a 360-basis. Thus, to obtain the dealer's break-even rate on a reverse to maturity, all we need to do is convert $y*$ to a 360-day basis.

Let

$$y* = \text{true yield to maturity}$$
$$r* = \text{dealer's break-even rate on a reverse to maturity}$$

then

$$r* = y* \frac{360}{365}$$

$$= (y \pm v_{32} \text{ as required}) \left(\frac{360}{2B}\right) \frac{t_{sm}}{t_{ss}}$$

Typically, a dealer doing a reverse to maturity will immediately sell the security reversed in to him. Then on the maturity date (or payout date if maturity occurs on a nonbusiness day), the dealer and investor will *pair off* (1) the amount owed by the dealer to the investor, which is accrued interest over the life of the reverse *plus* the amount of the discount at which the security was reversed in, against (2) the amount owed by the investor to the dealer, which is interest on the reverse borrowing.

Example. To illustrate, let us consider again the security N 6⅛ 6/30/79, which we showed in the preceding section would have offered a true yield to maturity of 10.03 if sold on 4/9/79 at the bid side of the market, that is, at the price at which the dealer reversing it to maturity would have sold it if the market had not moved. The dealer's break-even rate on a reverse to maturity on this security would have been

$$r* = y* \frac{360}{365} = 0.1003 \frac{360}{365} = 0.0989 = 9.89\%$$

To check that this is the true break-even, note that on this security, accrued interest on the settlement date equaled 0.016751 per $1 of face value, while the coupon at maturity equaled 0.030625. Thus, per $1 of face value,

> ## Calculating the break-even reverse repo rate on a reverse to maturity of a Treasury or agency note or bond *in its last coupon period*
>
> Let
>
> $$y^* = \text{true yield to maturity}$$
> $$r^* = \text{break-even reverse repo rate}$$
> $$t_{sm} = \text{days settlement to maturity}$$
> $$t_{ss} = \text{days settlement to payout}$$
> $$v_{32} = \text{yield value of } 1/32$$
> $$B = \text{basis, i.e., number of days in the coupon period}$$
>
> **Case I:** The security is a government note or bond:
>
> $$r^* = y^* \frac{360}{365}$$
>
> $$= (y \pm v_{32} \text{ as required}) \left(\frac{360}{2B}\right) \frac{t_{sm}}{t_{ss}}$$
>
> **Case II:** The security is a federal agency note or bond:† Let
>
> $$t'_{sm} = \text{assumed days from settlement to maturity}$$
>
> then
>
> $$r^* = y^* \frac{360}{365}$$
>
> $$= (y \pm v_{32} \text{ as required}) \left(\frac{t'_{sm}}{t_{sm}}\right) \frac{360}{365}$$
>
> † The formula for y^* on a short agency is derived later in the chapter. See the box on page 103.

$$\binom{\text{Repo interest earned by}}{\text{dealer at maturity}} = r^*(P + a_i) \frac{t_{ss}}{360}$$

$$= 0.0989 \left(\frac{99^2/_{32}}{100} + 0.016751\right) \frac{84}{360}$$

$$= 0.023247$$

while

$$\binom{\text{Balance owned by dealer}}{\text{to investor at maturity}} = (1 - P) + \left(\frac{c}{2} - a_i\right)$$

$$= \frac{30/_{32}}{100} + (0.030625 - 0.016751)$$

$$= 0.023250$$

The small discrepancy, 0.000003, between the two numbers we have just calculated is to be expected. It reflects the fact that yields were rounded to two decimal places. On a $1 million trade, this discrepancy would have amounted to only $3.

Normally a dealer who is doing a reverse to maturity will try to charge a reverse rate at least 10 basis points above his break-even rate. When a security's true yield to maturity—which measures the dealer's interest cost on the reverse—is significantly less than its yield to maturity on the quote sheet, the dealer will try for more. Thus, it is worth an investor's time to calculate a dealer's break-even reverse bid. When a short government is sold and the proceeds are reinvested in some higher-yielding instrument, there are $X of extra earnings that will be picked up; how many go to the dealer and how many to the investor depends on where the reverse rate is set.

In our calculation we assumed that the dealer who is reversing in securities to maturity would give the investor a loan equal to the full market value of these securities, that is, equal to the bid price in the market *plus accrued interest*. If, alternatively, the dealer lends only principal, he will generate capital equal to accrued interest at the time of the transaction. If he has some use for that capital—such as reducing his bank borrowing—that will return him *more than the reverse rate,* generating such capital will render a reverse to maturity even more attractive.

True return earned on a purchase and sale before maturity

In Chapter 7 we showed that an investor who sells a CD before maturity must sell his CD at a yield less than the purchase yield in order to earn the purchase yield over the holding period. The same is true for a short government.

Let

P_1 = purchase price
a_1 = accrued interest at purchase
y_1 = yield to maturity at which the security is purchased[2]
t_1 = days from purchase to maturity
P_2 = sale price
a_2 = accrued interest at sale
y_2 = yield to maturity at which the security is sold[2]
t_2 = days from sale to maturity
i = simple interest rate earned

From our formula for calculating a simple interest return, it follows that on a short government purchased and sold before maturity, the return earned by the investor over the holding period is given by

$$i = \left[\frac{(P_2 + a_2) - (P_1 + a_1)}{P_1 + a_1} \right] \frac{365}{t_1 - t_2}$$

This formula can be used directly. It can also be used to derive an expression for i in terms of y_1 and y_2. To get that formula, which eliminates the need to calculate accrued interest on two dates, we use the equation

$$y = \left(\frac{1 + \frac{c}{2}}{P + a_t} - 1 \right) \frac{2B}{t_{sm}}$$

to solve for $(P_1 + a_1)$ as a function of y_1 and for $(P_2 + a_2)$ as a function of y_2. We then

---

[2] Note that y_1 and y_2 are y values calculated as on a quote sheet; i.e., by using the industry formula on page 90.

substitute those expressions into the previous formula for i, which gives us an equation that reduces to

$$i = \left(\frac{1 + y_1 \dfrac{t_1}{2B}}{1 + y_2 \dfrac{t_2}{2B}} - 1 \right) \frac{365}{t_1 - t_2}$$

Example.   Consider an investor who buys a short government with 90 days to run at a yield to maturity of 9 percent and later sells it at 9 percent. Assume

$$y_1 = 0.09$$
$$y_2 = 0.09$$
$$t_1 = 90$$
$$t_2 = 60$$

Over the holding period, the investor will have earned not 9 percent but

$$i = \left(\frac{1 + 0.09 \dfrac{90}{2 \times 181}}{1 + 0.09 \dfrac{60}{2 \times 181}} - 1 \right) \frac{365}{90 - 60} = 0.0894 = 8.94\%$$

BREAK-EVEN PURCHASE RATE ON A SHORT

A trader who shorts a government in anticipation of a rise in interest rates and a fall in bond prices will want to calculate the rate at which he would have to purchase the securities shorted in order to break even. If we assume the short is covered by a *reverse*, i.e., that the dealer lends the sale proceeds at the reverse repo rate, a formula for this break-even yield can easily be calculated.

If a trader breaks even on a short, the interest he earns on the reverse will equal his loss on the short; that is,

Interest earned on reverse = Purchase price − Sale price

To derive a break-even sale price, we must restate this relationship in symbols. On a short sale, the sale occurs before the covering purchase; therefore, we use

Subscript 1 to denote all variables—P, a_j, y and t_{sm}—that describe the security *sale*
Subscript 2 to denote all variables that cover the security *purchase*.[3]

Using this notation, we can restate the break-even relationship as follows:

$$r(P_1 + a_1) \frac{t_1 - t_2}{360} = (P_2 + a_2) - (P_1 + a_1)$$

where

$$r = \text{reverse repo rate}$$

If we now solve this break-even equation for r and substitute expressions for price plus

---

[3] This is the precise opposite of the notation introduced on page 95, where we were talking about a purchase-resale transaction.

accrued interest as a function of yield and days to maturity, as we did in the preceding section, we get[4]

$$r = \left(\frac{1 + y_1 \frac{t_1}{2B}}{1 + y_2 \frac{t_2}{2B}} - 1 \right) \frac{360}{t_1 - t_2}$$

Let

y^* = break-even rate of purchase on a short covered by a reverse at the rate r

Obviously, when the above *break-even* relationship holds, $y_2 = y^*$. Thus, solving this relationship for y_2, we get

$$y^* = \left(\frac{1 + y_1 \frac{t_1}{2B}}{1 + r \frac{t_1 - t_2}{360}} - 1 \right) \frac{2B}{t_2}$$

In examining this equation, note that, as intuition suggests, y^* will be higher as y_1 is higher and r is lower.

Example. Assume that a trader sells short a government note or bond with 90 days to run at a yield to maturity of 9 percent; the security's basis is 182 days. To cover his short, the trader reverses in the security; and the rate he gets on the reverse is 8.50 percent. Thirty days later, the trader covers his short. In doing so, he must purchase the security shorted at a rate no lower than

$$y^* = \left(\frac{1 + 0.0900 \frac{90}{364}}{1 + 0.0850 \frac{30}{360}} - 1 \right) \frac{364}{60} = 9.14\%$$

BREAK-EVEN RATE ON A FORWARD SALE

Occasionally a customer will ask a dealer to do a *forward* transaction, to sell him x days hence, when he will have funds, some security at a fixed rate. A dealer faced with such a request will often choose to eliminate risk by buying the security immediately and financing it in the repo market. In that case, he must ask what would be the minimum rate at which he could commit to sell the security forward and not lose money.

Let

Subscript 1 denote variables associated with the *purchase* transaction
Subscript 2 denote variables associated with the *sale* transaction.

For the dealer to break even, the purchase price plus the cost of carry must equal the price at which the forward sale occurs; that is,

$$(\text{Purchase price}) \left(1 + r \frac{t_1 - t_2}{360} \right) = \text{Sale price}$$

Rewriting this expression, we get

---

[4] Note: This equation can be used to solve for r^*, the break-even reverse rate, when the security is sold at y_1 and the *anticipated* purchase rate is y_2.

$$P_2 + a_2 = (P_1 + a_1)\left(1 + r\frac{t_1 - t_2}{360}\right)$$

If we now substitute for $P + a_i$, as we did in the two preceding sections, and simplify the resulting expression, we get a break-even expression that can be solved for y_2. This y_2 value is

$$y* = \text{break-even rate on the forward sale}$$

Solving for $y_2 = y*$ we get

$$y* = \left(\frac{1 + y_1\frac{t_1}{2B}}{1 + r\frac{t_1 - t_2}{360}} - 1\right)\frac{2B}{t_2}$$

Note that this expression is identical with the one obtained in the preceding section for the break-even rate of purchase when a security is shorted. Actually, what we have is a single formula that is applicable to two situations that are the precise *opposites* of each other. In each case, we denote variables associated with the initiation of the transaction with subscript 1 and those associated with its termination with subscript 2. On a short sale, termination involves a *purchase*; on a forward sale, it involves a *sale* (see the box on page 99).

Example.   Suppose a customer wants to buy 30 days hence a government with 90 days to run. Currently this security is trading at 9 percent, and its basis in its current and final coupon period is 181 days. The security can be RPed at 8.50. Plugging these numbers into our formula for $y*$, the break-even sale rate, we get

$$y* = \left(\frac{1 + 0.09\frac{90}{362}}{1 + 0.085\frac{30}{360}} - 1\right)\frac{362}{60} = 9.16\%$$

A quick approximation based on the observation that a carry of approximately 50 basis points is being earned by the dealer over 30 days would suggest that $y*$ should be 9.25. It is actually lower (and the break-even sale price therefore higher) because the repo rate is a 360-day rate and, more important, because a purchase and sale before maturity of a short government tend, as showed earlier, to reduce the return earned by the holder.

In this respect, observe that—assuming our calculation is correct—if the dealer sold at the break-even rate, he would earn over the holding period a simple interest return i equal to the repo rate. To test this, we note that the required formula for i on a *360-day basis* is

$$i = \left(\frac{1 + y_1\frac{t_1}{2B}}{1 + y_2\frac{t_2}{2B}} - 1\right)\frac{360}{t_1 - t_2}$$

Inserting the numbers in our example into this formula, we obtain the result anticipated:

$$i = \left(\frac{1 + 0.0900\frac{90}{362}}{1 + 0.0916\frac{60}{362}} - 1\right)\frac{360}{30}$$
$$= 8.50\%$$

the dealer's assumed repo cost.

> ### Calculating two break-even rates for government notes and bonds in their last coupon period
>
> Let
>
> y = yield to maturity
> t = days settlement to maturity
> B = basis, i.e., days in the coupon period
> r = repo or reverse rate
>
> The formula is
>
> $$y^* = \left(\frac{1 + y_1 \frac{t_1}{2B}}{1 + r \frac{t_1 - t_2}{360}} - 1 \right) \frac{2B}{t_2}$$
>
> Subscript 1 refers to values at the initiation of the transaction, subscript 2 to values at the end of the transaction.
>
> **Case I:** y^* = break-even rate of *purchase* on a short covered by a reverse at the rate r
>
> Subscript 1 refers to sale variables.
> Subscript 2 refers to purchase variables.
>
> **Case II:** y^* = break-even rate of *sale* on a forward sale of a security financed by a repo at the rate r
>
> Subscript 1 refers to purchase variables.
> Subscript 2 refers to sale variables.

SHORT AGENCY SECURITIES
Accrued interest

Federal agency securities are, as Table 8–1 shows, quoted in the same way as governments.[5] In our discussion of price and yield calculations, we must treat short agencies separate from short governments, however, because they accrue interest in a different way. On agencies, *interest accrues as if the year has 360 days and every month has 30 days.* This method of accruing interest, which is also used on municipal securities, is referred to as a 30/360 basis.

To illustrate (1) how this method of accruing interest works and (2) how it affects the yield to maturity figures given on the quote sheet, let's consider the Federal Home Loan Bank security

FHLB 9½ 8/27/79

quoted in Table 8–1 for settlement on 4/9/79.

Recalling (1) that agencies accrue interest as if every month has 30 days and (2) the familiar rhyme, "Thirty days hath September, April, June, . . . ," it is easy to come up

---

[5] The one difference between quotes given in Table 6–1 and those given in Table 8–1 is that on the agency quote sheet the issue date is given. That is an important date to know because a few agency issues have an original maturity of approximately 9 months and pay coupon interest only at maturity.

Table 8–1
Selected quotes: Federal agency issues

DISCOUNT CORPORATION OF NEW YORK
58 Pine Street, New York, N. Y. 10005
Telephone 212-248-8900 • WUI Telex 620863 Discorp • WU Telex 125675 Discorp - NYK

QUOTATIONS FOR FEDERAL AGENCY ISSUES
Noon APR. 5, 1979
Ylds. for Del'y. APR. 9, 1979

Issue	Bid	Asked	Change from Prev. Day	Yield to Maturity or Call (1)	Yield after Tax (2)	Taxable Coupon Equiv.	Yield Value of 1/32	Current Markets	Amt. of Issue ($ Millions)	Issue Date
FEDERAL HOME LOAN BANKS										
7 1/2 5/25/79	99.20	99.22	--	9.71	5.24	9.71	.241	--------------------	1300	2/27/78
8.650 5/25/79	99.24	99.26	+ 1	9.82	5.30	9.82	.240	--------------------	499	10/25/74
8 3/4 5/25/79	99.24	99.26	--	9.91	5.35	9.91	.240	--------------------	393	5/28/74
7.200 8/27/79	98.26	98.30	+ 2	9.99	5.39	9.99	.084	--------------------	900	11/25/77
9 1/2 8/27/79	99.21	99.25	--	9.98	5.39	9.98	.083	--------------------	491	7/25/74
7 1/2 11/26/79	98.11	98.15	--	10.04	5.42	10.04	.053	--------------------	482	12/23/74
8.150 11/26/79	98.23	98.27	--	10.06	5.43	10.06	.053	--------------------	493	11/25/74
8.600 11/26/79	99.	99. 4	+ 1	10.03	5.42	10.03	.053	--------------------	700	7/25/78
7.050 2/25/80	97.12	97.16	+ 1	10.08	5.44	10.08	.039	--------------------	300	2/25/74
7 3/4 2/25/80	98.	98. 4	+ 1	10.01	5.41	10.01	.039	--------------------	350	3/25/70
8.100 2/25/80	98.12	98.16	+ 2	9.90	5.35	9.90	.038	--------------------	1200	5/25/78
6.650 5/27/80	96.16	96.24	+ 2	9.73	5.81	10.75	.030	--------------------	500	5/25/77
8.400 5/27/80	98.10	98.18	--	9.75	5.51	10.20	.030	--------------------	1000	8/25/78
7.300 8/25/80	96.20	96.28	--	9.77	5.72	10.59	.025	--------------------	700	8/25/76
9 3/4 8/25/80	99.28	100.	+ 1	9.73	5.25	9.73	.025	--------------------	900	11/27/78
7.800 10/15/80	97. 1	97. 9	+ 1	9.77	5.63	10.42	.023	--------------------	200	10/15/70
6.700 11/25/80	95.12	95.20	+ 2	9.66	5.75	10.64	.022	--------------------	500	11/26/76
7 3/4 11/25/80	96.30	97. 6	+ 4	9.65	5.55	10.28	.022	--------------------	600	11/25/75
7.600 2/25/81	96. 6	96.14	+ 2	9.71	5.62	10.41	.019	--------------------	500	2/25/76
9.550 5/26/81	99.21	99.25	+ 1	9.65	5.23	9.68	.017	--------------------	600	12/26/78
** 9.650 5/26/81	99.27	99.29	+ 1	9.69	5.24	9.70	.017	--------------------	800	2/26/79
7.050 8/25/81	94.12	94.20	--	9.63	5.66	10.49	.016	--------------------	800	8/25/77
8.650 11/25/81	97.22	97.30	--	9.55	5.32	9.85	.014	--------------------	400	10/25/74
6.600 11/27/81	93.10	93.18	--	9.41	5.59	10.34	.014	--------------------	200	10/27/71
7.950 2/25/82	96. 6	96.14	--	9.38	5.32	9.85	.013	--------------------	800	2/27/78
8 5/8 2/25/82	97.28	98. 4	--	9.38	5.20	9.63	.013	--------------------	500	8/25/75
7.450 2/25/82	94.20	94.28	--	9.37	5.41	10.01	.012	--------------------	700	11/25/77
8 1/4 11/26/82	96.16	96.24	+ 4	9.32	5.23	9.67	.011	--------------------	800	5/25/78
9.000 2/25/83	98.30	99. 2	--	9.29	5.07	9.38	.010	--------------------	700	11/27/78
7.300 5/25/83	92.26	93. 2	--	9.36	5.43	10.04	.010	--------------------	175	4/12/73
** 9.300 8/25/83	99.26	99.30	--	9.31	5.03	9.31	.009	--------------------	800	2/26/79
7 3/8 11/25/83	92.18	92.26	--	9.32	5.38	9.96	.009	--------------------	300	2/25/75
7 3/4 5/25/84	93.16	93.24	--	9.31	5.31	9.83	.008	--------------------	300	5/25/76
8 3/4 5/25/84	98. 8	98.16	--	9.12	4.99	9.24	.008	--------------------	300	5/28/74
7.850 8/27/84	93.20	93.28	--	9.32	5.30	9.81	.008	--------------------	500	8/25/76
7. 3/8 11/26/84	91.12	91.20	--	9.32	5.38	9.96	.008	--------------------	300	11/26/76
7 3/8 2/25/85	91.	91. 8	--	9.34	5.40	9.99	.007	--------------------	500	2/25/77
8 1/8 5/28/85	94. 8	94.16	--	9.32	5.25	9.71	.007	--------------------	500	2/27/78
** 9.350 8/26/85	99.30	100. 2	--	9.33	5.04	9.33	.007	--------------------	400	2/26/79
8.100 11/25/85	93.26	94. 2	--	9.32	5.25	9.72	.007	--------------------	400	11/25/75
7.650 5/26/87	90.16	90.24	--	9.29	5.31	9.83	.006	--------------------	300	5/25/77
7.600 8/25/87	90.	90. 8	--	9.30	5.33	9.86	.006	--------------------	400	P/25/77
7 3/8 11/26/93-83	85.20	85.28	--	9.14	5.25	9.72	.004	--------------------	400	10/25/73
7 7/8 2/25/97-87	88. 8	88.16	--	9.20	5.21	9.64	.004	--------------------	300	2/25/77

DENOTES MOST RECENT ISSUES, SEE BACK FOR ADDITIONAL FOOTNOTES

with the numbers in Table 8–2. As they show, because February has 28 days and seven other months have 31 days, significant discrepancies can arise between the number of days that is *assumed* to exist in a certain period for purposes of accruing interest on a agency security and the number of days that *actually* exists in that period.

To determine how much interest per dollar of face value had accrued on

FHLB 9½ 8/27/79

as of April 9, we divide the coupon rate by 360 (the assumed number of days in the year)

Table 8–2
FHLB 9% 8/27/79 for settlement 4/9/79

	Days from last coupon to settlement	Days from settlement to maturity
Assumed in calculating accrued interest	42	138
Actual	41	140

and then multiply by 42 (the assumed number of days from the last coupon date to the settlement date). This gives us

$$a_i = 0.095 \frac{42}{360} = 0.011083$$

To get a general formula for this procedure, we must introduce a new symbol. For all securities that pay interest on a 30/360-day basis, let

t'_{is} = days *assumed* to have elapsed from issue
or last coupon date to settlement date

Using this symbol, accrued interest, *i*, *on an agency* can be expressed as:[6]

$$a_i = c \frac{t'_{is}}{360}$$

From this formula and the figures in Table 8–2, it is clear that FHLB 9½ 8/27/79 accrued interest before settlement on April 9 on 2 days that did not exist (because February has 28 days), and failed to accrue interest on 1 day that did exist (March 31); it also failed to accrue interest on 2 days between settlement and maturity (because May and July have 31 days). Clearly, accruing interest on a 30/360-day basis must at times create serious distortions in the yield to maturity figures given for short agencies.

Yield to maturity on the quote sheet

In determining yield to maturity on a security that pays interest on a 30/360-day basis, the number of days from settlement to maturity is also calculated on an *assumed* as opposed to an *actual* day basis. Let

t'_{sm} = days *assumed* to elapse from settlement to maturity

Then the formula by which the industry calculates yield to maturity on an agency security that will mature on its next coupon date can be written as:

$$y = \left(\frac{1 + \frac{c}{2}}{P + c \frac{t'_{is}}{360}} - 1 \right) \frac{360}{t'_{sm}}$$

Most people on the street know that this yield to maturity figure is wrong, but many do not understand why or what adjustment must be made to correct it. A common misconception is to think that quote-sheet yield to maturity figures on agencies are not comparable to yield to maturity figures on governments because the former pay interest on a 360-day-year basis and the latter on a 365-day-year basis; that is, there is a discrepancy of the sort that exists between the repo rate and yield to maturity on a government. Actually yield to maturity on an agency *is* measured on a 365-day basis. The reason is that the calculation involves two offsetting errors: (1) a full 365-day year is assumed to have only 360 days, and (2) every month is assumed to have 30 days.

To prove the above, consider a 1-year agency that is issued on June 15 and matures on the following June 15. The security will pay coupon interest equal to $c/2$ per \$1 of face value on December 15 and again at maturity. Thus, over the full 365-day year stretching from the issue date, June 15, to the following June 15, the investor who

---

[6] In contrasting this formula with the one we gave for calculating a_i on a short government, note that on an agency the basis in the current coupon period is always assumed to be 180 days.

bought and held this security to maturity would earn, per \$1 of face value, interest payments equal to

$$\frac{c}{2} + \frac{c}{2} = c$$

that is, on a 365-day basis he would earn a rate of return of c, the coupon rate, on his investment. Note this is precisely the same outcome that would have occurred if, on its next to last coupon date, the investor had bought *at par* a government note or bond bearing a coupon c.

The yield to maturity figure given on a quote sheet for a short agency is often wrong not because it is quoted on a 360-day basis, as the repo rate is, but because

$$t'_{sm} \neq t_{sm}$$

that is, the number of assumed days to maturity t'_{sm} does not equal the number of actual days from settlement to maturity, t_{sm}.

Once this is understood, it is simple to obtain an expression for y^*, the *true* yield to maturity on a short agency. Since agencies never mature on nonbusiness days,[7] on a short agency

$$y^* = true \text{ yield to maturity on a short agency}$$
$$= y \frac{t'_{sm}}{t_{sm}}$$

Example. To illustrate, consider again FHLB 9½ 8/27/79. In Table 8–1 this security was quoted as offering a yield to maturity of 9.98 if sold at the offered price of 99–25 for settlement on 4/9/79. Plugging this price plus the values from Table 8–2 for t'_{is} and t'_{sm} into the industry formula for y, we get

$$y = \left(\frac{1 + \dfrac{0.095}{2}}{\dfrac{99^{25}/_{32}}{100} + \dfrac{0.095 \times 42}{360}} - 1 \right) \frac{360}{138} = 9.98\%$$

the yield value on the quote sheet.

The true yield to maturity offered by this security was, however, much lower because the true number of days from settlement to maturity was not 138, but 140. To determine how much this discrepancy affected yield, we insert these numbers into our equation for y^*. This gives us

$$y^* = 0.0998 \frac{138}{140} = 9.839\%$$

which is 21 basis points below the yield figure on the quote sheet.

A final note: Our formula for y^* as a function of y on a short agency assumes that the security is traded at the offered price on the quote sheet. If the security is traded at other than that price, y on the quote sheet must be adjusted by adding or subtracting yield values of $^1/_{32}$. This adjustment is made the way we did it when we calculated y^* on a short government.

---

[7] Their issue and maturity dates are set so this does not occur.

Calculating yield given price and price given yield on a federal agency security *in its final coupon period*†

Let

t'_{is} = assumed days from issue or last coupon to settlement

t'_{sm} = assumed days from settlement to maturity

y = quote sheet yield to maturity

y^* = *true* yield to maturity

P = price per \$1 of fare value

v_2 = yield value of $1/32$

I: Industry formulas:

1. Accrued interest:

$$a_i = c \frac{t'_{is}}{360}$$

2. Yield given price:

$$y = \left(\frac{1 + \frac{c}{2}}{P + c \frac{t'_{is}}{360}} - 1 \right) \frac{360}{t'_{sm}}$$

3. Price given yield:

$$P = \left(\frac{1 + \frac{c}{2}}{1 + y \frac{t'_{sm}}{360}} \right) - a_i$$

II: *True* yield to maturity:

1. At the offered price:

$$y^* = y \frac{t'_{sm}}{t_{sm}}$$

2. At some other price:

$$y^* = (y \pm v_{32} \text{ as required}) \frac{t'_{sm}}{t_{sm}}$$

---

† On an agency note that has an original maturity of more than 6 months and pays interest at maturity, $c/2$ in the formulas must be appropriately adjusted.

Other calculations

We have derived the industry formula for calculating yield given price on a short agency. Solving that equation for P as a function of y, we get the industry formula for calculating price given yield on a short agency:

$$P = \left(\frac{1 + \frac{c}{2}}{1 + y \frac{t'_{sm}}{360}} \right) - a_i$$

While short agencies are reversed to maturity less frequently than short governments, the transaction is sometimes done. On such a transaction, the dealer's break-even reverse rate is given by

$$r^* = y^* \frac{360}{365}$$
$$= (y \pm v_{32} \text{ as required}) \left(\frac{t'_{sm}}{t_{sm}} \right) \frac{360}{365}$$

MUNICIPAL NOTES

For investors who are in a position to benefit from tax-exempt income, municipal notes—which when issued with a short original maturity typically pay interest at maturity—are an important money market instrument.

Muni notes, unlike other instruments we have discussed, are usually held by investors from purchase to maturity. Also because of tax considerations, they are never RPed; because of the thin secondary markets in which they trade, they are rarely shorted.

Thus, the question an investor in muni notes is most likely to ask is what *true* yield to maturity a particular issue offers him. Since muni notes accrue interest on a 30/360-day basis, the true yield to maturity can be calculated on an interest-at-maturity muni note using the formula for y^* that we gave for short agencies. Only one obvious modification is needed; $c/2$ must be adjusted to reflect the security's original maturity, which often differs from 6 months. The same formula can also be used to calculate the true yield to maturity on a municipal bond in its last coupon period.

SWAPPING AND ARBITRAGING MONEY MARKET INSTRUMENTS

A common question asked by portfolio managers and by securities salespeople is how one should evaluate a swap. We have said very little about this directly and a great deal indirectly. A swap is worthwhile when an investor can move from one security into another that possesses greater *relative value* measured in terms of his parameters.

A security's relative value is a function of its risk, liquidity, and return. The key aid a book on money market calculations can give a portfolio manager who is searching for relative value is the means to compare the yields on different money market instruments correctly. That is something we have spent many pages discussing both directly and indirectly.

As one astute portfolio manager noted, "Once you get all the rates on a *strictly* comparable basis, there is nothing more to say about the mathematics of swaps. In that situation, swapping boils down to a question of where the portfolio manager perceives there is relative value."

A similar comment applies to the mathematics of evaluating money market arbitrages. When the eventual gain or loss on an arbitrage is locked in at the time the transaction is initiated, e.g., a reverse to maturity of one security to invest in another of the same maturity, figuring the gain on the arbitrage is trivial once all the relevant rates are put on a strictly comparable basis. On an arbitrage with an uncertain outcome, e.g., buying one security and shorting another because the rates look out of line or are expected to move, the key first step for the trader is to measure correctly all costs and all potential losses and gains. Once that is done, he must determine on the basis of his own rate or spread forecast whether the gamble, which such a loosely defined arbitrage involves, is favorable enough for him to undertake. There is no magic formula to make that forecast for him.

APPENDIX: CALCULATING ACCRUED INTEREST OVER AN IRREGULAR FIRST COUPON PERIOD

Irregular first coupons

Occasionally government notes and bonds are issued with an irregular first coupon period. If the first coupon period is *short,* interest accrued as of the first coupon date is calculated as follows:

$$a_i = \frac{c}{2} \frac{(\text{Days from assumed normal last})}{\left(\begin{array}{l}\text{Days from issue to}\\\text{first coupon date}\end{array}\right)}$$

$$a_i = \frac{c}{2} \frac{\left(\begin{array}{l}\text{Days from issue to}\\\text{first coupon date}\end{array}\right)}{\left(\begin{array}{l}\text{Days from assumed normal last}\\\text{coupon to first coupon date}\end{array}\right)}$$

Note the amount of coupon interest paid on the first coupon date will be a fraction of the normal payment. To illustrate consider a 7 percent Treasury note issued on 5/20/78, due on 10/31/80, and having a first coupon on 10/31/78. On this note

$$\left(\begin{array}{l}\text{Short first}\\\text{coupon payment}\end{array}\right) = \frac{0.07}{2}\left(\frac{5/20/78 \text{ to } 10/31/78}{4/30/78 \text{ to } 10/31/78}\right)$$

$$= \frac{0.07}{2}\left(\frac{164}{184}\right) = 0.031196$$

The more common form of irregular first coupon is the *long* first coupon. In this case a partial first coupon is deferred until the next full coupon payment. The amount of coupon paid on the first coupon date will equal the normal payment plus a fractional payment for the beginning period. It is calculated as follows:

$$a_i = \frac{c}{2}\left[\frac{\left(\begin{array}{l}\text{Days from issue to beginning}\\\text{of normal coupon period}\end{array}\right)}{\left(\begin{array}{l}\text{Days from assumed normal last coupon}\\\text{to beginning of first coupon period}\end{array}\right)} + \frac{\left(\begin{array}{l}\text{Days in first}\\\text{coupon period}\end{array}\right)}{\left(\begin{array}{l}\text{Days in first}\\\text{coupon period}\end{array}\right)}\right]$$

$$a_i = \frac{c}{2}\left[\frac{\left(\begin{array}{l}\text{Days from issue to beginning}\\\text{of normal coupon period}\end{array}\right)}{\left(\begin{array}{l}\text{Days from assumed normal last coupon}\\\text{to beginning of first coupon period}\end{array}\right)} + 1\right]$$

To illustrate consider a 8¼ percent note issued on 8/29/75, due on 8/31/77 and having a first coupon on 2/29/76. On that data accrued interest per dollar of face value is given by

$$\binom{\text{long first}}{\text{coupon payment}} = \frac{0.0825}{2}\left(\frac{8/29/75 \text{ to } 8/31/75}{2/28/75 \text{ to } 8/31/75} + \frac{8/31/75 \text{ to } 2/29/76}{8/31/75 \text{ to } 2/29/76}\right)^{[1]}$$

$$= \frac{0.0825}{2}\left(\frac{2}{184} + \frac{182}{182}\right) = 0.041698$$

Once the irregular first coupon payment is made, all subsequent accrued interest calculations are based on regular coupon periods.

---

[1] Because 1976 is a leap year, the normal coupon period is 8/31/75 to 2/29/76.

9

Notes and bonds—One or more coupons from maturity

A note or bond that at issue is scheduled to pay interest on two or more dates passes through two distinct phases. Initially it is a security that pays *periodic interest*. Then in its last coupon period it becomes a special breed of *interest-at-maturity* security. In Chapter 8 we considered notes and bonds in this latter stage. In this chapter we focus on the same securities in their initial stage, that is, when they are scheduled to make at least one coupon payment before maturity and therefore offer the investor periodic interest.

CALCULATING PRICE GIVEN YIELD

In Chapter 6 we pointed out that the street prices securities that pay periodic interest at the present value of the stream of dollar flows—coupon interest plus redemption value at maturity—that they offer the investor.[1] We also noted that the rate of discount used in this calculation is the yield to maturity at which the security is offered.

Our remarks in Chapter 6 were intended only to introduce the principle underlying the pricing of notes and bonds, and for this reason we considered only securities traded *on a coupon date*. Our task here is to use the street's approach to develop a general formula that will permit us to calculate accurately the price at which any existing long coupon would sell if it were traded at a specific yield for settlement on *any* date.

When we move from the general introductory discussion presented in Chapter 6 to calculating the price at which an actual security would trade, we must deal with two complications. First, an investor who buys a note or bond always pays the dollar price at which it is quoted *plus* accrued interest as of the settlement date. Thus, the first complication is calculating accrued interest. The procedure for doing this for government, agency, and municipal securities was described in Chapter 8.

The second complication that arises when a security is traded on an *off-coupon date* is that the future dollar flows generated by the security must be discounted not over some *whole* number of coupon periods, as in the examples in Chapter 6, but over some

---

[1] See pages 63–66.

number of coupon periods *plus a fraction* of a coupon period. The best way to show this is with an example.

    Example. The quote sheet reproduced in Table 6–1 shows the Treasury note

N 7⅛ 12/31/79

as being offered for settlement on April 9, 1979, at a yield to maturity of 9.92.[2] Using this information, we want to derive the corresponding dollar price at which this security must be offered.

    To do so, we first look at the time framework in which the dollar flows associated with an investment in the security would occur. Part A of Figure 9–1 pictures this.

Figure 9–1
Calculating price given yield on a coupon security on its next to last coupon period: An example

A. To determine price, future dollar flows produced by the security are discounted back to t_s, the settlement date.

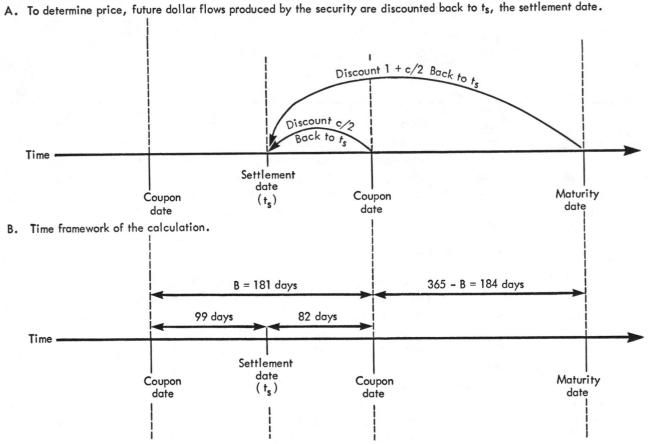

Specifically, it shows that the settlement date is slightly more than halfway through the security's next to last coupon period. The figure also correctly indicates that, to calculate the present value of the dollar flows generated by this security, we must discount the approaching coupon payment and the maturity value of the security *back to the settlement date.* To do this requires that precise numbers be put on the time periods involved; this is done in part B of the figure.

---

[2] See page 62.

April 9 is 82 days before the next coupon date, and the basis B, in the settlement period is 181 days. Thus, to receive the approaching coupon payment, the investor must wait a *fraction*, $82/181$, of a coupon period. Give that yield to maturity at the offered price is 9.92, the factor by which the next to last coupon must be discounted is

$$\left(1 + \frac{0.0992}{2}\right)^{82/181}$$

To obtain the maturity value of the security, the investor must wait the full final coupon period plus a fraction, $82/181$, of the next to last coupon period, i.e., $1 + 82/181$ coupon periods. Thus the factor by which the security's maturity value must be discounted is

$$\left(1 + \frac{0.0992}{2}\right)^{1+(82/181)}$$

Since the investor pays a *dollar price*, P, plus accrued interest for the security, and since this amount equals the present value of the coupon payments it will yield plus the security's value at maturity, the offered price per \$1 of face value must be P in the following expression:[3]

$$P + a_i = \left[\frac{\dfrac{0.07125}{2}}{\left(1 + \dfrac{0.0992}{2}\right)^{82/181}}\right] + \left[\frac{1 + \dfrac{0.07125}{2}}{\left(1 + \dfrac{0.0992}{2}\right)^{1+(82/181)}}\right]$$

which reduces to

$$P = 1.000149 - a_i$$

We next note that the settlement date is 99 days after the last coupon date (Figure 9–1, part B). Therefore, at settlement

$$a_i = \frac{0.07125}{2}\left(\frac{99}{181}\right) = 0.019485$$

and

$$P = 1.000149 - 0.019485$$
$$= 0.980664$$

This P value is the price per \$1 of face value. Multiplying it by 100 and rounding to the nearest $1/32$, we get a dollar price of 99–2. We have thus concluded that, since the security is offered at a 9.92 yield, the *dollar price* asked for it must be 99–2. Checking back to Table 6–1, we find that this is in fact the case.

Price given yield in the next to last coupon period

The example we have just worked is a specific case of a general problem—calculating the price of a note or bond in its next to last coupon period when yield to maturity is known. Generalizing from the example, we can easily write a formula for solving this problem. Let

t_{sc} = days from settlement to next coupon
B = basis (number of days) in the coupon period in which *settlement* occurs

---

[3] In decimal form, the coupon rate is

$7\frac{1}{8}$ percent = 0.07125

then

$$P = \left[\frac{c/2}{\left(1 + \frac{y}{2}\right)^{t_{sc}/B}} \right] + \left[\frac{1 + (c/2)}{\left(1 + \frac{y}{2}\right)^{1+(t_{sc}/B)}} \right] - a_i$$

The summation sign Σ

The procedure we used to calculate price given yield on a note or bond in its next to last coupon period can easily be extended to cover the calculation of price given yield on securities any number of coupon periods from maturity. The only problem is that each time current maturity is extended by one coupon period, a new term is added to the expression for P; thus, on a bond with a long current maturity, P could become an unwieldly expression. Fortunately, it need not because a shorthand device can be used to represent the discounted value of *all* future coupon payments as a single term.

This device is the summation sign Σ. Let

$$n = \text{some indefinite positive number}$$

then Σ is defined as follows:

$$\sum_{k=1}^{n} x_k = x_1 + x_2 + x_3 + \cdots + x_n$$

Note that in this expression the three consecutive dots represent omitted ordered terms.

While Σ is a simple concept, it may appear confusing to those who are encountering it for the first time. To dispel such confusion, we present two examples:

$$\sum_{k=1}^{4} x^k = x + x^2 + x^3 + x^4$$

and

$$\sum_{k=1}^{2} \frac{a}{(1+x)^k} = \frac{a}{1+x} + \frac{a}{(1+x)^2}$$

Let us now apply Σ to the problem at hand. First we restate the equation derived earlier for price given yield on a security in its next to last coupon period so that the present value of each coupon payment is a separate term. Doing so gives us

$$P = \left[\frac{1}{\left(1 + \frac{y}{2}\right)^{1+(t_{sc}/B)}} \right] + \left[\frac{c/2}{\left(1 + \frac{y}{2}\right)^{t_{sc}/B}} \right] + \left[\frac{1}{\left(1 + \frac{y}{2}\right)^{1+(t_{sc}/B)}} \right] - a_i$$

Once the equation is written in this form, it is obvious that a pattern exists in the power to which $[1 + (y/2)]$ is raised in the discounting of coupon payments. This pattern permits us to rewrite the equation using Σ as follows:

$$P = \left[\frac{1}{\left(1 + \frac{y}{2}\right)^{1+(t_{sc}/B)}} \right] + \left[\sum_{k=1}^{2} \frac{c/2}{\left(1 + \frac{y}{2}\right)^{k-1+(t_{sc}/B)}} \right] - a_i$$

The general formula for price given yield

The manipulations we have just gone through may seem pointless since the expression for P that we derived using Σ looks neither shorter nor simpler than the one we started with, and in fact it is not. The payoff from introducing Σ lies elsewhere. Specifically, using Σ permits us to write a *short general formula* for calculating the price given the yield of any note or bond that is one or more coupons from maturity. Let

$$N = \text{number of remaining coupon payments}[4]$$

Generalizing from our formula for P when $N = 2$, i.e., when the security being priced is in its next to last coupon period, we note that on a security with a longer current maturity, the maturity value will be discounted by a factor of

$$\left(1 + \frac{y}{2}\right)^{N-1+(t_{sc}/B)}$$

We also note that each future coupon payment will be discounted by a factor of

$$\left(1 + \frac{y}{2}\right)^{k-1+(t_{sc}/B)}$$

where

$$k - 1 = \text{number of } whole \text{ coupon periods, hence the} \\ \text{coupon payment will be received}$$

Thus the general formula for calculating price given yield on a coupon security one or more coupon payments from maturity can be written as follows:

$$P = \left[\frac{1}{\left(1 + \frac{y}{2}\right)^{N-1+(t_{sc}/B)}}\right] + \left[\sum_{k=1}^{N} \frac{c/2}{\left(1 + \frac{y}{2}\right)^{k-1+(t_{sc}/B)}}\right] - a_i$$

YIELD GIVEN PRICE

We have with some effort established a formula for determining price given yield on a long coupon. Now we want to do the opposite, namely, solve for *yield to maturity* given price.

The yield value corresponding to any dollar price at which a long note or bond might trade is the y value in the equation for calculating price P given yield.

Thus, to obtain an expression for yield given price, we must solve the price equation to obtain y as a function of P. Unfortunately there is no simple way to do this, because y in the price equation is part of a term, $[1 + (y/2)]$, that is raised to a number, N, of different powers.

To solve for y given P on a long coupon, one must begin by approximating y and then apply one of several possible *iteration methods*, the most common being *Newton's*

---

[4] To keep the exposition simple, in the discussion of discounting in Chapter 6 we used the symbol n where

$$n = \text{number of compounding (coupon) periods}$$

Here we use the symbol N where

$$N = \text{number of remaining coupons}$$

To avoid possible confusion, note that

$$n = N - 1 + \frac{t_{sc}}{B}$$

and if $t_{sc} = B$, i.e., if the trade occurs on a coupon date,

$$n = N$$

method. We relegate the description of this arduous procedure to the appendix of this chapter because traders and investors can quickly calculate yield given price for securities that are any number of coupons from maturity simply by using one of the preprogrammed bond calculators that are standard equipment in any trading room. In effect the only people who need be concerned with iteration methods are those who want to program a computer to make this calculation.

Price and yield calculations on coupon securities scheduled to pay one or more coupons before maturity, i.e., on securities paying *periodic* interest

Case I: Price given yield to maturity: Let

y = yield to maturity
c = coupon rate
a_i = accrued interest per dollar of face value
P = price per dollar of face value
N = number of remaining coupons
t_{sc} = days from settlement to next coupon
B = basis (number of days) in the coupon period in which settlement occurs

Then

$$P = \left[\frac{1}{\left(1 + \frac{y}{2}\right)^{N-1+(t_{sc}/B)}} \right] + \left[\sum_{k=1}^{N} \frac{c/2}{\left(1 + \frac{y}{2}\right)^{k-1+(t_{sc}/B)}} \right] - a_i$$

Case II: Yield to maturity given price:

$y = y$ in the above equation for P

The procedure for solving for y is described on pages 136–138.

True yield to maturity

When we discussed *short* coupons, we noted that a considerable discrepancy could exist between a security's *true* yield to maturity and its yield to maturity as calculated by the industry and recorded on a quote sheet. For securities *more than one coupon from maturity,* discrepancies may also exist between yield to maturity as calculated according to the industry formula and true yield to maturity.

For example, the holding period corresponding to a Treasury security's last coupon period might be as short as 181 days. Alternatively, it might be as long as 187 days if the basis in that coupon period were 184 days and if the security matured on the first day of a long weekend. However long this holding period is, it will be represented by 1 in the exponent of the factor by which the maturity value of the security is discounted. Also on agency and municipal securities, the 30/360-day basis on which interest is accrued can distort yield to maturity figures.

The important thing to note in this respect is, however, that as a security's current maturity increases to more than 6 months, discrepancies between true and calculated yield to maturity created by such problems are amortized over an increasingly long period and consequently diminish in size. A day-count problem that would noticeably distort yield to maturity on a security 7 months from maturity would have no noticeable effect on the yield to maturity of a security 2 years, not to speak of 10 years, from maturity.

A second important point is that a trader who makes a *short-term* play because he expects a move of 25 basis points in rates and who is off 14 basis points (the difference at 10 percent between a 360- and a 365-day rate) in his calculation has cut his potential profit in half. In long bonds, in contrast, the exactitude of the yield to maturity calculation is less important. An investor who buys long bonds because he thinks yields on them are going to move from 9 to 8.5 cares little whether he buys the securities at a yield to maturity of 9.01 or 8.97. Whether he is right or wrong in his interest rate forecast, this difference in yield will have little effect on the outcome of his investment.

Another point worth noting is that it may be more valuable to the investor in long bonds to stay in a current issue—on which every dealer will give him a bid and offer—than to pick up a few basis points by getting into a higher-yielding, off-the-run issue.

The reinvestment rate revisited

The yield to maturity that any note or bond offers is a function of three key variables:

1. The known (or assumed) cash flows the security will generate.
2. The frequency of compounding.
3. The reinvestment rate.

On most of the securities—governments, agencies, and municipals—that a typical money market portfolio holds, the cash flows that the security will generate are known; so too is the frequency of compounding, which is semiannual. The interesting questions arise with respect to the third variable, the reinvestment rate.

The pricing formula we derived earlier in the chapter suggests the following definition of a security's yield to maturity. It is the rate such that, if all the future dollar flows generated by the security were discounted with semiannual compounding at this rate, the sum of the values thus obtained minus accrued interest on the security would equal the price at which the security is offered. This definition is useful but it tends to mask the assumptions with respect to the reinvestment of coupon interest and the reinvestment rate that are implicit in the definition.

To focus on these, it is best not to look at the pricing formula but rather at the relationship from which it is derived. The equation we gave in Chapter 6 tells us that the price per \$1 of face value of a 1-year security paying semiannual interest and offered at a yield to maturity of y is P in the expression.[5]

$$P\left(1 + \frac{y}{2}\right)^2 = \frac{c}{2}\left(1 + \frac{y}{2}\right) + \left(1 + \frac{c}{2}\right)$$

What this equation says is that, if P were invested at a yield y for 1 year with semiannual compounding, P plus interest earned at the yield of y at the end of the year equals the sum of the dollar flows thrown off by the security plus the interest that could

---

[5] See page 65. Note here we consistently assume F-1.

be earned by reinvesting the first coupon payment for half a year at the rate y. *Any change in the rate y at which coupon interest is reinvested would, of course, destroy this equality and thereby change yield to maturity.*

The reinvestment rate implied in the calculation of yield to maturity is referred to as an *internal rate of return* because it is internal to the yield calculation as opposed to being *externally* specified. There is, of course, no rule that says the reinvestment rate will in fact equal y or, more important, that an investor should assume it will. An investor who entertains definite notions as to how he will invest coupon interest and/or where interest rates are headed should, in calculating the yield to maturity offered by a note or bond, incorporate an expected (i.e., *externally specified*) reinvestment rate, r_e, and use it to calculate an expected yield to maturity that will necessarily differ (unless he anticipates a reinvestment rate y) from yield to maturity on the quote sheet.

Yield to maturity with r_e externally specified

As noted, the calculation of yield to maturity is complicated when coupon interest is assumed to be reinvested at y. When the reinvestment rate is assumed not to be this internal rate of return, but rather an *externally* specified rate, the calculation of yield to maturity becomes a simple algebraic operation.

To calculate yield given price when the reinvestment rate is externally specified, we first calculate the *future value* of the security, which equals the value of all intermediate coupon payments *plus* the interest that would be earned if these coupon payments were reinvested with semiannual compounding at the assumed reinvestment rate *plus* the security's value at maturity. Next we determine the yield at which the security's future value would have to be discounted over the period from settlement to maturity in order that the resulting discounted value equal the price plus accrued interest paid for the security.

Put more succinctly, we obtain

y' = yield to maturity when the reinvestment rate is externally specified

by solving an expression of the general sort,

$$P + a_i = \left(\frac{\text{Future value of the security}}{\substack{\text{A discount factor that} \\ \text{is a function of } y'}} \right)$$

for y'.

To illustrate, let's work an example. Specifically, let us consider again the security we worked with earlier in the chapter, N 7⅛ 12/31/79.[6] As noted, if this security were purchased for settlement on 4/9/79 at a price of 99–2 plus accrued interest and if coupon interest were reinvested at the *security's yield to maturity*, 9.92, the yield to maturity actually realized by the investor would be 9.92.

Let us now alter the reinvestment assumption. Specifically, suppose the investor is operating in an environment in which the yield curve peaks in the 6-month area and he anticipates reinvesting coupon interest short term in a higher-yielding instrument at 10.75 percent. The *future value, FV,* of the dollar flows generated by the security will be the first coupon payment times a factor—1 plus the reinvestment rate divided by 2—plus the value of the security at maturity; to state this relationship in symbols, let

r_e = externally specified reinvestment rate

---

[6] See pages 108–9.

then

$$FV = \frac{c}{2}\left(1 + \frac{r_e}{2}\right) + \left(1 + \frac{c}{2}\right)$$

Plugging the numbers in our example into this equation, we get

$$FV = \frac{0.07125}{2}\left(1 + \frac{0.1075}{2}\right) + \left(1 + \frac{0.07125}{2}\right)$$

$$= 1.073165$$

Since the number of periods over which the future value of our security must be discounted is $1 + (82/181)$, and since

$$P + a_i = 1.000149$$

the yield to maturity offered by the security when $r_e = 10.75$ percent must be y' in the expression

$$1.000149 = \frac{1.073165}{\left(1 + \dfrac{y'}{2}\right)^{1+(82/181)}}$$

Solving this equation for y' gives us

$$y' = 9.94\%$$

As would be expected, assuming a reinvestment rate higher than the internally implied reinvestment rate raises yield to maturity in this case from 9.92 to 9.94. If, alternatively, a reinvestment rate lower than y had been assumed, the result would have been a lower yield to maturity.

In our example a rather dramatic change in the assumed reinvestment rate, from 9.92 to 10.75, altered yield to maturity by only 2 basis points. This should not be taken to indicate that the reinvestment rate is of minor importance. If the security had been selling at par so that the discount earned was a smaller element in yield and if the current maturity of the security had been longer, a change of this magnitude in the assumed reinvestment rate would have affected more strongly *anticipated* yield to maturity; we say *anticipated* because the reinvestment rate is typically an expected as opposed to a certain rate.

A general formula

Since portfolio managers often find it useful to calculate yield to maturity on a coupon security when the reinvestment rate is externally specified, we will now derive a formula for calculating this value. Let

c = coupon rate
r_e = *externally* specified reinvestment rate
FV = *future value* of the dollar flows generated by a security when coupon interest is reinvested at r_e with semiannual compounding
y' = yield to maturity when the reinvestment rate is r_e
N = number of remaining coupons
P = price per \$1 of face value
a_i = accrued interest per \$1 of face value
t_{sc} = days from settlement to next coupon
B = basis, i.e., days in the settlement coupon period

then

$$FV = \left(\sum_{k=1}^{N} \frac{c}{2} \left(1 + \frac{r_e}{2}\right)^{N-k} \right) + 1$$

and yield to maturity is y' in the expression

$$P + a_i = \left[\frac{\left(\sum_{k=1}^{N} \frac{c}{2} \left(1 + \frac{r_e}{2}\right)^{N-k} \right) + 1}{\left(1 + \frac{y'}{2}\right)^{N-1+(t_{sc}/B)}} \right]$$

which, when solved gives[7]

$$y' = 2 \left[\frac{\left(\sum_{k=1}^{N} \frac{c}{2} \left(1 + \frac{r_e}{2}\right)^{N-k} \right) + 1}{P + a_i} \right]^{\frac{1}{N-1+(t_{sw}/B)}} - 2$$

Figuring yield to maturity on a note or bond when the reinvestment rate is externally specified

Let

c = coupon rate
r_e = externally specified reinvestment rate
y' = yield to maturity when the reinvestment rate is r_e
N = number of remaining coupons
t_{sc} = days from settlement to next coupon
a_i = accrued interest per \$1 of face value
P = Price per \$1 of face value
B = basis, i.e., days in the settlement coupon period

then

$$y' = 2 \left[\frac{\left(\sum_{k=1}^{N} \frac{c}{2} \left(1 + \frac{r_e}{2}\right)^{N-k} \right) + 1}{P + a_i} \right]^{\frac{1}{N-1+(t_{sc}/B)}} - 2$$

Often a portfolio manager will find it convenient to assume a series of reinvestment rates. For example, he might reason that in the short run coupon interest will be invested in some money market instrument and that in the long run, 6 months or more hence, it will go into bonds. In that case, to calculate yield to maturity, he would use the same general approach outlined above, but because the assumed reinvestment rate is not constant, the calculation would be more complex. Any portfolio manager who invests large sums and who needs to make this sort of calculation often should develop a program so that the calculation can be done on a computer. Besides saving time, such a

---

[7] The only tricky part of this calculation is that the $1/[N - 1 + (t_{sc}/B)]$ root of a number must be taken. This procedure cannot be done on a bond market calculator, but it can be done on any cheap scientific calculator. First divide 1 by $N - 1 + (t_{sc}/B)$; then raise the amount inside the brackets to that power. The mathematical acumen involved in the latter operation is that one must push a single correct button, typically one labeled y^x.

program would permit the portfolio manager to test quickly how sensitive yield to maturity on a security is to the assumptions he makes about the reinvestment rate over time.

REVERSES TO MATURITY ON LONG COUPONS

The majority of securities reversed out to maturity have a current maturity of 6 months or less because it is in this maturity range that the security holder is most likely to find attractive arbitrages. Longer-term reverses to maturity are done, however; and the question arises as to how to calculate the dealer's break-even reverse rate r^* on them.

The usual, but by no means only, way a reverse to maturity on a long coupon is set up is for the dealer to lend to the security holder an amount equal to the price of the security or to that price minus some margin, haircut in street jargon. Then, on coupon dates, the dealer and the investor pair off coupon interest against interest on the reverse, that is, the borrower pays the dealer on each coupon date the difference between the repo interest he owes the dealer and the coupon payment the dealer owes him.

Dollar flowing a reverse to maturity

If the reverse transaction is done this way, it will generate a series of dollar inflows and outflows for the dealer. Assuming for the moment that *no haircut* is taken, these flows on a security with N remaining coupons will be those recorded in Table 9–1. Note in the table that the vertical lines of three dots represent omitted ordered terms.

One way to approximate the dealer's break-even rate on a long reverse to maturity is to say that it is the rate such that on the transaction

$$\text{Total dollars in} = \text{Total dollars out}$$

Table 9–1
Dollar flowing a reverse to maturity on a security with N remaining coupons; no haircut taken

Date	Dollars in to lender	Dollars out from lender
Settlement	$P + a_i$	P
First coupon	$r\dfrac{t_{sc}}{360}P$	$\dfrac{c}{2}$
Second coupon	$r\dfrac{182.5}{360}P$	$\dfrac{c}{2}$
.	.	.
.	.	.
.	.	.
$(N-1)$th coupon	$r\dfrac{182.5}{360}P$	$\dfrac{c}{2}$
Nth coupon	$r\dfrac{182.5}{360}P + P$	$F + \dfrac{c}{2}$
Total	$2P + a_i + \dfrac{rP}{360}[t_{sc} + (N-1)182.5]$	$P + N\dfrac{c}{2} + F$

that is, such that (Table 9–1)

$$2P + a_i + \frac{rP}{360}[t_{sc} + (N-1)182.5] = P + N\frac{c}{2} + F$$

which reduces to

$$\frac{rP}{360}[t_{sc} + (N-1)182.5] = (F - P - a_i) + N\frac{c}{2}$$

This relationship states that the dealer breaks even when the total interest he receives on the reverse (the left side of the equation) equals his cost of doing the transaction, which is the discount, $F - P$, at which he takes in the security plus all coupon interest he must pay out minus accrued interest at the time the transaction is initiated.

Solving this break-even expression for r, which when the relationship holds equals r^*, the break-even reverse rate, we get

$$r^* = \left[\frac{F - P + N\frac{c}{2} - a_i}{t_{sc} + (N-1)182.5}\right]\frac{360}{P}$$

This formula for r^* is an *approximation because it does not allow for compounding of interest, and therefore the timing of dollar inflows and outflows in no way affects the value obtained for r^*.*[8]

Ignoring the timing of dollar inflows and outflows in the calculation of r^* creates, a predictable bias in the calculation of r^* if the transaction is set up as we have assumed. Specifically, if the security reversed in is trading *at a discount*, r^* will be overestimated because net the transaction will generate capital for the dealer from the day it is put on until it terminates, and because of this the ignored interest on interest the dealer receives will exceed the ignored interest on interest he pays out.[9]

As noted later, the best way to estimate r^* is typically *not* by using the formula we have just developed. Our major purpose in dollar flowing an example of a reverse to maturity and in deriving an expression for dollars in equal to dollars out was to create a framework for showing (1) the importance of dating dollar flows and (2) the economics for a dealer of generating capital when a haircut is taken.

---

[8] Also, as noted later, the formula assigns *no* value to the capital, a_i, generated from settlement to the first coupon date. Finally and least importantly the basis used in calculation repo interest in each coupon period is assumed for simplicity to be precisely one half a year.

[9] To show this, assume that the transaction occurs on a coupon date. In that case the earlier expression for

$$\text{Dollars in} = \text{Dollars out}$$

reduces to

$$(F - P) = \frac{N}{2}(rP - c)$$

and since

$$(F - P) > 0$$

then

$$rP > c$$

If $a_i > 0$, this relationship still holds. It must because the fact that $P < F$ implies that, when the security matures, the dealer will have to make a balloon payment equal to the discount at which he took in the security.

Dating dollar flows

To show the importance of *dating dollar flows,* let us alter in an extreme fashion the way the reverse transaction is assumed to be done. Specifically, we assume that coupon interest is paid out to the borrower on each coupon date but that all interest on the reverse is paid at the termination of the transaction. Note this change does not affect the equality of dollars in and dollars out. It does, however, create a situation in which the dealer is net putting out capital, and the size of his capital deficit will increase steadily over the life of the transaction. In this extreme case, a dealer who did a reverse at the r^* value given by the earlier formula would lose money equal to the cost of the capital used by the transaction. This observation suggests two key points.

First, any formula for calculating r^* is sensitive to the way the transaction is done. Thus, on a transaction that deviates from the standard form—the security is trading at a discount and interest is paired on coupon dates—the effect on the dealer's capital must be checked and the expression for r^* may have to be reformulated.

Second, on any money market transaction that involves dollars in and dollars out in different time periods, the dating of these flows and thus their effect on the trader's capital position must be taken into account. Dollars in equal to dollars out does not suffice to guarantee that a trader will break even on a given transaction if the dollar flows occur in different time periods.

Generating capital

Whenever a dealer takes a haircut on a reverse to maturity, he generates capital because the amount he lends is less than the price at which he sells the security. This capital is, however, not free. By taking a haircut the dealer incurs an *opportunity cost* equal to the interest he forgoes by not making a larger loan to the security holder. If

$$H = \text{haircut}$$

then the amount of interest forgone, i.e., the opportunity cost of the capital generated, equals

$$\frac{r}{360} H [t_{sc} + (N - 1)182.5]$$

So long as the value of that capital to the dealer exceeds the reverse rate, this cost is acceptable, and the haircut will raise the dealer's profit on the transaction.

Presumably in the short run the value of capital to the dealer will always exceed the reverse rate. However, on a long reverse to maturity, the desirability to the dealer of generating capital will depend on his interest rate forecast. If he expects rates to decline sharply, he will want to minimize the haircut, whereas if he anticipates a rise in rates, he will desire the opposite.

Solving for r^*

As noted, when the problems that cause discrepancies between y and y^* on short coupons are amortized over a longer time period, these rates converge. Thus, on a long coupon a quick and quite accurate way to estimate r^*, assuming interest is paired on coupon dates, is simply to convert yield to maturity on the quote sheet to a 360-day-year basis, i.e.,

$$r^* = y \, \frac{360}{365}$$

Note, however, that if the dealer reverses in a long coupon to maturity at $r*$ and then sells out the security, as is normal practice, he will assume some reinvestment risk. The reason is that, in entering into the transaction, he is committing himself to make a series of payments over time to the security seller, the monies for which must, if the transaction is to be profitable to him, be generated by his investment of the sale proceeds, $P + a_i$, and his reinvestment of interest earned on that investment.

$r*$ on relatively short coupons

For a dealer seeking opportunities to make profitable deals others do not see, the above calculation is too obvious to be interesting. What such a dealer seeks is a security that has a true yield to maturity that is substantially lower than the quote sheet yield and on which he can therefore offer, on a basis profitable to him, what appears to be an especially attractive reverse rate. On securities one or more coupons from maturity, the maturity range in which a dealer is most likely to find such a security is the 6- to 12-month area. Securities in their next to last coupon period are close enough to maturity so that factors such as a long last coupon period and maturity on a nonbusiness day can cause significant discrepancies between y and $y*$. On such a security, the dealer can estimate $r*$—assuming interest is paired on the coupon date—by using a modified version of the formula for $r*$ that we derived by dollar flowing the transaction.

Example. To illustrate, we consider a Treasury note that is in its next to last coupon period. The note carries a 10 percent coupon and is priced at 99–10 to yield 11 percent to maturity. It will pay its next coupon 60 days hence, the basis in its final coupon period is 184 days, and it matures on a Saturday preceding a Monday holiday. Obviously we have constructed an extreme case in which the holding period corresponding to the security's last coupon period is 187 days; because of this, the security's true yield to maturity must be significantly less than 11 percent.

If we estimate for this security $r*$ using y, yield to maturity on the quote sheet, we get

$$r* = 0.11\frac{360}{365} = 0.1085 = 10.85\%$$

If, alternatively, we estimate $r*$ using the dollars-in-dollars-out formula we derived on pages 117–18, we get[10]

$$r* = 10.93\%$$

The latter rate is higher because we constructed our formula for $r*$ on the assumption that the transaction generated from settlement to the first coupon date an amount of capital equal to accrued interest at the time of the trade; we assigned, however, *no* value to that capital. When time to maturity is long or accrued interest is small, this omission will have little effect on the value obtained for $r*$. In situations where that is not so, the assumption can be made that an amount $P + a_i$ is lent to the security holder. In that case, the formula for estimating $r*$ when $N = 2$ becomes, as the reader can verify,

$$r* = \frac{360(F - P + c - a_i)}{P(182.5 + t_{sc}) + a_i t_{sc}}$$

Using this formula, the value we obtain for $r*$ on a reverse to maturity of the security in

---

[10] In this and following calculations, the price $P = 0.993447$, which precisely corresponds to $y = 11$ percent, was used. Also $a_i = 0.033425$.

our example is

$$r* = 10.84\%$$

a number close to the one we obtained when we approximated $r*$ by converting y to a 360-day-year basis.

Nothing we have done so far takes into account the unusually long holding period corresponding to our security's last coupon period. To do that, we modify the last formula given for $r*$ when $N = 2$ as follows:

$$r* = \frac{360(F - P + c - a_i)}{Pt_{ss} + a_i t_{sc}}$$

where

$$t_{ss} = \text{days in the holding period}$$
$$t_{sc} = \text{days from settlement to first coupon}$$

(Note $t_{ss} = t_{sm}$ if the security matures on a business day. If not, $t_{ss} = $ days from settlement to payout.) This formula gives us

$$r* = 10.64\%$$

which tells us that the dealer can break even on a reverse to maturity even if he quotes a reverse rate 36 basis points below to security's quoted yield to maturity.

TAXES

In Tables 6–1 and 8–1, which give quotes for selected Treasury and agency notes and bonds, there are two columns we have not yet discussed, "Yield after Tax" and "Taxable Coupon Equivalent."

Yield after tax

Corporations pay one tax rate on ordinary income, which includes coupon interest, and a much lower rate on *long-term* capital gains, that is, on capital gains earned over a holding period of 1 year or more. What is important to an institution with income that is taxable is *after-tax* as opposed to *pretax* income. Therefore quote sheets always include, in addition to yield to maturity, a second yield figure—*yield after tax.*

The taxation of corporate income and in particular of capital gains and losses is complex, and the rates at which a corporation will be taxed on security income—interest, gains, and losses—will depend in part on the size and composition of its current and sometimes its past earnings. Thus, to calculate yield after tax and taxable coupon equivalent, issuers of quote sheets must make arbitrary assumptions. These are:

1. The investor is taxed as an ordinary corporation.
2. Coupon interest on taxable securities is taxed as ordinary income.
3. Long-term capital gains are taxed at the long-term capital gains rate.
4. Premiums paid for securities are deducted, as amortized over the life of the security, from ordinary income.

Let

$$T = \text{corporate tax rate on ordinary income}$$
$$y_T = \text{yield after tax}$$

On any security that has a current maturity of less than 1 year and/or is selling at par or at a premium, the street calculates yield after tax as follows:

$$y_T = (1 - T)y$$

Example. The first security quoted in Table 9–2,

FHLB 9.65 2/26/79

was offered for settlement on 2/23/79 at a yield to maturity of 8.29. Currently ordinary corporate income is taxed at a rate of 46 percent, so the security's quoted yield after tax, 4.48, was calculated as follows

$$y_T = (1 - 0.46)0.0829 = 0.0448 = 4.48\%$$

Table 9–2
Selected quotes for Federal Home Loan Banks securities for settlement February 23, 1979

DISCOUNT CORPORATION OF NEW YORK
58 Pine Street, New York, N. Y. 10005
Telephone 212-248-8900 • WUI Telex 620863 Discorp • WU Telex 125675 Discorp - NYK

QUOTATIONS FOR FEDERAL AGENCY ISSUES
Noon FEB.21, 1979
Ylds. for Del'y. FEB.23, 1979

	Issue		Bid	Asked	Change from Prev. Day	Yield to Maturity or Call (1)	Yield after Tax (2)	Taxable Coupon Equiv.	Yield Value of 1/32	Current Markets	Amt. of Issue ($ Millions)	Issue Date
	FEDERAL HOME LOAN BANKS											
	8.650	2/26/79	99.28	100.	--	8.29	4.48	8.29	3.597	-------------------	588	6/21/74
	9.450	2/26/79	99.28	100.	--	9.03	4.88	9.03	3.589	-------------------	596	9/25/74
	7 1/2	5/25/79	99.10	99.14	+ 2	9.58	5.17	9.58	.123	-------------------	1300	2/27/78
	8.650	5/25/79	99.17	99.21	--	9.82	5.30	9.82	.123	-------------------	499	10/25/74
	8 3/4	5/25/79	99.17	99.21	--	9.92	5.36	9.92	.123	-------------------	393	5/28/74
	7.200	8/27/79	98.12	98.16	--	10.28	5.55	10.28	.065	-------------------	900	11/25/77
	9 1/2	8/27/79	99.17	99.21	--	10.20	5.51	10.20	.064	-------------------	491	7/25/74
	7 1/2	11/26/79	97.28	98.	--	10.28	5.55	10.28	.044	-------------------	482	12/23/74
	8.150	11/26/79	98.10	98.14	--	10.31	5.57	10.31	.044	-------------------	493	11/25/74
	8.600	11/26/79	98.23	98.27	+ 1	10.19	5.50	10.19	.044	-------------------	700	7/25/78
	7.050	2/25/80	96.26	97. 2	--	10.20	6.08	11.25	.034	-------------------	300	2/25/74
	7 3/4	2/25/80	97.14	97.22	--	10.23	5.97	11.05	.034	-------------------	350	3/25/70
	8.100	2/25/80	97.28	98. 4	--	10.11	5.82	10.78	.034	-------------------	1200	5/25/78
	6.650	5/27/80	95.28	96. 4	--	9.98	5.99	11.09	.028	-------------------	500	5/25/77
	8.400	5/27/80	97.28	98. 4	--	10.00	5.69	10.53	.027	-------------------	1000	8/25/78
	7.300	8/25/80	96. 8	96.16	--	9.86	5.79	10.71	.023	-------------------	700	8/25/76
	9 3/4	8/25/80	99.22	99.26	--	9.89	5.37	9.93	.023	-------------------	900	11/27/78
	7.800	10/15/80	96.20	96.28	- 2	9.89	5.72	10.58	.021	-------------------	200	10/15/70
	6.700	11/25/80	94.22	94.30	- 2	9.90	5.92	10.96	.020	-------------------	500	11/26/76
	7 3/4	11/25/80	96.12	96.20	- 2	9.88	5.72	10.59	.020	-------------------	600	11/25/75
	7.600	2/25/81	96.	96. 8	- 4	9.70	5.62	10.40	.018	-------------------	500	2/25/76
	9.550	5/26/81	99.22	99.26	- 4	9.63	5.21	9.65	.016	-------------------	600	12/26/78
WI	9.650	5/26/81	99.28	99.30	- 2	9.67	5.23	9.67	.016	-------------------	800	2/26/79
	7.050	8/25/81	94.	94. 8	--	9.69	5.71	10.57	.015	-------------------	800	8/25/77
	8.650	11/25/81	97.24	98.	- 4	9.48	5.27	9.75	.013	-------------------	400	10/25/74
	6.600	11/27/81	92.30	93. 6	- 4	9.45	5.62	10.40	.014	-------------------	200	10/27/71

FOOTNOTES:
The foregoing quotations are not to be construed as offerings and are subject to change without notice. All quotations are for delivery and payment in New York City.
(1) The calculations are to maturity date for issues selling below par and to earliest call date for issues selling above par.
(2) Yields after tax have been computed by using rates based upon the Tax Revenue Act of 1978. For ordinary income tax purposes we have used a rate of 46% and for long term capital gains purposes 28%.

Long-term capital gains. When a note or bond with a current maturity of 1 year or more is selling at a *discount,* it offers the investor who buys it and holds it to maturity both coupon interest *and* a long-term capital gain. In that case, to calculate the after-tax yield that the security offers, it is necessary *to split its yield to maturity into two components, coupon interest and capital gain.* The way the street makes this calculation is as follows: Of the total yield to maturity, y, offered by the security, an amount c, the coupon rate, is taken to represent interest income, while the remainder, $y - c$, is taken to represent the rate of capital gain earned.

Let

$$T_G = \text{tax rate on long-term capital gains}$$

then yield after tax on a discount bond with a current maturity of 1 year or more is calculated by the street as follows:

$$y_T = c(1 - T) + (y - c)(1 - T_G)$$

This calculation has the virtue of simplicity but, like many other street calculations, the disadvantage that it is only an approximation.

Recalling the formulas we gave earlier for price and yield calculations on notes and bonds (page 112), it is obvious that *true* after-tax yield, y_T, on a discount bond with a current maturity of a year or more is the y value that would be obtained by solving the following equation for y:

$$P = \left[\frac{1 - (1 - P)T_G}{\left(1 + \frac{y}{2}\right)^{N-1+(t_{sc}/B)}} \right] + \left[\sum_{k=1}^{N} \frac{c/2\,(1 - T)}{\left(1 + \frac{y}{2}\right)^{k-1+(t_{sc}/B)}} \right] - a_i$$

Such a solution can, as noted, be carried out efficiently only on a computer programmed to make it by using an iterative procedure (see the appendix to this chapter).

Taxable coupon equivalent

Because coupon interest received by a corporation is taxed at a much higher rate than long-term capital gains, a security that is a year or more from maturity and that is priced to yield x percent to maturity will be worth *more* to a corporation if it is trading at a *discount* than if it is trading at *par*. In the former case some of the income on the security will come in the form of low-taxed capital gains, while in the latter case all the income will come in the form of high-taxed coupon interest.

This observation raises the question: What coupon rate would a security selling at par and having a current maturity of more than one year have to pay in order to return the same *after-tax* yield offered by a note or bond of similar maturity that is selling at a discount, i.e., a note or bond whose yield consists in part of a long-term capital gain? The yield value thus calculated is called the security's *taxable coupon equivalent*.

Muni notes. To understand the rationale behind the street's estimate of this number, let's start with municipal notes. Interest income on municipal securities is *not* subject to federal taxation;[11] therefore on a muni note trading at par, after-tax yield is given by

$$y_T = c$$

To get the same after-tax yield on a taxable security that is selling at par, the investor would have to receive a coupon,

$$c_T = \text{taxable coupon equivalent}$$

such that

$$(1 - T)c_T = c$$

---

[11] The Internal Revenue Service Code prohibits, except for specifically exempted institutions such as banks, the expensing of interest on funds borrowed for the purchase or carry of tax-exempt securities. For corporations that have borrowed long term to finance capital investments and have surplus short-term funds, this raises the question of whether interest income on muni notes is tax exempt for them. The answer is uncertain because the IRS has issued few definitive rulings.

Solving for c_T, we get

$$c_T = \frac{c}{1 - T}$$

To illustrate, consider a muni note offered at par and carrying a 5.40 percent coupon. On this note

$$c_T = \frac{0.054}{1 - 0.46} = 0.10 = 10\%$$

The contrast between the 5.4 percent and 10 percent rates explains the major attraction of municipal securities.

Taxable securities.   Bearing the above in mind, let us return to taxable securities. The way the street calculates *taxable coupon equivalent* on taxable securities that sell at a discount and offer a long-term capital gain is as follows. First, yield to maturity, y, is separated, as in the calculation of after-tax yield, into two components: coupon interest, c, and a second portion, $y - c$, which measures the capital gain offered. Next, the capital gain portion of yield is multiplied by a factor, $1 - T_G$, to obtain its after-tax value; since this amount is not subject to further taxation, and in particular not to taxation at the ordinary tax rate T, it is (like the coupon on a muni note) divided by a factor, $1 - T$, to make it directly comparable to the coupon rate c paid by the security. In symbols, the street's method of calculating *taxable coupon equivalent*, c_T, on a *taxable security* is

$$c_T = c + (y - c)\frac{1 - T_G}{1 - T}$$

Example.   Consider the security

FHLB 7.050 2/25/80

Tax calculations used on industry quote sheets

Let

y = yield to maturity
c = coupon rate
T = corporate tax rate on ordinary income
T_G = corporate tax rate on long-term capital gains
y_T = yield after tax
c_T = taxable coupon equivalent

Case I: Security is taxable; its current maturity is less than 1 year and/or it is selling at a premium:

$$y_T = y(1 - T)$$
$$c_T = y$$

Case II: Security is taxable; its current maturity is 1 year or more and it is selling at a discount:

$$y_T = c(1 - T) + (y - c)(1 - T_G)$$

$$c_T = c + (y - c)\frac{1 - T_G}{1 - T}$$

which, as Table 9–2 shows, was offered for settlement on 2/23/79 at a price of 97– 2 to yield 10.20 to maturity. Using the corporate tax rates based on the Tax Revenue Act of 1978—*46 percent for ordinary income and 28 percent for long-term capital gains*—we calculate that on this security

$$y_T = 0.0705(1 - 0.46) + (0.1020 - 0.0705)(1 - 0.28)$$
$$= 0.0608 = 6.08\%$$

and

$$c_T = 0.0705 + \frac{(0.1020 - 0.0705)(1 - 0.28)}{1 - 0.46}$$
$$= 0.1125 = 11.25\%$$

which are the figures given in Table 9–2.

The 1-year boundary

In Table 9–2, note that the security considered in our example was the first FHLB security quoted with a current maturity of 1 year or more, i.e., the first that offered the investor an opportunity to realize a long-term capital gain. On all securities with a shorter current maturity, taxable coupon equivalent yield was quoted as identical with yield to maturity, even though these securities were trading at a discount.

Fairyland

After-tax yield and taxable coupon equivalent yield, as calculated on a quote sheet, are approximations based on another (at least on shorter-term coupons) approximation, yield to maturity. The resulting possible inaccuracy in these figures is much more forgivable than that in the yield to maturity figure on which it is based. The reason is that different types of institutions are taxed in different ways and at different rates. Banks, for example, must pay the same tax rate on long-term capital gains realized on security holdings as they pay on ordinary income. Also institutions of the same type may find themselves in very different tax situations because of their past and/or present earnings positions. (See the example below.) In effect after-tax yield and taxable coupon equivalent yield are numbers that are almost unique to an institution, especially when state taxes are taken into account; they are therefore numbers an astute institution will calculate for itself.

Example. To illustrate what an extreme discrepancy can exist between (1) quote sheet figures for after-tax yield and taxable coupon equivalent and (2) the rates realized by an actual corporation, let us consider a transaction that—fanciful as it may sound—is done in huge size by a few corporations in a position to benefit from it.

Consider a corporation that has incurred a sizable long-term capital loss and that, for the purpose of calculating net taxable long-term gains, may carry this loss forward. For such a corporation long-term capital gains during the carry-forward period will be taxed up to the amount of the capital loss carried at a *zero* tax rate. This tax situation sets the stage for the following profitable and, if all niceties (such as the securities must exist) are observed, legal operation.

The corporation buys for settlement on 2/23/79 $1 million of the security considered above: FHLB 2/25/80, which carries a coupon of 7.05 and offers a yield to maturity of 10.20, a yield after tax of 6.08, and a taxable coupon equivalent yield of 11.25. Ignoring accrued interest that is paid out at settlement and received 2 days later on the security's coupon date, the corporation must pay out $970,625 to make this purchase. To do so, it puts up $20,625 of its own money and borrows $950,000 by repoing the security to maturity at 11.50. At first this transaction appears unattractive because the corporation will earn over the year (plus the 2 days we neglect) during which the transaction is on $70,500 of coupon interest and pay out $110,767 in repo interest, for a net loss of $40,267 of interest.

Now tax fairyland: Assuming the corporation has taxable ordinary income, the interest loss of $40,267 will reduce its tax on current income by $18,523. Also, by holding the security to maturity, the corporation will realize a long-term capital gain of $29,375, which, because of its capital loss carry-forward, will be taxed at a *zero* rate. Thus, *net after taxes* the corporation will realize over the 1-year life of the transaction a *loss* equal to $40,267 − $18,532 and a *gain* equal to $29,375. These sum to a net gain of $7,631.

To earn that gain, the corporation invested $20,625. Thus, over the year on this amount

$$\text{Yield after tax} = \frac{\$7,631}{\$20,625} = 37\%$$

and

$$\text{Taxable equivalent coupon} = 68.5\%$$

For purposes of illustration, we worked with $1 million of securities. A corporation that is carrying a big capital loss forward would do this transaction in *very* large size. Also it would be more likely to do the transaction in Treasury issues, if appropriate ones were available, because markets for agency issues are more likely to be thin than those for Treasury issues.

Dual tax exempts

Interest income on any state or local security is exempt from *federal income taxes*. A municipal security held by investors in the state in which it is issued offers a *dual tax exemption*, that is, interest income on it is exempt not only from federal taxes, but also from state and local income taxes.

Most institutional investors in judging the relative value of a tax-exempt security will calculate its *taxable coupon equivalent yield*. This yield value, discussed above, reflects the impact on the after-tax yield offered by the municipal security of the fact that interest income on it is exempt from federal taxation. The same investor may, however, ignore the impact on after-tax yield offered by local tax exempts that give it a *dual* tax exemption. That can be a serious mistake in this era of rising state and local taxes.

To illustrate, consider again the example we gave on page 123–24. There we showed that for a corporation taxed at a marginal rate of 46 percent on ordinary income, the taxable coupon equivalent yield, c_T, offered by a municipal note carrying a 5.4 percent coupon would be 10 percent.

Let us now assume that the municipal note in question would offer the buyer a *dual* tax exemption and that, in the buyer's state, state and local taxes total 15 percent. Then the security's taxable coupon equivalent yield would be not 10 percent but

$$c_T = \frac{0.054}{1 - (0.46 + 0.15)} = 13.85\%$$

that is, 385 basis points higher.

Catching all the subtleties

So far we have focused essentially on basics. A firm investing a sizeable amount of short-term money will want to do an in depth analysis of the impact of *all* the taxes it pays on the after-tax yields offered by *all* the types of securities in which it would consider investing.

To illustrate consider a large corporation that does business in a number of states and thus pays taxes to more than one state as well as to the federal government. Such a firm should begin by calculating a table that shows the total tax rate it would pay on each type of paper in which it might invest, given

1. Its current taxable earnings.
2. The allocation of those earnings among different states.
3. Any quirks that exist in the rates at which states tax interest income derived from different sorts of short-term paper.[12]

To illustrate, we reproduce in Table 9–3 a tax rate table constructed some years ago by a corporation with national operations. In studying this table, note that the list of securities that a firm should include in such a table will vary from firm to firm because different firms have different investment parameters. Note also that the list appropriate for any one firm will change over time as new securities are introduced. Finally note that the numbers in such a table must be periodically updated as the sources of the firm's income vary and/or changes occur in tax laws and rates.

Table 9–3
Total Tax Rates Applicable to Different Types of Securities

Type of security	*Total tax rate* %
1. Local tax exempts	1.600
2. Other state tax exempts	5.837
3. Treasury securities	48.832
4. Commercial paper, FNMA paper	51.187
5. Bank CDs	50.467

Once a firm has constructed a table of the sort illustrated in Table 9–3, it should then use this table to construct a second table that will allow its traders to engage in *tax arbitrage,* that is, to choose among and/or swap securities so as to maximize after-tax earnings. This second table gives for each type of security in which the firm would consider investing *yield equivalent factors,* that is, factors that show the *multiple* by which yield on each type of security would have to exceed or could be less than yield on some other type of security in order that the two types of securities offer the firm the same after-tax yield. Naturally before these factors can be applied yields on the different types of securities must be *stated on the same basis,* i.e., made directly comparable.

Table 9–4, which was constructed using the numbers in Table 9–3, illustrates what we mean by a yield equivalent factor table. To interpret this table, let's look at line 1. The second entry in this line says that, if the firm could purchase a security free of all taxes, a local muni note would be as attractive an investment only if it yielded 1.0163 times as much as the free-of-all-taxes security. The 1.0163

---

[12] In New York State, for example, interest income derived from BAs is taxed at a higher rate than that derived from CDs, a fact which naturally discourages local firms from investing in BAs.

Table 9–4
Yield Equivalent Factors

Security	(1) Free	(2) Local state	(3) Other state	(4) Treasury	(5) CP/ FNMA	(6) CDs
1. Free of all taxes	—	1.0163	1.0620	1.9543	2.0486	2.0187
2. Local tax exempts	.984	—	1.0450	1.9231	2.0159	1.9864
3. Other state tax exempts	.9416	.9569	—	1.8403	1.9288	1.9008
4. Treasury securities	.5117	.5200	.5434	—	1.0482	1.0329
5. Commercial paper, FNMA paper	.4881	.4961	.5184	.9540	—	.9854
6. Bank CDs	.4953	.5034	.5261	.9681	1.0148	—

number is calculated using the tax rate given in Table 9–3 on local tax exempts, 1.6%, as follows:

$$\frac{1}{1 - 0.016} = 1.0163$$

Looking at the second line of Table 9–4, we see (column 1) that, given the firm's tax rates, a free-of-all-taxes security would be as attractive as a local tax exempt if it yielded only 0.984 times as much and (column 6) that a CD would have to yield 1.9864 times as much as a local tax except to provide the same after-tax yield.

The free-of-all-taxes securities category is introduced to provide a standard frame of reference. Also for a firm that is losing money or has large foreign tax credits it may be applicable.

A numerical example: The way a firm's trader should use a table such as Table 9–4 is straight forward. Suppose that he can purchase a CD yielding 9 percent and Treasury bills that yield on an *equivalent* basis 8.5 percent. Which is the better buy? Looking at line 4 of Table 9–4, we see that the CD had to yield 1.039 times as much as the Treasury security to yield the same after-tax return. Since

$$1.0329(8.5\%) = 8.78\%$$

and since the CD is available at 9 percent, on a straight after-tax yield basis the CD is the more attractive investment.

ARBITRAGES

Strictly defined, the term *arbitrage* means to buy at a low price in one market and simultaneously resell at a higher price in another market. Some arbitrages in this strict sense do occur in the money market. For example, when a Canadian agency bank accepts an overnight Eurodollar deposit from a U.S. corporation and resells the funds at ⅛ markup in the Fed funds market, it is (besides offering the corporation backdoor entry to the funds market) also engaging in arbitrage in the strict sense of the term. So too are U.S. and foreign banks that engage in weekend arbitrage between Fed funds and Euros. Still another example of pure arbitrage would be a dealer who takes in collateral on a reverse for a fixed period and RPs it at a lower rate for precisely the same period, that is, a matched transaction in repo.

Money market participants use the term *arbitrage* to refer not only to such pure arbitrages, but also to various transactions in which they seek to profit by *exploiting anomalies* either in the yield curve or in the pattern of rates established between different instruments. Typically the anomaly is that the yield spread between two similar instruments is too wide or too narrow; that is, one instrument is priced too generously relative to the other. To exploit such an anomaly, the arbitrager *shorts* the expensive instrument and goes *long* in its underpriced cousin; in other words, he shorts the instrument that has an abnormally low yield relative to the yield on the instrument in which he goes long.

If the arbitrager is successful, he will be able to unwind his arbitrage at a profit because the abnormal yield spread will have narrowed in one of several ways: (1) the security shorted will have fallen in price and risen in yield, (2) the security purchased will have risen in price and fallen in yield, or (3) a combination of the two will have occurred.

In the money market, yield spread arbitrages are often done (1) between identical instruments of similar maturity (one government is priced too generously relative to another government of similar maturity) and (2) between different instruments of the same maturity (an agency issue is priced too generously relative to a government issue of the same maturity).

Note that in a strictly defined yield spread arbitrage (the long and the short positions in similar maturities), the arbitrager exposes himself to *no market risk.* If rates rise, the resulting loss on his long position will be offset by profits on his short position; if rates fall, the reverse will occur. Thus the arbitrager is not basing his position on a prediction of the direction of market rates, and he is concerned about a possible move up or down in interest rates only insofar as such a move might alter yield spreads in the money market.

An arbitrage in the purest sense of the term involves *no* risk of any sort since the sale and purchase are assumed to occur simultaneously or almost so. An arbitrage based on a yield spread anomaly involves, as noted, no market risk. But it does involve risk of another sort; the arbitrager is in effect speculating on yield spreads. If he bets that a given spread will narrow and it in fact widens, he will lose money. Thus, even a strictly defined yield spread arbitrage offers no locked-in profit.

Most money market dealers, with the exception of commercial paper and muni note dealers, are active players of the arbitrage game. They have stored in a computer all sorts of information on historical yield spreads and have programmed the computer to identify anomalies in prevailing spreads as they feed data on current yields into it. Dealers use the resulting "helpful hints to the arbitrager" both to set up arbitrages themselves and to advise clients of profitable arbitrage opportunities.

Generally in a dealer shop arbitrage is done in an account that is separate from the *naked trading* account. The reason is that arbitrage and naked trading are distinctly different lines of business. The trader who seeks to profit from a naked position long or short in a specialist in one narrow sector of the money market, and the positions he assumes are based on a prediction of interest rate trends and how they are likely to affect yields in his particular sector of the market. The arbitrager, in contrast, has to track yields in a number of market sectors, and if he engages in strictly defined yield spread arbitrage, he is not much concerned with whether rates are likely to rise or fall.

Anomalies in yield spreads that offer opportunities for profitable arbitrage arise due to various temporary aberrations in market demand or supply. For example, if the Treasury brings a big 4-year note issue to market, it might trade for a time at a higher rate than surrounding issues because investors were loath to take the capital gains or losses they would have to in order to swap into the new issue. In this case the cause of the out-of-line yield spread would be, for the time it persisted, that the new issue had not been fully distributed. Alternatively, an anomaly might be created by a particular issue being in extremely scarce supply.

Example of an arbitrage

Here's an example of an arbitrage *along the yield curve* based on supply conditions. The Treasury markets a new 2-year note at the end of each month. In contrast it offers 3-year notes only in connection with quarterly financings; thus a new 3-year note comes to market at most once a quarter.

In late January 1978, the yield curve in the 2- to 3-year area was relatively flat, partly because the Treasury had not offered a new 3-year note for 3 months. The market anticipated, however, that the Treasury would include a 3-year note in its February financing and that this new offering would widen yield spreads in the 2- to 3-year area. Thus, buying the current 2-year note and shorting the current 3-year note appeared to be an attractive arbitrage.

Here's how one dealer did this arbitrage. On January 30, for settlement on January 31, he bought the current 2-year note, N 7½ 1/31/80, at a yield to maturity of 7.44. At the same time he shorted the current 3-year note, N 7⅛ 11/15/80, at a yield to maturity of 7.51.

The current 2-year note was trading at a dollar price of 100– 3+, and the yield value of ¹/₃₂ on it was 0.0171.[13] The current 3-year note was trading at a dollar price of 99– 1, and the yield value of ¹/₃₂ on it was 0.0127. The smaller yield value of ¹/₃₂ on the 3-year note meant that, for a given movement up or down in interest rates, the 3-year note would move 135 percent as far up or down in price as the 2-year note would.[14] This in turn meant that, if the arbitrage were established on a dollar-for-dollar basis, that is, if the amount of 3-year notes shorted equaled the amount of 2-year notes purchased, the arbitrage would expose the dealer to market risk. In particular, if rates should fall while the arbitrage was on, the dealer would lose more on his short position in the 3-year note than he would gain on his long position in 2-year note. To minimize market risk, the dealer set the arbitrage in a *ratio* based on the yield values of ¹/₃₂ on the two securities. Note that this procedure insulated the arbitrage against general movements up or down in yields but not against a relative movement between yields on the two securities.

Table 9–5 shows precisely how the arbitrage worked out. The dealer bought for January 31 settlement $1.35 million of the current 2-year note and financed these securities by RPing them at 6.65 percent. Simultaneously he reversed in $1 million of the 3-year note at the lower 6.20 reverse repo rate and sold them. Sixteen days later, when the Treasury was offering a new 3-year note in connection with its February financing, the dealer was able to unwind his arbitrage, which he put on at a *7-basis-point* spread, at a *9-basis-point* spread (Step 2, Table 9–5). The dealer's total return on the arbitrage was, as Step 3 in Table 9–5 shows, $375 per $1 million of securities arbitraged.

On an arbitrage of this sort, risk is limited to the spread relationship, so the size in which dealers do such arbitrages depends only on their ability to finance the securities purchased and to borrow the securities shorted. In practice such arbitrages are commonly done for $50 or $100 million.

Risk: The unexpected occurs

When a strictly defined yield spread arbitrage fails to work out, the reason is usually that something unexpected has occurred. Here's an example. On several occasions in

---

[13] The + in the quote equals ¹/₆₄.

[14] The calculation is

$$\frac{0.0171}{0.0127} = 135\%$$

Table 9–5
An arbitrage along the yield curve

Step 1: Set up the arbitrage for settlement on January 31, 1978.

    A. *Buy* $1.35 million of the current 2-year note, N 7½ 1/31/80, at 100–3+ (7.44 yield):

Principal..................	$1,351,476
Accrued interest	0
Total purchase price	$1,351,476

    Repo these securities at 6.65.

    B. Reverse in and *sell* $1 million of the current 3-year note, N 7⅛ 11/15/80, at 99– 1 (7.51 yield):

Principal..................	$ 990,312
Accrued interest	15,155
Total sale price	$1,005,467

    Reverse rate 6.20.

Step 2: Unwind the arbitrage for settlement on February 16, 1978.

    A. Sell out the long position in the 2-year note at 99–28 (7.57 yield):

Principal..................	$1,348,312
Accrued interest	4,475
Total sale price	$1,352,787

    Pay financing cost at 6.65 repo rate for 16 days: $3,994.

    B. Cover the short position in the 3-year note at 98–22 (7.66 yield):

Principal..................	$ 986,875
Accrued interest	18,304
Total purchase price	$1,005,179

    Receive return on reverse at 6.20 for 16 days: $2,770.

Step 3: Calculate net return on arbitrage.

    Return on short position in the 3-year note:

Sale price	$1,005,467
Purchase price	−1,005,179
Income on reverse	2,770
Total return..............	$ 3,058

    Return on long position in the 2-year note:

Purchase price	$−1,351,476
Sale price................	1,352,787
Cost of repo..............	− 3,994
Total return	$− 2,683

    Net return on overall arbitrage:

Return on short position.......	$3,058
Return on long position	−2,683
Net return on the arbitrage	$ 375

the spring of 1977, the old 7-year note and the current 7-year note, whose maturities were only 3 months apart, traded at a 10-basis-point spread. This made no sense since it implied that, at the 7-year level, the appropriate spread between securities differing by 1 year in maturity was 40 basis points—an impossible yield curve. One dealer successfully arbitraged this yield spread three times by shorting the high-yield current note and going long in the old note. On his fourth try the unexpected occurred. In his words: "We stuck our head in the wringer. We put on the 'arb' at 10 basis points and, while we had it on, the Treasury reopened the current 7-year note. That did not destroy the productive nature of the arbitrage but it did increase the time required before it will be possible to close it out at a profit. The costs of shorting the one issue and being long in the other (especially delivery costs on the short side) are high so at some point we will probably have to turn that arbitrage into a loss trade. Had the Treasury reopened some other issue, we would have made $20,000 bang. Instead we're looking at a $40,000 paper loss."

The arbitrage in this example comes close to being a strictly defined yield arbitrage. Many money market arbitrages do not. Dealers will often go long in an issue of one maturity and short another issue of quite different maturity. An arbitrage of this sort resembles a strictly defined yield spread arbitrage in that it is a speculation on a yield spread. But it is more risky than such an arbitrage, because if interest rates move up or down, the price movement in the longer-maturity security will normally exceed that in the shorter-maturity security; thus the arbitrage exposes the investor who puts it on to a *price risk*.

Dealers are not unaware of this, and they attempt to offset the inherent price risk in an arbitrage involving securities of different maturities by adjusting the sizes of the two sides of the arbitrage, as in the previous arbitrage example. If, for instance, the arbitrage involves shorting the 2-year note and buying the 7-year note, the arbitrager will short more notes than he buys. Such a strategy, however, cannot completely eliminate market risk; a movement in interest rates may be accompanied by a change in the slope of the yield curve, and the difference in the price movements the two issues would undergo if interest rates changed can therefore only be estimated.

Bull and *bear market arbitrages* are based on a view of where interest rates are going. A bull market arbitrager anticipates a fall in interest rates and a rise in securities prices. Thus he might, for example, short 2-year Treasuries and go long in 10-year Treasuries on a one-for-one basis, hoping to profit when rates fall from the long coupon appreciating more than the short coupon. If, alternatively, the arbitrager were bearish, he would do the reverse: short long governments and buy short ones.

An arbitrage can also be set up to profit from an anticipated change in the slope of the yield curve. For example, an arbitrager who anticipated a flattening of the yield curve might buy notes in the 7-year area for high yield and short notes in the 2-year area, not necessarily on a one-to-one basis. If the yield curve flattened with no change in average rate levels, the 7-year note would appreciate, the 2-year note would decline in price, and the arbitrage could be closed out at a profit.

Money market practitioners are wont to call any pair of long and short positions an arbitrage, but it is clear that as the maturities of the securities involved in the transaction get further and further apart, price risk increases, and at some point the "arbitrage" becomes in reality two separate speculative positions, one a naked long and the other a naked short.

Money market arbitragers normally put on both sides of an arbitrage simultaneously, but they rarely take them off simultaneously. As one dealer noted: "The compulsion to *lift a leg* [unwind one side of an arbitrage before the other] is overwhelming. Hardly anyone ever has the discipline to unwind both sides simultaneously. Instead they will first unwind the side that makes the most sense against the market. If, for example, the trader thinks the market is going to do better, he will lift a leg by covering the short."

VISUAL AIDS

For a coupon trader, as for a bill trader, *visual aids* can be a big help. Here is an example. In a dealership or large trading operation, obvious arbitrages between different coupons are sometimes not spotted for one or both of two reasons. First, traders in a fast-moving market tend to focus on the *prices* of different issues and in the process lose track of *yields*. Second, different traders may be responsible for different market sectors.

Under these circumstances, it is quite possible that trading will create a situation in which, for example, the 5-year note trades at a higher yield than the 8-year note. Under normal yield curve conditions, that creates an obvious arbitrage—buy the underpriced 5-year note and sell the overpriced 8-year note. Whatever happens to the general level of coupon prices, the 5-year note is bound to rise in value relative to the 8-year note.

A useful aid for spotting such arbitrages is a computer printout that gives a price-yield matrix of the sort shown in Table 9–6. Glancing at it, a trader can immediately spot the relationship at the current *moment*'s prices that prevails between yields on two issues. What issues a trader will want to include in such a table and how finely he will want to gradate price will depend on his area of interest, on the general condition of the market, and in particular on current price volatility in the market.

MAGIC NUMBERS

For the trader of notes and bonds, as for the trader of short instruments, being aware of subleties and knowing magic numbers can be useful. Here are two examples.

Rolling the 2-year note

A strategy pursued by some investors in 2-year notes is to roll into the new note at each monthly auction. This keeps the investor in the current issue. Also, such investors hope that, for the new 2-year note to be digested by the market, it will have to sell slightly below the old 2-year note and that rolling will therefore enable them to pick up yield.

In fact a favorable spread between the prices of the old and new issues is *not* required for the investor to achieve at least a small yield pickup on such a roll. The reason lies in a familiar friend, the importance of dating and compounding.

To illustrate, assume an investor buys at par in the auction a new 2-year note carrying a 9.5 percent coupon. Assume also that 1 month later he is able to swap—selling at par and buying at par—into the new 2-year note, which also carries a 9.5 percent coupon. Since governments trade at the quoted price plus interest accrued at the coupon rate, our investor must earn 9.5 percent on his investment on the first note over his 1-month holding period. The Treasury, however, will not pay coupon interest on that security for another 5 months. Therefore the buyer of the security must earn slightly less than 9.5 percent on his investment over the remainder of the coupon period, which in fact he does.

The way our investor picks up yield is that by rolling he is in effect turning a

Table 9–6
Visual aid for a coupon trader: Price-yield matrix for Treasury Issues

Coupon Maturity Price*	10.125 11/94 95		10.750 11/89 97		9.000 2/87 88		9.250 5/84 91	
	32nds	Yield	32nds	Yield	32nds	Yield	32nds	Yield
	0	10.804	15	11.174	0	11.356	15	11.725
	1	10.799	16	11.169	1	11.349	16	11.715
	2	10.795	17	11.163	2	11.343	17	11.706
	3	10.790	18	11.158	3	11.336	18	11.696
	4	10.786	19	11.153	4	11.329	19	11.687
	5	10.782	20	11.147	5	11.323	20	11.677
	6	10.777	21	11.142	6	11.316	21	11.667
	7	10.773	22	11.137	7	11.309	22	11.658
	8	10.768	23	11.131	8	11.303	23	11.648
	9	10.764	24	11.126	9	11.296	24	11.639
	10	10.760	25	11.121	10	11.289	25	11.629
	11	10.755	26	11.115	11	11.283	26	11.620
	12	10.751	27	11.110	12	11.276	27	11.610
	13	10.746	28	11.105	13	11.269	28	11.600
	14	10.742	29	11.099	14	11.263	29	11.591
	15	10.738	30	11.094	15	11.256	30	11.581
	16	10.733	31	11.089	16	11.250	31	11.572
	17	10.729	0	11.083	17	11.243	0	11.562
	18	10.724	1	11.078	18	11.236	1	11.553
	19	10.720	2	11.073	19	11.230	2	11.543
	20	10.716	3	11.068	20	11.223	3	11.534
	21	10.711	4	11.062	21	11.216	4	11.524
	22	10.707	5	11.057	22	11.210	5	11.515
	23	10.703	6	11.052	23	11.203	6	11.505
	24	10.698	7	11.046	24	11.197	7	11.496
	25	10.694	8	11.041	25	11.190	8	11.486
	26	10.690	9	11.036	26	11.183	9	11.477
	27	10.685	10	11.030	27	11.177	10	11.467
	28	10.681	11	11.025	28	11.170	11	11.458
	29	10.676	12	11.020	29	11.164	12	11.448
	30	10.672	13	11.015	30	11.157	13	11.439
	31	10.668	14	11.009	31	11.150	14	11.429
	0	10.663	15	11.004	0	11.144	15	11.420
	1	10.659	16	10.999	1	11.137	16	11.410
	2	10.655	17	10.994	2	11.131	17	11.401
	3	10.650	18	10.988	3	11.124	18	11.392
	4	10.646	19	10.983	4	11.117	19	11.382
	5	10.642	20	10.978	5	11.111	20	11.373
	6	10.637	21	10.972	6	11.104	21	11.363
	7	10.633	22	10.967	7	11.098	22	11.354
	8	10.629	23	10.962	8	11.091	23	11.344
	9	10.624	24	10.957	9	11.085	24	11.335
	10	10.620	25	10.951	10	11.078	25	11.325
	11	10.616	26	10.946	11	11.072	26	11.316
	12	10.611	27	10.941	12	11.065	27	11.307
	13	10.607	28	10.936	13	11.058	28	11.297
	14	10.603	29	10.930	14	11.052	29	11.288
	15	10.598	30	10.925	15	11.045	30	11.278
	16	10.594	31	10.920	16	11.039	31	11.269

* To nearest dollar.

security that offers an opportunity for *semiannual* compounding of interest into one that offers *monthly* compounding. To see the effect of this on return, observe that if rates were so stable that each of 12 consecutive 2-year notes were issued with a 9.5 percent coupon, and if our investor were able to swap from each into the next, selling at par and buying at par, the return he would earn over 1 year would be

$$\left(1 + \frac{0.095}{12}\right)^{12} - 1 = 9.92\%$$

which is 20 basis points more than the rate,

$$\left(1 + \frac{0.095}{2}\right)^{2} - 1 = 9.72\%$$

that the security offers when compounding occurs only semiannually.

wi price

Between its auction and issue dates, a note or bond will trade *wi, when issued.* When the issue auctioned is a reopening of an existing issue, there will exist for 5 days two prices for that issue—the price in the cash market and the wi price. The latter is a price for *future* delivery, and as such should be spread from the cash price by an amount equal to the *cost of* or *return on* carrying the cash security over the wi period.

To calculate the correct spread, a handy magic number is 1,140. To show why, let's work an example. Assume the structure of rates is such that over the 5-day wi period a 200-basis-point carry can be earned by owning and RPing the cash security. This equals per $1 of face value a profit of

$$2\% \left(\frac{5}{365}\right)$$

To determine what this profit is worth in terms of 32nds, we divide it by the value of $\frac{1}{32}$ per $1 of face value, which is 0.003125. This gives us

$$\frac{2\% \left(\dfrac{5}{365}\right)}{0.003125} = 0.9$$

Carry profit is worth $\frac{9}{10}$ of $\frac{1}{32}$, so the cash security should trade approximately $\frac{1}{32}$ below the wi price at the beginning of the wi period.

Let's now derive the magic number. To do so, we rewrite our expression for carry profit in 32nds as follows:

$$\frac{2\% \ (5)}{0.1140} = 0.9$$

Next, since traders think of carry in terms of basis points, not decimals, we multiply both the numerator and the denominator of the fraction by 10,000. This gives us

$$\frac{200(5)}{1,140} = 0.9$$

From this expression we can generalize as follows:

$$\begin{pmatrix} \text{Value of wi} \\ \text{carry in} \\ \text{32nds} \end{pmatrix} = \frac{\begin{pmatrix} \text{Carry earned in} \\ \text{basis points} \end{pmatrix}\begin{pmatrix} \text{Days carry} \\ \text{is earned} \end{pmatrix}}{1,140}$$

If carry is *negative,* the magic number 1,140 can be used to determine at how much of a *premium* the wi note should trade to the cash security.

Finally note that if a trader shorts an issue by reversing it in, he can, using the 1,140 number, calculate in his head what his break-even rate on a covering purchase *x* days hence will be, that is, his true give-up yield.

APPENDIX: CALCULATING YIELD GIVEN PRICE ON A SECURITY PAYING PERIODIC INTEREST

The algorithm for calculating yield to maturity given price on a security that pays periodic interest involves three basic calculations, the second two of which are repeated in the iteration method described below.[15]

Calculation I.   Yield to maturity, *y,* is estimated on the basis of the security's known price, coupon, and current maturity. Let

$$P = \text{known price}$$
$$y_1 = first \text{ estimate of yield to maturity}$$
$$Y = \text{security's current maturity in years}$$

then[16]

$$y_1 = \frac{cY + 1 - P}{Y - (1 - P)\left(\frac{2Y + 1}{4}\right)}$$

Calculation II.   Calculate price as a function of yield. To facilitate computation, we rewrite the formula derived in Chapter 9 for P given y as follows:

$$P = \left(1 + \frac{y}{2}\right)^{-t_{sc}/B}\left[\left(1 + \frac{y}{2}\right)^{1-N} + \frac{c}{2}\sum_{k=1}^{N}\left(1 + \frac{y}{2}\right)^{1-k}\right] - a_i$$

Calculation III.   Calculate $dP/dy,$ the derivative of price with respect to yield. Let

$$P' = \frac{dP}{dy}$$

The formula is:

$$P' = \left(1 + \frac{y}{2}\right)^{-N-(t_{sc}/B)}\left[\frac{1 - N - \frac{t_{sc}}{B}}{2} - \frac{c}{4}\sum_{k=1}^{N}\left(k - 1 + \frac{t_{sc}}{B}\right)\left(1 + \frac{y}{2}\right)^{-k}\right]$$

The algorithm

We will describe the method for calculating yield *y* given price *P* as a series of steps.

Step 1:   Calculate $y_1,$ the first estimate of *y,* using Calculation I.
Step 2:   Calculate $P_1,$ the price at which the security would be offered if it were priced to yield $y_1,$ using Calculation II.

---

[15] The notation used in this appendix is consistent with the usage elsewhere in the book. In particular, P is price per \$1 of face value and c is the coupon rate expressed as a decimal.

[16] This formula applies whether the security is selling at a premium or at a discount. An illustration of its use is given at the end of the appendix.

Step 3: Calculate P_1', the value of dP/dy when $y = y_1$, using Calculation III.

Step 4: Calculate y_2, the second estimate of y, as follows:

$$y_2 = y_1 + \frac{P - P_1}{P_1'}$$

where

$$P_1 = P \text{ evaluated at } y_1$$
$$P_1' = dP/dy \text{ evaluated at } y_1$$

Step 5: Repeat Step 2 using y_2 to obtain P_2, the price at which the security would be offered if it were priced to yield y_2.

Step 6: Repeat Step 3 using y_2 to obtain P_2', that is, dP/dy evaluated at y_2.

Step 7: Calculate y_3, the third estimate of y as follows:

$$y_3 = y_2 \frac{P - P_2}{P_2'}$$

The iteration method outlined in Steps 2–7 should be continued until the absolute value of the last increment or decrement in the estimated value of y (that is, $|y_{n+1} - y_n|$) is smaller than some initially specified value.

The general formula for calculating each new estimate of y (Steps 4 and 7) can be written as follows:

$$y_{n+1} = y_n + \frac{P - P_n}{P_n'}$$

The method of iteration we have described is known as *Newton's method*. Normally the successive estimates of y it produces will converge on the security's actual yield to maturity, y. There are, however, situations in which they will diverge, so care should be taken. Other iteration methods described in calculus texts can also be used to solve for a bond's yield to maturity.

Example

Calculations II and III are straightforward but arduous. Calculation I, which provides an initial estimate, y_1, of yield to maturity is simple, surprisingly accurate, and deserves an example.

Consider

FHLB 6.60 11/27/81

which, as Table 9–2 shows, was offered for settlement on 2/23/79 at a price of 93–6. We want to *estimate* this security's yield to maturity using the formula given earlier in this appendix:

$$y_1 = \frac{cY + 1 - P}{Y - (1 - P)\dfrac{2Y + 1}{4}}$$

To do so, we first calculate Y, the security's current maturity in years. On 2/23/79 the security was 2 years and 277 days from maturity (recall that agencies accrue interest on a 30/360-day basis). Thus the security's current maturity in years was

$$Y = 2 + \frac{277}{360} = 2.769444$$

Inserting this value, the security's coupon, and its price into the formula for y_1, we get

$$y_1 = \frac{0.066(2.769444) + (1 - 0.931875)}{2.769444 - (1 - 0.931875)\dfrac{2(2.769444) + 1}{4}}$$

$$= 0.094395$$

$$= 9.44\%$$

As Table 9–2 shows, our estimate, $y_1 = 9.44$, differs from the security's actual yield to maturity, which was 9.45, by only 1 basis point.

10

Tracking portfolio performance

Institutions measure performance on their short-term portfolios in various ways. We will start with the method that is most widely used, namely, measuring performance in terms of historic purchase prices and yields and current book value. Then we will discuss how the *true* yield realized over any holding period can be measured by marking a portfolio to market. Finally, in the appendix to this chapter, we introduce a new concept, average daily yield—a useful tool for measuring both offered yields and performance achieved.

WEIGHTED AVERAGES

Many performance measures make use of weighted averages. To illustrate, we give two examples. Consider first an investor who invests over a 30-day holding period $100 at 10 percent and $50 at 9 percent. Over that period his average return on capital invested will be the following weighted average:

$$\frac{\$100(0.10) + \$50(0.09)}{\$100 + \$50} = 9.67\%$$

Let

V_j = amount invested in the jth security
i_j = rate of interest on the jth security
$\bar{i}_t$ = average rate of interest over the investment period of t days

then in symbols the formula for calculating the average return earned when all securities are held for the full investment period t is:[1]

---

[1] When it is clear over what values a summation is being taken, an expression such as

$$\sum_{j=1}^{n} x_j y_j$$

139

$$\bar{i}_t = \frac{\sum_j V_j i_j}{\sum_j V_j}$$

Suppose now that our investor invests $100 at 10 percent over the full 30-day holding period and $50 at 9 percent over the last 15 days of this period. Then over the whole period his average return on capital invested will be the following weighted average:

$$\frac{\$100(0.10)(30) + \$50(0.09)(15)}{\$100(30) + \$50(15)} = 9.80\%$$

Let

t_j = days during the holding period that the jth security is held

In symbols the formula for calculating the average return earned when securities are held for various portions of the full investment period t is:

$$\bar{i}_t = \frac{\sum_j V_j i_j t_j}{\sum_j V_j t_j}$$

MEASURING PERFORMANCE ON THE BASIS OF HISTORIC AND BOOK VALUES

Institutions frequently measure performance on a monthly or quarterly basis using historic yield at purchase as the value for i and purchase price or book value at the beginning of the investment period as the value for V.

If all yields are on a comparable basis, the last formula we gave suffices for measuring performance using this approach, provided, that is, that the portfolio does not use leverage.

If yields are *not* on a comparable basis, either they must be restated on some uniform basis, e.g., as simple interest rates on a 365-day-year basis, or total interest accrued over the period must be divided by the amount invested and the resulting rate must be annualized. Let

R_j = dollars of interest accrued on the jth security over the investment period

t = days in the investment period

then, using the latter approach, we can write the formula for measuring average return over the investment period, dt days, as follows:

$$\left[\bar{i}_t = \frac{\sum_j R_j}{\sum_j V_j t_j} \frac{365}{t} \right]$$

is often written more simply as

$$\sum_j x_j y_j$$

By eliminating the need to introduce and define new symbols, this practice contributes to both brevity and clarity; for that reason we use it here.

$$\bar{i}_t = \frac{\sum_j V_j i_j}{\sum_j V_j}$$

Note, if the portfolio has interest-bearing securities bought at prices other than par, it will typically *accrete discounts* and *amortize premiums* over time so that a security's book value will equal its par value at maturity. If that procedure is followed, *any such accretions and amortizations should be included in R.* So too should any *realized capital gains or losses* that occur because securities are sold at a price that differs from their book value.

Allowing for leverage

Even conservative portfolio managers sometimes reverse out securities as part of an arbitrage and less conservative managers sometimes consciously lever their positions. If leverage is used, accrued interest on debt over the investment period should be subtracted from the return earned on the portfolio in calculating average yield. Also the amount invested, i.e., the denominator of the expression for performance, should be adjusted to reflect the amount of its own capital the portfolio has invested. Let

r_k = rate on a 360-day basis on the kth borrowing
L_k = amount of the kth borrowing (loan)
t_k = days the kth loan is outstanding during the investment period

then the average return earned over the investment period is given by

$$\bar{i}_t = \left[\frac{\sum_j R_j - \sum_k r_k L_k \dfrac{t_k}{360}}{\sum_j V_j t_j - \sum_k L_k t_k} \right] \frac{365}{t}$$

MARKING THE PORTFOLIO TO MARKET

The approach we have just described for measuring portfolio performance is common; it is also fallacious. If a portfolio manager has just bought 6-month CDs at a yield of 10 percent and then rates go to 11 percent, he has made a bad market judgment and his true current yield is not 10 percent but—given prevailing market prices—some *negative* number. Measuring return earned on the basis of historic yields at purchase insulates the portfolio manager's record from subsequent price movements in a way such that it fails to reflect either good judgments—he extends in maturity and rates fall— or bad judgments—he extends and rates rise.

To measure performance validly, an institution should *mark its portfolio to market* each time performance is evaluated. Trading portfolios always do this; investment accounts rarely do it.

If a portfolio is marked to market each time performance is evaluated, then the return figure R should reflect both *realized* and *unrealized* capital gains and losses. Also, the figure for the amount invested as of the beginning of the period should be based on the *market value* of the securities held at that time. Let us *redefine* V_j and R_j as follows:

V_j = Beginning-of-period market value of the jth security *or* its purchase price if it is purchased during the investment period

R_j = All interest accrued on the jth security during the investment period plus (minus) any realized or unrealized capital gains (losses), where the latter are measured as the difference between the end-of-period market value or sale price of the jth security and its beginning-of-period market value or purchase price if it was purchased during the investment period

Using these definitions for V_j and R_j, the formula we gave earlier,

$$\bar{i}_t = \left[\frac{\sum_j R_j - \sum_k r_k L_k \frac{t_k}{360}}{\sum_j V_j t_j - \sum_k L_k t_k} \right] \frac{365}{t}$$

becomes an accurate measure of performance.

Measuring performance on a mark-to-market basis gives a portfolio manager a true idea of what yield he has earned over the investment period. To determine how good that yield is, he should compare it with some external yardstick. What yardstick is best—average yield on the 90-day bill, yield achieved by money market funds, or what—depends on his investment parameters, e.g., how long in maturity he can extend, what instruments he can purchase, etc. Naturally, no yardstick will be perfect, and because of this, a few portfolio managers compare the performance they actually achieve with what they could have achieved—given their parameters—had they invested with perfect foresight with respect to interest rate movements over the period.

When a portfolio manager's performance is measured on a mark-to-market basis, no valid evaluation of how well he does relative to the market can be made unless his performance is compared with some yardstick over a relatively long period—6 months or more. A portfolio manager who makes trading and maturity choices is bound to make some good ones and some bad ones. Thus, gauging performance accurately requires a time period sufficiently long to determine whether the good judgments outweigh the bad ones.

APPENDIX: AVERAGE DAILY YIELD

Average daily yield is an extremely useful concept for measuring both the yields at which different securities are offered and the total return earned by a portfolio over some period. Specifically, measuring offered rates in terms of average daily yield provides two important advantages: first, the calculation is simple; and second, the yield figures obtained for different securities are *all directly comparable.* In effect measuring yields on the basis of average daily yield eliminates the problem of noncomparability of rates that arises because securities differ with respect to: (1) the number of days on which annual return is based (360 versus 365), (2) whether they pay interest or are sold at a discount, and (3) how, in the case of interest-bearing securities, they accrue interest.

The major disadvantage of measuring yield in terms of average daily yield is that this rate, because it is a *daily* rate, is an extremely small number that has little intuitive meaning to an investor or trader who is unaccustomed to working with it. The solution to this problem is to annualize the rate.

The concept

The *average daily yield* offered by a security is a rate such that, if that rate were paid and compounded daily on the principal invested in the security, the future value of the investment would equal the security's value at maturity or, on securities paying periodic interest, the security's future value.

That may sound complicated but when the concept is applied to individual types of securities, it is easily understood and easily calculated. We begin with discount securities.

Discount securities

Let

$$\alpha = \text{average daily yield}$$

On a discount security that is purchased at a price P and will be redeemed at a face value F some number of days, t_{sm}, hence, average daily yield, as defined above, is α in the expression

$$P(1 + \alpha)^{t_{sm}} = F$$

This expression can be solved for α as follows:

$$(1 + \alpha)^{t_{sm}} = \frac{F}{P}$$

$$1 + \alpha = \left(\frac{F}{P}\right)^{1/t_{sm}}$$

$$\alpha = \left(\frac{F}{P}\right)^{1/t_{sm}} - 1$$

Example. Suppose an investor buys a 90-day bill at an 8 percent rate of discount. The price he pays will be \$98 per \$100 of face value, and the average daily yield he earns will be

$$\alpha = \left(\frac{100}{98}\right)^{1/90} - 1$$
$$= 0.000224$$

Annualizing α. The number we have just obtained, $\alpha = 0.000224$, is meaningless to anyone who is not used to working with daily yield. To obtain an intuitively meaningful number, we must annualize α. This can be done in two ways. We can multiply α by 365, i.e.,

$$\alpha_{\text{annualized}} = 365\alpha$$

or we can calculate the annual rate of return obtained when α is compounded daily over 1 year, i.e.,

$$\alpha_{\text{annualized}} = (1 + \alpha)^{365} - 1$$

Of these two approaches, the latter is preferable. It is more consistent with the basic calculation of daily yield. Also it is a more appropriate basis for comparing yields on short-term securities that offer the opportunity for frequent or—in the case of Fed funds and overnight RP— compounding of interest on every business day.

Example. We showed earlier that on a 90-day bill offered at an 8 percent rate of discount, $\alpha = 0.000224$. Of the two methods we can use to annualize this rate

$$365\alpha = 365(0.000224)$$
$$= 8.18\%$$

and

$$(1 + \alpha)^{365} - 1 = (1 + 0.000224)^{365} - 1$$
$$= 8.52\%$$

the latter approach yields the more realistic number.

To see this, note that multiplying α by 365 produces an annual rate that is *less than* the bill's bond equivalent yield, which is

$$d_b = \frac{0.08(365)}{360 - 0.08(90)} = 8.28\%$$

Annualizing α on a daily compounded basis produces a rate close to the one obtained by appropriately compounding the bill's bond equivalent yield; that rate is

$$i^* = \left(1 + \frac{0.0828}{\frac{365}{90}}\right)^{365/90} - 1$$

$$= 8.54\%$$

Because the second method given for annualizing α is clearly preferable, *we will define α on an annualized basis as follows:* Let

$$\alpha^* = \alpha \text{ annualized on a 365-day-year basis}$$

then

$$\alpha^* = (1 + \alpha)^{365} - 1$$

Securities that pay interest at maturity

On a security that pays interest at maturity, a CD, or a note or bond in its last coupon period, average daily yield is calculated as follows:

$$\alpha = \left(\frac{\text{Maturity value}}{\text{Price including accrued interest}}\right)^{1/t_{sm}} - 1$$

To illustrate, consider a 90-day CD that carries an 8 percent coupon. If purchased at issue, this CD will offer a daily yield:

$$\alpha = \left(\frac{102}{100}\right)^{1/90} - 1$$

$$= 0.000220$$

and an annualized yield:

$$\alpha^* = (1 + 0.000220)^{365/90} - 1$$
$$= 8.36\%$$

We know that an 8 percent rate of discount is worth more over 90 days than an 8 percent coupon. The α^* values we calculated for a 90-day bill selling at an 8 percent discount and for a 90-day CD carrying an 8 percent coupon reflect this fact: on the bill α^* is 8.52 percent, and on the CD it is only 8.36 percent.

The value obtained for α^* also reflects the frequency of compounding that an instrument would permit if rolled over 1 year. To show this, note that on a 180-day CD, i.e., one that if rolled would permit compounding half as frequently as a 90-day CD, α^* would, if the CD carried an 8 percent coupon, equal 8.28 percent, which is 8 basis points less than the α^* rate on an 8 percent, 90-day CD.

Securities that pay periodic interest

On a note or bond one or more coupons from maturity, yield to maturity is y in the expression

$$P = \left[\frac{1}{\left(1 + \frac{y}{2}\right)^{N-1+(t_{sc}/2B)}} \right] + \left[\sum_{k=1}^{N} \frac{c/2}{\left(1 + \frac{y}{2}\right)^{k-1+(t_{sc}/2B)}} \right] - a_i$$

To measure yield to maturity as an average daily rate α, we divide y in all discount factors in the above equation by 365 instead of 2 and multiply the exponents of these discount factors by 182.5. The first operation converts y to a daily rate, and the second gives the number of days, as opposed to coupon periods, over which each payment is discounted. These two operations yield the following expression in which α is the *internal rate of return on a daily basis* offered by the security:

$$P = \frac{1}{(1 + \alpha)^{182.5(N-1)+t_{sm}}} + \sum_{k=1}^{N} \left[\frac{c/2}{(1 + \alpha)^{182.5(k-1)+t_{sm}}} \right] - a_i$$

If the reinvestment rate r_e is *externally specified*, then using the equation for y when r_e is externally specified and repeating the two operations we did above, we conclude that the average daily yield offered by the security is:[2]

$$\alpha = \left[\frac{\sum_{k=1}^{N} \frac{c}{2}(1 + r_e)^{\frac{182.5(N-k)}{365}} + 1}{P + a_i} \right]^{\frac{1}{182.5(N-1)+t_{sm}}} - 1$$

Note in this equation that the exponent of $(1 + r_e)$ is divided by 365; the reason is that r_e is assumed to be an annual, not a daily, rate.

Measuring performance in terms of α^*

The concept of average daily yield can be applied to measuring not only offered rates, but also the *total return* earned on a portfolio over some period of time. In this second role, as in the first, the concept of average daily return is a convenient one to use because the α figures calculated for securities of different types and maturities are all directly comparable.

Measuring performance on a daily basis. To begin our discussion, we will assume that the portfolio is marked to market each day and that total return achieved is also calculated daily.

A *single security.* The total return earned over a 1-day holding period on a single security is easily calculated. Let

V_n = market value of the security (accrued interest, if any, included) on day n

V_{n+1} = market value of the security on day $n + 1$

Then the return earned over the period day n to day $n + 1$ on a daily basis is:

$$\alpha = \left(\frac{V_{n+1}}{V_n}\right) - 1$$

and on an annual basis is:

$$\alpha^* = \left(\frac{V_{n+1}}{V_n}\right)^{365} - 1$$

---

[2] The equation for y as a function of r_e is given on page 116.

Formulas for calculating the annualized value of average
daily yield on different types of securities†

Let

$$\alpha = \text{average daily yield}$$
$$\alpha^* = \text{annualized value of } \alpha$$

The formula for α^* is

$$\alpha^* = (1 + \alpha)^{365} - 1$$

Case I: A security (e.g., overnight RP) that pays daily interest on a 360-day basis at a rate i:

$$\alpha^* = \left(1 + \frac{i}{360}\right)^{365} - 1$$

Case II: A discount security:

$$\alpha^* = \left(\frac{F}{P}\right)^{365/t_{sm}} - 1$$

Case III: A CD that pays interest at maturity:

$$\alpha^* = \left(\frac{1 + c\,\dfrac{t_{im}}{360}}{P}\right)^{365/t_{sm}} - 1$$

where

P = price per \$1 of face value, *accrued interest included*

Case IV: A note or bond in its last coupon period:

$$\alpha^* = \left(\frac{1 + \dfrac{c}{2}}{P + a_i}\right)^{365/t_{ss}} - 1$$

---

† If the investor chooses to recognize that compounding occurs in
practice only on business days, he can do so by making simple
adjustments in the formulas given here.

A number of securities. On a portfolio that contains a number of securities, the annualized return α^* earned over a 1-day holding period is

$$\alpha^* = \left(\frac{\text{Value of the portfolio on day } n + 1}{\text{Value of the portfolio on day } n}\right)^{365} - 1$$

To state this relationship in symbols, let

$$V_{n,j} = \text{market value on day } n \text{ of the } j\text{th security}$$
$$V_{n+1,j} = \text{market value on day } n + 1 \text{ of the } j\text{th security}$$

Then the total return earned on the portfolio over the period day n to day $n + 1$ is given by

where

P = price per \$1 of face value

t_{ss} = days from settlement to settlement, i.e., days from settlement to payout

If the security matures on a nonbusiness day, t_{ss} will exceed t_{sm}. Otherwise, $t_{ss} = t_{sm}$.

Case V: A note or bond paying periodic interest:

A. Reinvestment is assumed to occur at the internal rate of return; the value of α is obtained by solving the following expression for α:

$$P = \frac{1}{(1 + \alpha)^{182.5(N-1)+t_{sm}}} + \sum_{k=1}^{N} \left[\frac{c/2}{(1 + \alpha)^{182.5(k-1)+t_{sm}}} \right] - a_i$$

where

$$P = \text{price per \$1 of face value}$$

B. Reinvestment is assumed to occur at an externally specified rate of return, r_e:

$$\alpha = \left[\sum_{k=1}^{N} \frac{(c/2)(1 + r_e)^{\frac{182.5(N-k)}{365}} + 1}{P + a_i} \right]^{\frac{1}{182.5(N-1)+t_{sm}}} - 1$$

where

r_e = reinvestment rate expressed as an *annual* rate

The α values calculated under A and B for securities paying periodic interest can be annualized by using the formula for α^* given above.

$$\alpha^* = \left(\frac{\sum_j V_{n+1,j}}{\sum_j V_{n,j}} \right)^{365} - 1$$

where the symbol $\sum_j$ indicates that the sum is to be taken over all securities, first to jth, in the portfolio.

A change in money invested. On day n, as a result of money inflows and outflows the amount invested in the portfolio may increase or decrease. If it does, another term must be added to the expression for α^*. Let

Δ = *net* change on day n in the amount invested in the portfolio

then

$$\alpha^* = \left(\frac{\sum_j V_{n+1,j}}{\Delta + \sum_j V_{n,j}} \right)^{365} - 1$$

Borrowings. Even a conservative portfolio is likely to occasionally reverse out securities as part of an arbitrage. When a portfolio borrows, the impact of this on earnings must be taken into account in calculating α^*. Let us consider first the case of a single security financed in part with debt. Let

> L = amount of the investor's loan, i.e., borrowing
> r = reverse or other borrowing rate on a 360-day basis

then

$$\alpha^* = \left(\frac{(V_{n+1} - V_n) - \frac{r}{360}L}{V_n - L} \right)^{365} - 1$$

If a portfolio contains a number of securities and has more than one borrowing outstanding, then

$$\alpha^* = \left(\frac{\sum_j (V_{n+1,j} - V_{n,j}) - \sum_k \frac{rk}{360}L_k}{\sum_j V_{n,j} - \sum_k L_k} \right)^{365} - 1$$

where r_k and L_k are, respectively, the rate on and the amount of the kth borrowing.

Measuring performance over a longer period

So far we have derived formulas for measuring performance when the measurement was done daily. More typically performance is measured monthly or even quarterly. In that case, the length of the holding period must be taken into account in calculating α^*. To illustrate, let

> t = days in the investment period over which performance is measured

then, on a security held over the entire period,

$$\alpha^* = \left(\frac{V_{n+t}}{V_n} \right)^{365/t} - 1$$

The major problem when performance is measured over a period longer than 1 day is, as noted in Chapter 10, that during the period securities may mature, new securities may be purchased, and net dollars may flow into and out of the portfolio on different days. To account for the resulting changes during the period in securities held and in the amount invested, weighted averages of the sort described in Chapter 10 can be used.

Futures contracts

part IV

Financial futures

The most dramatic and successful innovation in the money market in recent years has been the introduction of trading in futures contracts for financial instruments. This innovation has enabled market participants of all types—dealers, investors, and primary borrowers—to engage in a wide range of transactions that were hitherto impossible or all too often unproductive because of high transactions costs. The introduction of futures trading also required money market participants to learn a new set of calculations.

BILL FUTURES

In January 1976 the *International Monetary Market (IMM)*, which is now part of the Chicago Mercantile Exchange (CME), opened trading in futures contracts for 3-month Treasury bills. The initial reception of T bill futures by the street was marked by uncertainty and coolness. Nevertheless, the volume of contracts traded in the T bill futures market rose rapidly and dramatically; in fact, the market in T bill futures came to be used more widely and more rapidly than any futures market ever had been.

The contract

The basic contract traded on the IMM is for $1 million of 90-day Treasury bills. Currently a contract matures once each quarter—in the third weeks of March, June, September, and December. There are eight contracts outstanding, so when a new contract starts to trade, the furthest delivery date stretches 24 months into the future. Since the initiation of trading in T bill futures by the IMM, other exchanges have initiated trading in similar contracts for other delivery dates.

Price quotes

Bills trade and are quoted in the *cash market* on a yield basis. Because of this, the bid is always higher than the offer. Also, when yield rises, price falls, and vice versa. All this seems reasonable to a person accustomed to trading money market instruments, but it is confusing to an individual who is used to trading either commodities or stocks. The IMM therefore decided not to quote bill contracts directly in terms of yield. Instead it developed an *index* system in which a bill is quoted at a "price" equal to 100.00 minus yield; a bill yield of 8.50 would thus be quoted on the IMM at 91.50. Note that in this system, when yield goes down, the index price goes up; and the trader with a long position in futures profits. This conforms to the relationship that prevails in other commodity futures markets, where long positions profit when prices rise and short positions profit when prices fall.

Price fluctuations

Price fluctuations on a bill futures contract are in multiples of an 01, one basis point. Because the contract is for delivery of 90-day bills, each 01 is worth $25.

A LONG HEDGE

The existence of a market in bill futures permits investors in money market instruments and firms that know they must borrow or will lend short term in the future *to reduce the interest rate risk inherent in their position by hedging, that is, by taking an equal and offsetting position in futures.* Specifically the existence of a market in bill futures permits investors in bills to reduce the price risk to which their long position in securities exposes them by selling an equivalent amount of bill futures. It also permits firms that know they will need to borrow short term in the future to hedge the interest rate risk inherent in their future short position in cash by buying bill futures. Finally the market permits firms that know they will be long cash at some future date to lock in a lending rate by buying bill futures. We begin our discussion with an example of that third type of hedge.

Suppose that an investor's cash flow projections tell him that he will have a large sum of cash to invest short term in the future; that is, he is going to be *long* in investable cash. He can simply wait to invest that cash until he gets it and take whatever rate is prevailing then, or as soon as his projections tell him how much cash he is going to have, he can lock in a lending rate by buying T bill futures contracts.

Table 11–1 illustrates how this works. We assume that our investor knows in June that he will have $10 million of 3-month money to invest in September, and we assume additionally that when September arrives, he intends to invest that money in bills. In June, the September bill contract is trading at 5.50. If our investor buys 10 of these contracts, he will earn 5.50 on the money he invests in September regardless of the rate at which the cash 3-month bill is then trading.

One way he could get the 5.50 rate would be to take delivery in September of the bills he purchased at 5.50. But, to see the nature of the hedge, let's assume he does not do this. Instead, when his cash comes in, he closes out his futures position and buys cash bills.

The first thing to note is that, as the September contract approaches maturity, it must trade at a yield close to and eventually equal to the rate at which the 3-month cash bill is trading. The reason is that if any divergence existed between these two rates as trading terminated in the contract, there would be a potential for a profitable arbitrage. For example, if a few days before the September bill contract matured, it was trading at a significantly higher yield than the cash bill, traders would buy the contract, sell cash bills wi or wi wi, then take delivery to cover their short position in the cash bill, and make a profit on the transaction.[1]

---

[1] For the distinction between wi and wi wi trading, see the glossary.

In practice a maturing bill futures contract will trade during the last few days of its life at a yield 1 to 3 basis points higher than the deliverable cash bill. The difference reflects the extra commission and other transactions costs that an investor would incur if he bought bill futures and took delivery instead of purchasing new 3-month bills in the cash market.

Table 11–1
A long hedge in T bill futures for bills with a $10 million face value

Step 1 (Thursday, third week of June): Purchase ten September bill contracts at 5.50.

Put up security deposit.
Pay roundturn commission.

Step 2 (Wednesday, third week of September): Sell ten futures contracts, buy cash bills.

Outcome 1: Cash 91-day bill trading at 5.20.
Sell September contracts at 5.20.

Delivery value at sale	$9,870,000
−Delivery value at purchase.........................	−9,862,500
Profit on futures transaction	$ 7,500

Buy 91-day bills at 5.20.

Purchase price	$9,868,555
−Profit on future transaction........................	− 7,500
Effective price of 91-day bills	$9,861,055

Calculate effective discount at which bills are purchased.

Face value	$10,000,000
−Effective purchase price	−9,861,055
Discount at purchase.................................	138,945

Calculate effective discount rate d at which bills are purchased.

$$d = \frac{D(360)}{F(91)} = \frac{\$138,945(360)}{\$10,000,000(91)}$$
$$= 0.055$$
$$= 5.50\%$$

Outcome 2: Cash 91-day bill trading at 5.80.
Sell September contracts at 5.80.

Delivery value at sale	$9,855,000
−Delivery value at purchase	−9,862,500
Loss on futures transaction	−$ 7,500

Buy 91-day bills at 5.80.

Purchase price	$9,853,389
+Loss on futures transaction	+ 7,500
Effective price of 91-day bills.........................	$9,860,889

Calculate effective discount at which bills are purchased.

Face value	$10,000,000
−Effective purchase price	−9,860,889
Discount at purchase	$ 139,111

Calculate effective discount rate d at which bills are purchased.

$$d = \frac{D(360)}{F(91)} = \frac{\$139,111(360)}{=10,000,000(91)}$$
$$= 0.055$$
$$= 5.50\%$$

In Outcome 1 in Table 11–1, we assume that as the September contract is maturing, the 91-day cash bill is trading at 5.20 and the futures contract is consequently also trading at 5.20. At this time our investor sells his September contracts and buys the cash 3-month bill. He purchases his futures contracts at 5.50 and sells them at 5.20, a lower rate. Since the delivery value of the contracts is higher the lower the yield at which they trade, our investor makes, as Table 11–1 shows, a $7,500 profit on his futures transaction.

When his profit on the futures transaction is deducted from the price at which he buys cash bills, he ends up paying an effective price for his cash bills that is $7,500 less than the actual price he pays. And this lower effective price implies that the yield he will earn on his investment is not 5.20, the rate at which he buys cash bills, but 5.50, the rate at which he bought bill futures (see Table 11–1).

Because the prevailing yield at which the cash 3-month bill was trading in September was lower than the rate at which our investor bought bill futures contracts in June, he made money by engaging in a long hedge; that is, he earned a higher yield than he would have if he had not hedged.

There is, however, a counterpart to this. As Outcome 2 in Table 11–1 shows, if in September the cash 3-month bill were trading at 5.80, our investor would have lost so many dollars on his hedge that he would in effect earn only 5.50 on the money he invested then.

Calculating in basis points

It is instructive to work out a hedge example in dollars and cents. However, it is quicker to follow what is going on in terms of basis points earned and lost. In our example, the investor buys September contracts at 5.50 and, according to Outcome 1, sells them at 5.20. On this transaction he earns on each contract for $1 million of bills 30 90-day basis points. By buying the 3-month bill at 5.20 and maturing it, he earns 520 90-day basis points per $1 million of bills purchased. So *net* he is going to earn 550 90-day basis points per $1 million of bills purchased—a yield of 5.50 over 90 days.

Actually the basis points earned on the cash bill are 91-day basis points and those earned on the futures contract are 90-day basis points. This difference, however, which is reflected in the numbers in Table 11–1, affects yield earned only in the third decimal place and then only in a minor way.

The example we have just worked through was a *perfect hedge*, because our investor bought a futures contract for precisely the instrument and precisely the maturity of the instrument he intended to buy. Note in the case of a perfect hedge, the investor eliminates *all* risk.

Speculating on spread variation

Most investors who use the T bill futures market to hedge an anticipated long position in cash will find that the hedge they establish is *imperfect* for one or both of two reasons:

1. Their projected investment period does not precisely match that of any futures contract or series of contracts.
2. They anticipate investing in some money market instrument other than a Treasury bill, e.g., a CD or term Fed funds.

When a hedge is imperfect, the hedger does not eliminate *all* risk. Instead he shifts the nature of his speculation from *rate level* speculation to speculation on *spread variation*.

Example.   Returning to our example, we now suppose that our investor's cash inflow will occur 1 month *before* the June contract expires. This means that, in closing out his hedge, he will be selling the June contract 1 month before it expires, and simultaneously he will be buying the new cash bill.

At the time our investor sells his futures contract, he will in effect be selling the right to take delivery 1 month hence of the then 4-month bill, while he will be buying a 3-month bill. Typically some spread exists between the rates yielded by the 3- and 4-month bills; the futures contract, because of arbitrage, should trade nearer the 4-month than the 3-month rate.

The arbitrage that causes this rate relationship is dual. If the futures contract yielded *less than* the 4-month bill 1 month before it expired, a profit could be made by buying that bill, selling a futures contract, and then unwinding this arbitrage when the futures contract expired. Note that at that time the rate on the futures contract and the rate on the deliverable bill must be equal because they are both prices for next-day delivery of the same cash bill. This arbitrage would tend to lower the yield on the cash bill and to raise the yield on the futures contract, thereby eliminating the discrepancy between the rates on these two instruments. If, alternatively, the rate on the futures contract were greater than that on the 4-month bill, it would be profitable to buy the futures contract and short the cash bill—an arbitrage that would also tend to close the divergence between these two rates. The profitability of the two arbitrages we have just described depends in the first instance on the repo rate and in the second on the reverse rate. Since these rates vary in relationship to bill rates, it is uncertain how close the futures contract 1 month from maturity will trade to the 4-month bill.

To continue our example, we next assume that at the time our investor enters into his hedge, the yield curve is upward sloping and the spread between the 3- and 4-month bill rates is 5 basis points. Assuming (1) that there is no change in that spread and (2) that the futures contract trades 1 month before expiration at a rate equal to the rate on the 4-month bill, the rate our investor will actually earn as a result of his hedge will be 5.45, that is, the 5.50 rate at which he bought the futures contract *minus* the 5-basis-point spread between the rate at which he sold it and the rate on the new 3-month bill. Note, moreover, that so long as our two spread assumptions hold, this result will occur whether the investor sells his futures contract at a low yield (Case 1, Table 11–1) or at a high yield (Case 2, Table 11–1).

In practice of course spreads, like rate levels, are not written in stone; they change. What our investor cares about is what happens to the spread between the rate at which he sells his futures contract and the rate on the new 3-month bill. If this spread *widens* by 5 basis points from the level assumed above, i.e., from 5 to 10 basis points, the yield our investor earns will *decrease* by a like amount, from 5.45 to 5.40. If, alternatively, the spread *narrows* by 5 basis points, i.e., from 5 basis points to 0, the yield he earns will *rise* by a like amount, from 5.45 to 5.50.

To sum up:

An investor who hedges a future long position in cash must take spread relationships into account in estimating the yield he will earn as a result of his hedge. These relationships, however, are subject to variation. Therefore the investor cannot know with certainty what return an imperfect hedge will yield him, and it is in that sense that *a hedger shifts his risk from rate level speculation to speculation on spread variation.*

Earlier we said that a second reason why a long hedge is likely to be imperfect is that the investor who hedges intends to buy an instrument other than a T bill. Suppose the investor in our example intended to buy a 3-month CD and that CDs were trading at the time he bought his futures contract at a 30-basis-point spread to bills. Then, in establishing a long hedge, our investor would be exchanging a natural speculative position on rate levels (generated by his anticipated cash inflow) for a speculation on the spread x months hence between either (1) the rates on cash 3-month bills and cash 3-month CDs or (2) the rates on an unexpired bill futures contract and cash 3-month CDs.

When a short futures position in one instrument (e.g., bills) is used to hedge a long position in some *other* instrument (e.g., CDs), the hedge is called a *cross hedge.*

SHORT HEDGES

The T bill futures market can also be used to hedge either a long position in money market securities or a future borrowing need. To illustrate, we begin with a perfect *short* hedge.

Consider an investor who has money to invest for 3 months and who is unwilling to accept any market risk. We assume that the 6-month bill yields more than the 3-month bill, and that the 6-month bill 3 months hence will be the 3-month bill deliverable when the nearest futures contract expires. In the absence of a futures market, our investor would have no choice but to buy the 3-month bill and mature it. However, given the existence of this market, he should investigate the relationship among the rates on the 3-month bill, the 6-month bill, and the nearest futures contract. This relationship may be such that, without incurring any market risk, he could earn more by buying the 6-month bill and selling the nearest futures contract than by buying and maturing the cash 3-month bill. Note that buying the 6-month bill and selling the nearest futures contract against it effectively converts this bill into a 3-month bill, but the return on that bill will differ from that on the 3-month cash bill.

Most short hedges are *imperfect* for one or both of the two reasons that apply to long hedges: (1) a discrepancy exists between the period over which the hedge is needed and the life of any futures contract or series of such contracts; and (2) the instrument or borrowing need being hedged does not correspond to the instrument traded in the futures market.

Examples of imperfect short hedges are easy to find: (1) Because of rate expectations, an investor wants to swap out of a long bill into a shorter bill, but for tax or other reasons he does not want to do the swap in the cash market. He can obtain essentially the same result by selling bill futures against the long cash bill, but there is a maturity mismatch. (2) An investor or dealer uses the sale of T bill futures to hedge a long position in CDs or BAs against a rise in interest rates. (3) A corporation sells T bill futures to hedge an anticipated need to borrow short term from its bank.

In each of these cases, the outcome of the hedge will depend on what happens to spread relationships. Thus the short hedger, like the long hedger, is shifting his risk from rate level speculation to speculation on spread variation.

MORE IMAGINATIVE HEDGING STRATEGIES

To hedge is to assume a position in futures equal and opposite to an existing or anticipated position, which may be negative or positive, in cash or cash instruments. This definition does *not* imply that the best way to hedge a cash position is necessarily to sell (buy) the futures contract that most nearly corresponds in maturity to the long (short) position being hedged.

Consider for example, a corporate treasurer who knows he must borrow 3 months hence. He fears that the Fed might tighten and believes on the basis of past experience that, if it does, the yield curve will steepen. Given this fear and this assumption, his best hedge would be to sell not the futures contract that matures in 3 months, but a longer contract. The reason is that the latter would fall more in value than the nearest contract would if the eventuality feared by the treasurer occurred, namely, tightening by the Fed and a consequent steepening of the yield curve.

For a second example of imaginative hedging, consider an investor who will be long cash 3 months hence and wants to invest then in the 2-year maturity range. The investor fears that the Fed might ease credit shortly and believes that, if it did, the yield curve would flatten. For him the best hedge is not to buy a *strip* of eight consecutive futures contracts, i.e., a synthetic 2-year note, but rather to buy eight of some long futures contract. Note that if his fears are realized, the value of a long contract will rise more than that of shorter contacts.

PROFITING FROM SPECULATION ON SPREAD VARIATION

To say that speculation on spread variation arises from "imperfect" hedges perhaps suggests that it is unfortunate that there are not sufficient numbers and types of futures contracts so that the hedger could always eliminate risk by entering into a perfect hedge. This view corresponds with the academic view of hedging, which is that the purpose of hedging is to eliminate or minimize price risk, not to create an opportunity to profit from a different sort of speculation. Hedging in textbooks is viewed as a form of insurance that has a cost that, like the electric bill, is part of normal business operating expenses.

For an investor or borrower, to hedge a position—negative or positive—in cash does in fact insulate his business activity from price level speculation. However, it also *retains for him the opportunity to speculate on spread variation.*

Moreover, as our earlier examples suggest, such speculation can itself become a source of profit as opposed to a cost. In this respect two important comments should be made. First, speculation on spread variation did not arise in the money and bond markets after and as a result of the introduction of trading in financial futures. Quite to the contrary, it has long been a common practice. A dealer who anticipates a fall in rates and buys a 10-year Treasury bond and simultaneously shorts—to minimize risk—an 8-year issue is doing an "arbitrage" that is nothing more or less than speculating on spread variation. Many other transactions commonly done by dealers and investors are also essentially speculation on spread variation. What the introduction of futures trading did was not to create such speculation, but to provide a vastly more efficient and less costly mechanism than had previously existed for taking forward positions long and short. Equally important, the introduction of futures trading provided a liquid market in which such forward positions could be traded.

A second important point is that the use of hedging to minimize price level speculation while simultaneously speculating on spread variation is not an innovation fathered by money market participants. Firms that produce, process, or use commodities for which futures markets exist have long understood that speculation on spread, which they refer to as *the basis,* is a potential source of profit, and they have worked hard to profit from it.

Once speculation on spreads is viewed as a potential source of profit, it becomes clear that hedging should not be viewed as an automatic and thoughtless operation; for example, an investor has money coming in 3 months hence so he buys the most nearly corresponding futures contract. Instead hedging is an intricate activity. To succeed at it, the participant must have considerable knowledge of what spreads have been historically and of the factors that cause them to change. In establishing a hedge, he must, moreover, look into the future and try to predict how events are most likely to affect the spreads involved in his hedge. Finally, if an unanticipated change in conditions occurs, he must be prepared to alter his hedge.

If the suggestion that investors, dealers, and borrowers should consider hedging as a form of potentially profitable speculation offends the reader's sense of what is proper, he should note that any institution that holds a portfolio or any firm that anticipates a borrowing need is unescapably speculating on changes in rate level, since it is impossible to be long or short cash and do otherwise. To hedge and thus speculate on spread variations is only to trade one form of speculation for another typically less risky form of speculation.

RELATIONSHIP OF CASH TO FUTURES RATES

The first thing anyone using the bill futures market wants to know is what relationship exists between cash and futures rates and what forces create it. The answer in brief is that these rates are related but the relationship varies over time depending on the structure of rates, including term repo rates, and on the stance taken by dealers and investors. To understand the relationship of cash to futures rates, it is useful to track the values of two variables, bill parity and the "implied repo rate."

Bill parity revisited

In Chapter 5 we introduced the concept of bill parity.[2] As noted there, academics and others have argued that the yield curve in the cash market for bills provides an implicit prediction of future interest rates. To illustrate, consider part A of Figure 11–1. On 12/17/79 the 3-month (94-day) bill was trading at 12.25 and the 6-month (185-day) bill at 11.95. Using our formula for bill parity, we can determine that on that date, in order to earn the 6-month rate, which was 11.95, by investing in two consecutive 3-month bills, an investor would have had to receive a rate of 12.02 on the 3-month bill 3 months hence. Since many investors were holding the 3-month bill on 12/17/79, they must—so the argument goes—have anticipated that 3 months hence the 3-month bill would in fact yield 12.02. In the academic literature bill parity is referred to as a *forward rate* (i.e., a rate for *forward delivery*); in our discussion we will use both terms.

Using the same technique we used to calculate an implied forward rate for delivery of a 3-month bill 3 months hence on the basis of the cash 3- and 6-month rates, we can also calculate implied forward rates for delivery of a 3-month bill 6 months hence and 9 months hence. This is done in part A of Figure 11–1.

If the theory were true that the forward rates implied by the yield curve in the cash market accurately reflect investors' rate expectations, and if investors—operating on the same set of expectations—were the dominant force in the futures market, then, because of arbitrage by investors, rates in the forward and futures markets should at any time be identical; that is, rates in the futures market should be the forwards implied by the yield curve in the cash market.

To illustrate the potential for arbitrage by investors between the cash and futures markets when forward and futures rates are out of line, note that if the futures rate on a bill deliverable 3 months hence were 9.92 and the corresponding forward rate were 9.82, investors would have a rate incentive to buy the cash 3-month bill and the nearest futures contract in preference to the 6-month bill. Their doing so would, moreover, drive up the rate on the 6-month bill and thereby the forward rate; it would also drive

---

[2] See pages 54–57.

Figure 11–1
Bill rates, existing and implied
(December 17, 1979)

A. Rates in the market for <u>cash</u> bills imply <u>forward</u> rates (i.e. values of bill parity)

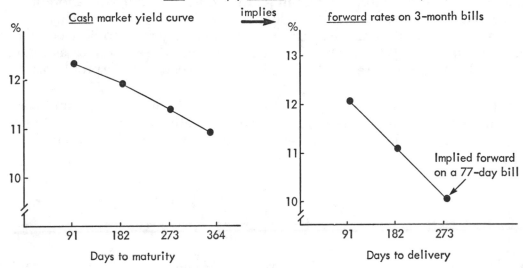

B. Rates in the <u>futures</u> market imply a <u>strip</u> yield curve

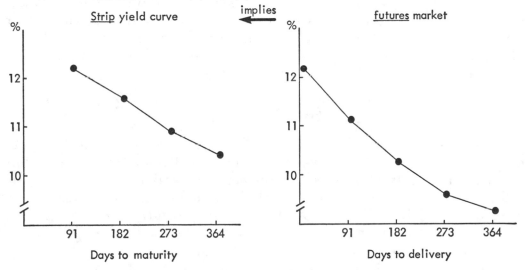

down the futures rate, and the gap between these two rates would thus be closed. If, alternatively, the forward rate implied by the rates on the 3- and 6-month bills were 9.92 and the corresponding futures rate were 9.82, investors would have an incentive to buy the 6-month bill and sell the overpriced futures contract. By lowering the price of the 6-month bill and thereby the implied forward rate and by raising yield on the futures contract, this operation would tend to close the gap between the forward and futures rates.

The strip yield curve

In practice, futures and forward rates are not identical, but before we talk about why, it is useful to introduce a new concept. Since the yield curve for the cash market implies a set of forward rates, futures rates must also imply their own yield curve. They do, and that synthetic yield curve is referred to by the street as the *strip yield curve*.

To estimate values along the strip yield curve one could use a simple averaging technique; but, as our discussion of bill parity implies, this approach would not yield accurate figures. To derive a formula for calculating true values along the strip yield curve, we first recall the nature of the bill parity problem. In deriving a formula for bill parity, we asked: If the yields on a given long bill, bill 1, and on a given short bill, bill 2, are known, what rate must an investor earn over the maturity gap between these two bills in order that a roll of the short bill will yield him the same rate as buying and maturing the long bill? (Figure 5–2 illustrates clearly the nature of the problem. See pages 54–57.)

We denoted the bill that covered the maturity gap between bills 1 and 2 as bill 3, and our solution to the bill parity problem involved finding a break-even rate on bill 3. Specifically, we concluded that the investor would break even if d_3, the yield on bill 3, were given by

$$d_3 = \left(1 - \frac{1 - \frac{d_1 t_1}{360}}{1 - \frac{d_2 t_2}{360}}\right) \frac{360}{t_1 - t_2}$$

To derive a rate on the strip yield curve, we need only solve a simple variant of the bill parity problem. The futures market gives us rates for two short bills, and we want to find the break-even rate on the corresponding long bill. In terms of the notation used in Chapter 5, the futures market gives the yields on bills 2 and 3 (d_2 and d_3), and we want to solve for the break-even yield on the corresponding long bill, bill 1.

This yield value, d_1, is obviously d_1 in the preceding equation for d_3. Solving that equation for d_1 as a function of d_2 and d_3, we get

$$d_1 = \left\{\left(1 - \frac{d_2 t_2}{360}\right)\left[d_3\left(\frac{t_1 - t_2}{360}\right) - 1\right] + 1\right\} \frac{360}{t_1}$$

Example. To illustrate, let us use this formula to calculate from the price data in Table 11–2 the rates on the *strip* yield curve shown in Figure 11–1. Since on 12/17/79 a futures contract matured 3 days hence, we take d_2, the rate on the first short bill, to be the rate on the *cash* 3-month (94-day) bill, and we take d_3, the rate on the second short bill, to be the rate on the second *futures* contract, i.e., on the March contract. These rates were, respectively, 12.25 and 11.16. Plugging them into our equation for d_1, we get

$$d_1 = \left\{\left(1 - \frac{0.1225 \times 94}{360}\right)\left[0.1116\left(\frac{185 - 94}{360}\right) - 1\right] + 1\right\} \frac{360}{185}$$
$$= 11.54\%$$

The futures market implies that the 6-month bill should yield 11.54 percent.

To calculate the value of the strip yield curve for the 9-month bill, we use the same procedure except that now we take the 6-month bill (the implied yield on which we have just calculated) to be the first short bill, and we take the third futures contract to be the second short bill. This procedure can be continued over as many futures contracts as desired.

To say that forward and futures rates in the bill market should be identical, as the expectations theory implies, is equivalent to saying that the strip yield curve should be identical with the yield curve in the cash market. In other words, it should be that an investor who creates a *synthetic* bill by buying a short cash bill and a strip of consecutive futures contracts will earn the same return on that synthetic bill as an investor who buys and holds to maturity a long *cash* bill of equivalent maturity.

Table 11–2
Cash and futures rates
(December 17, 1979)

Cash bills			Values on strip yield curve implied by futures prices		
Maturity	Rate (percent)	Days to maturity	Rate (percent)		Days to maturity
3/20/80	12.25	94	12.25 (cash bill)		94
6/19/80	11.95	185	11.54		185
9/18/80	11.45	276	10.90		276
12/4/80	10.95	353	10.38		367

Futures contracts			Forward 3-month rates implied by the cash market		
Expiration date	Rate (percent)	Days to expira- tion	Delivery date	Rate (percent)	Days to delivery
12/20/79	12.23	3			
3/20/80	11.16	94	3/20/80	12.02	94
6/19/80	10.20	185	6/19/80	11.12	185
9/18/80	9.60	276	9/18/80*	10.04	276
12/18/80	9.33	367			

* A 77-day bill.

The rate relationship in practice

The relationship pictured in Figure 11–1 between forward and futures rates is typical. After the nearest futures contracts, there is often a marked divergence between futures and forward rates. This creates opportunities for arbitrages because eventually cash and futures rates must converge.

One reason for the divergence between forward and futures rates is that the expectations theory of investor behavior is oversimplified. Some of the normal upward slope of the yield curve reflects a liquidity premium. Also the expectations theory ignores the fact that many institutional investors operate under severe restraints, such as they may not extend beyond 3 months in maturity, they may not assume market risk, and they may not use the futures market. The expectations theory also ignores the fact that many institutions that invest cash short term are primarily concerned that their portfolio manager preserve capital and offer him no incentive to maximize return. Finally, economic theories concerning maximization, of which the expectations theory is one, consistently ignore the transactions costs in terms of learning and information gathering that maximization requires.

THE IMPLIED REPO RATE

By concentrating on investor behavior the expectations theory also tends to ignore the impact on rates of a very important group of market participants, namely dealers, many large bank portfolios, and others who finance any bill positions they take wholly or largely in the repo market, i.e., with borrowed money. For such investors, financing rates are more crucial than bill parity in purchase decisions.

This observation leads us to a new concept, the *implied repo rate*. For a levered investor, an attractive tactic is to buy a cash bill, finance it with term RP, and cover the

---

Formulas for calculating the implied forward rate (bill parity), a rate on the strip yield curve, and the implied repo rate

I. Implied forward rate (bill parity): Let

Subscript 1 denote a long cash bill, bill 1
Subscript 2 denote a short cash bill, bill 2
Subscript 3 denote a short bill that covers the maturity gap between bills 1 and 2

Then the formula for calculating *bill parity*, which is the *implied forward rate* on bill 3, is:†

$$d^* = \left(1 - \frac{P_1}{P_2}\right)\frac{360}{t_1 - t_2}$$

$$= \left(1 - \frac{1 - \dfrac{d_1 t_1}{360}}{1 - \dfrac{d_2 t_2}{360}}\right)\frac{360}{t_1 - t_2}$$

II. A rate on the strip yield curve: Let

Subscript 1 denote an implied long cash bill, bill 1
Subscript 2 denote an existing short cash bill, bill 2
Subscript 3 denote the futures bill (contract) that covers the maturity gap between bills 1 and 2

Then the formula for calculating a rate on the strip yield curve is:‡

---

rate risk on the resulting tail by selling that tail in the futures market.[3] Whether doing so will be profitable depends on the relationship of the term RP rate and the rate on the long cash bill and the futures rate. Clearly, there is some term RP rate at which a dealer who does the above transaction will just break even; this break-even rate has been dubbed the *implied repo rate.*

In Chapter 5 we derived a formula for the break-even sale rate on a bill tail, given the financing rate and the rate on the long cash bill. Developing a formula for calculating the implied repo rate involves solving a variant of that problem: If we know the sale rate on the tail, which is the futures rate, and also the rate on the cash bill, what is the break-even financing rate?

For a dealer to just break even on the creation and sale of a bill tail in the futures market, the dollars he receives from the future sale must precisely equal the dollars he pays out, which is the price he pays for the cash bill plus the cost of financing it.

Let

$$P = \text{price}$$
$$d = \text{rate of discount}$$
$$t = \text{days to maturity}$$

---

[3] Bill tails were discussed on pages 41–45, 47–51.

$$d_1 = \left\{ \left(1 - \frac{d_2 t_2}{360} \right) \left[d_3 \left(\frac{t_1 - t_2}{360} \right) - 1 \right] + 1 \right\} \frac{360}{t_1}$$

This procedure may be continued to find other strip rates by using rates on farther-out futures contracts.

III. The implied repo rate: Let

Subscript f denote a futures contract
Subscript c denote the deliverable (i.e., corresponding) cash bill

and let

t_{ss} = days from settlement to sale, i.e., the financing period

Then the formula for calculating the implied repo rate, r_t^*, is:§

$$r_t^* = \left(\frac{P_f}{P_c} - 1 \right) \frac{360}{t_{ss}}$$
$$= \left(\frac{d_c t_c - d_f d_f}{360 - d_c t_c} \right) \frac{360}{t_{ss}}$$

---

† See pages 54–57.
‡ See pages 159–61.
§ See pages 161–64.

and let

Subscript f denote the nearest futures contract
Subscript c denote the deliverable cash bill

Also let

r_t = term repo rate
t_{ss} = days from settlement to sale, i.e., the *financing* period

Then in symbols the condition that the dealer breaks even can be written as follows:

$$P_f = P_c \left(1 + r_t \frac{t_{ss}}{360} \right)$$

Let

$$r_t^* = \text{implied repo rate}$$

Since r_t^* is defined as the break-even financing rate, it is r_t in the preceding break-even relationship. Solving that relationship for r_t, we get

$$r_t^* = \left(\frac{P_f}{P_c} - 1 \right) \frac{360}{t_{ss}}$$

which, substituting $[1 - (dt/360)]$ for P, gives us

$$r_t^* = \left(\frac{d_c t_c - d_f t_f}{360 - d_c t_c} \right) \frac{360}{t_{ss}}$$

Example.   Assume that a cash bill 201 days from maturity is trading at 9.48 and that the corresponding futures contract is trading at 9.39. Then the implied repo rate is

$$r_t^* = \left(\frac{0.0948(201) - 0.0939(91)}{360 - 0.0948(201)}\right)\frac{360}{110}$$

$$= 10.09\%$$

The implied repo rate is a useful concept for explaining the behavior not only of levered investors but also of cash investors. If the actual term RP rate is *less than* the implied repo rate, it will pay the levered investor to create and sell tails in the futures market, whereas the cash investor will find that buying the cash bill yields him more than he would earn by buying a futures contract and investing in term repo over the interim period of t_{ss} days. If, alternatively, the prevailing term repo rate *exceeds* r_t^*, then levered investors will not be able to profit from creating a tail and selling it in the futures market, whereas the cash investor will earn more by buying a futures contract and doing a term repo over the invervening period, t_{ss} days, than he would by simply buying and maturing the cash bill.

To prove that if the term RP rate exceeds r_t^*, the cash investor is better off doing term RP and buying a futures contract than investing in the available cash bill, note that if

$$r_t = r_t^*$$

then

$$P_f = P_c\left(1 + r_t\frac{t_{ss}}{360}\right)$$

which implies that

$$1 - P_c = (1 - P_f) + r_t\left(\frac{t_{ss}}{360}\right)P_c$$

that is, that the discount on the cash bill precisely equals the interest on a term repo for t_{ss} days plus the discount on the future bill.

If, alternatively, the prevailing term repo rate exceeds r_t^*, that is, if

$$r_t > r_t^*$$

then

$$r_t\left(\frac{t_{ss}}{360}\right)P_c + (1 - P_f) > 1 - P_c$$

FUTURES AND FORWARD RATES

The expectations theory suggests that futures rates should equal forward rates. As our discussion of the implied repo rate shows, there are also other forces at work in determining futures rates. In recent years, the growth of the Fed funds market and of the closely related repo markets has been such that rates in these markets sometimes may dominate bill rates rather than the other way around.

The dollars-in-equal-dollars-out approach we used to derive a formula for the *implied repo rate* tells us that *this rate equals the holding-period yield an investor would earn if he bought a cash bill and sold it for delivery t_{ss} days hence at the futures rate.* In other words, the repo rate implied by a nearby futures contract and the deliverable cash bill equals the yield on a simple interest basis on a bill with a relatively short current maturity. Obviously much of the time in recent years, the term repo rate has been well above yields on short bills. To expect levered investors to be able to borrow on a term basis at such a low rate is therefore unrealistic, at least under prevailing market conditions. This means levered investors cannot profitably offer tails to investors at a rate equal to bill parity. They need to be able to sell at a higher price, and when futures rates are lower than forward rates (as in Table 11–2), one cause is likely to be that high financing costs are impinging on futures rates.

Table 11–3
Actual and implied rates

Inputs	Output[||]	Spread	Days	Other
Actual term repo rate, r_t	Implied term repo rate,[†] r_t^*	$r_t - r_t^*$	The financing period, $t_c - 91$	r_t on a discount basis
Actual futures rate, d_f	Implied futures rate,[‡] d_f^*	$d_f - d_f^*$	91	d_f^* on a simple interest, 360-day basis
Actual rate on the deliverable cash bill, d_c	Implied cash bill rate,[§] d_c^*	$d_c - d_c^*$	t_c	d_c^* on a simple interest, 360-day basis

[†] The *implied repo rate*, r_t^*, is the repo rate such that, if the rates inputed for d_f and d_c prevailed, a trader would break even by selling a futures contract and delivering a tail created by financing the deliverable cash bill.

[‡] The *implied futures rate*, d_f^*, is the futures rate such that, if the rates inputed for r_t and d_c prevailed, a trader would break even by selling a futures contract and delivering a tail created by financing the deliverable cash bill.

[§] The *implied cash bill rate*, d_c^*, is the cash bill rate such that, if the values inputed for r_t and d_f prevailed, a trader would break even by selling a futures contract and delivering a tail created by financing the deliverable cash bill.

[||] To derive formulas for calculating these implied rates, we let

t_{ss} = Days in the financing period
Subscript f denote the futures bill
Subscript c denote the cash bill

From the break-even relationship,

$$P\left(1 + r_t \frac{t_{ss}}{360}\right) = P_f$$

it follows that

$$r_t^* = \left(\frac{P_f}{P_c} - 1\right)\frac{360}{t_{ss}}$$

$$d_f^* = \frac{360}{91}\left[1 - P_c\left(1 + r_t \frac{t_{ss}}{360}\right)\right]$$

$$= \frac{360}{91}\left[1 - \left(1 - \frac{d_c t_c}{360}\right)\left(1 + r_t \frac{t_{ss}}{360}\right)\right]$$

$$d_c^* = \left(1 - \frac{P_f}{1 + r\frac{t_{ss}}{360}}\right)\frac{360}{t_c}$$

$$= \left(1 - \frac{1 - \frac{d_f t_f}{360}}{1 + \frac{r t_{ss}}{360}}\right)\frac{360}{t_c}$$

A MAGIC TABLE

Every trader of cash and futures bills should design a computer program to give a table of the sort described in Table 11–3. As the table entries and accompanying footnotes explain, data on three actual rates, a term repo rate, a futures rate, and the rate on the deliverable cash bill, are used to calculate and display *implied,* i.e., *break-even,* levels for each of these variables given the values of the other two variables.

Numerical examples

To illustrate, consider first the rate structure pictured in Table 11–4. The actual repo rate for the financing period, which is 59 days, is less than the implied repo rate; this indicates that a dealer could profitably buy the deliverable cash bill, finance it, and sell the tail in the futures market. The same numbers also tell the investor that he could earn more over the next 59 days by buying the cash bill and selling a futures contract than by investing in term repo.

Table 11–4
Actual and implied rates: an example
(see Table 11–3)

Inputs	Output	Spread (basis points)	Days	Other
$r_t = 13.375$	$r_t^* = 13.61$	−23.5	59	13.31
$d_f = 11.40$	$d_f^* = 11.54$	−14	91	11.89
$d_c = 12.00$	$d_c - d_c^* = 11.92$	8	150	12.54

The opposite situation is illustrated by the rate structure in Table 11–5. The numbers there tell a dealer that creating tails would not be profitable. They also tell an investor that he could earn more over the 41-day period from the present until the next futures contract expires by investing in term repo than by buying the deliverable cash bill and selling a futures contract.

Table 11–5
Actual and implied rates: An example
(see Table 11–3)

Inputs	Output	Spread (basis points)	Days	Other
$r_t = 12.75$	$r_t^* = 12.20$	55	41	12.04
$d_f = 12.15$	$d_f^* = 11.91$	24	91	12.28
$d_c = 12.00$	$d_c - d_c^* = 12.16$	−16	132	12.73

SPREADING

Earlier in the chapter we noted that a hedger is typically shifting his risk from a speculation on rate levels to a speculation on spread variation. A speculator with no cash position to hedge can also speculate on spread variation. Such speculation, which is referred to as *spreading,* calls for the trader to short one contract and go long in a neighboring contract on the expectation that the spread between the two contracts will either narrow or widen.

Example. An investor observes that the nearest futures contract, which is the March contract, is selling at 8.60 and the June contract at 9.00. He also observes that in the cash market the spread between 3- and 6-month bills has been averaging around 30 basis points. This implies that the forward rate for delivery of a 3-month bill 3 months hence should be 60 basis points above the current rate on the 3-month bill. The spread of 40 basis points between the March and June futures contracts thus looks narrow. The investor believes that, because of the impact of financing costs on rates, the spread may not rise to 60 basis points but it should go well above 40.

To speculate on the discrepancy between the spread of the forward rate to the cash rate and the spread of the two nearest futures contracts, the trader buys the March contract and sells the June contract. If he is correct in thinking that the spread between the March and June contracts will widen, he might end up unwinding his spread trade by selling the March contract at 8.45 and buying the June contract at 8.95. If so, he will earn 15 90-day basis points on his long position in the March contract and lose 5 90-day basis points on his short position in the June contract, for a net gain of 10 90-day basis points.

Evaluating a spread in nearby contracts

Method I. Traders use several approaches to evaluate potential spread trades. One is to *compare spreads between futures and forward rates.*

To illustrate, we assume that the rates and maturities on cash and futures bills are those given in Table 11–5. To determine whether a spread trade involving the September and December futures contracts would be attractive, the trader first calculates the two forward rates (bill parity values) implied by the three cash bills. He next observes that the spread between the two futures rates is 50 basis points but that the spread between the forward rates is only 38.8 basis points. The futures spread appears to be too wide, which suggests that he should sell the September contract and go long the December contract. If he does and if the spread between the futures contracts in fact narrows to 40 basis points, he will earn 10 90-day basis points.

Method II. The above spread should be considered attractive only if the December contract would be considered to have value as a long position. To test whether it does requires another calculation.

The trader asks: What does a 5.50 rate on the 3-month bill coupled with a 6.00 rate on the futures contract imply about the yield on the 6-month bill that would accompany the September 3-month bill? Note that answering this question involves calculating a value on the strip yield curve—a formula for this was given earlier.[4] Making this calculation, the trader determines that a cash 3-month rate of 5.50 and a futures rate of 6.00 together imply a 6.71 rate on the 6-month bill. In other words, the relationship of the two nearest futures contracts implies a spread of only 21 basis points between the 3- and 6-month bills along the strip yield curve. In the situation at hand, that spread seems narrow and the December contract is therefore of dubious value as a long position. Note the knowledge that the spread of 50 basis points between the futures contracts implies a spread of only 21 basis points between the

---

[4] See pages 163–64.

Table 11–6
Rates in the cash and futures bill markets

Cash bills			Futures bills		
Days to maturity	Ma-turity date	Rate (percent)	Maturity date	Futures rate (percent)	Forward rate (percent)
118	9/23	5.10	9/23	5.50	5.537
209	12/23	5.25	12/23	6.00	5.925
300	3/23	5.40			

cash 3-month and cash 6-month bills cautions the trader against assuming a spread that looks attractive, when evaluated by Method 1.

Arbitraging rates on different exchanges

Anyone who does spread trades in futures would be well advised to look at the rates prevailing on different exchanges. It has happened that the March contract traded on one exchange was 30 basis points higher in yield than the February contract traded on another exchange. Spreads of this sort, which reflect a lack of attention span by traders, create a golden profit opportunity for the arbitrager. He sells the February contract, buys the March contract, and waits for the spread to narrow as it must.

Another way to take advantage of this spread involves something called *roll theory.* The arbitrager might decide in the preceding situation to take delivery on the February contract and stay short the March contract. He could then roll, via the Fed's weekly auctions, the May bill, which he acquires by taking delivery on the February contract, into the June cash bill, which he is short because he sold a March future. To lose money on this transaction, he would have to lose more than 7.5 basis points on each roll. That, however, is not going to happen. If the futures bill is worth 7.5 basis points more than the cash bill, then it must be that financing is tough and expensive; and, if it is, then the price on the cash bill will get knocked down to reflect that situation.

Value of distant futures

We have described two theories of value for nearby contracts. The only theory that explains the value of a distant future is *yield curve shift.*

To illustrate, note that the value of a contract that is three futures out and matures with the present cash year bill will change by *1* basis point if the rates on the year bill and the 9-month bill both change by *1* basis point in the same direction. If, however, the rate on the year bill moves by *1* basis point while that on the 9-month bill remains unchanged, the rate on the contract three futures out will change by *4* basis points.

For a trader who is speculating on a fall in rates, the only rationale for buying three consecutive futures contracts, as opposed to three of the nearest futures contract, is a belief that the yield curve will shift.

This observation leads back to a point we made earlier. The hedger who anticipates a fall in rates and wants to protect himself by going long futures should make the most attractive speculation on rate spreads possible, which in the case at hand means incorporating into his calculations any likely shift in the yield curve.

TREASURY BOND FUTURES

T bill futures are useful for hedging short-term positions and for speculating on changes in short-term interest rates and/or the shape of the yield curve at the short end. For the manager of a portfolio of long-term bonds, there is a second interesting set of financial futures contracts, namely—the several contracts for Treasury bonds of varying maturities that are traded on different exchanges.

Hedging with T bond futures

Our remarks about the usefulness of T bill futures as a *hedging* device all apply to T bond futures as well. The latter can be used to hedge an anticipated cash inflow or, if the portfolio manager anticipates a rise in interest rates, to hedge a long position in bonds, governments, or corporates.

Here are a few examples. A portfolio manager who anticipates an inflow of cash and fears a fall in interest rates could buy T bond futures to lock in a future long-term lending rate. Alternatively, a portfolio manager who holds bonds and fears tightening by the Fed could liquidate his portfolio to prevent a capital loss, but a preferable course of action might be to hedge his long position in bonds by selling T bond futures. Doing the latter would protect his long position against a rise in interest rates while simultaneously permitting him to retain a portfolio of bonds, which he had carefully selected for properties such as credit risk and call provisions. This obviates the need for him to scramble during a subsequent market rally to purchase securities with similar properties. The T bond futures market can also be useful to the portfolio manager who is seeking to minimize taxes. Consider a portfolio manager who owns long bonds in which he has a short-term capital gain that will become a *long-term* gain 2 months hence. The portfolio manager fears a rise in interest rates, but if he were to liquidate his position immediately, he would incur a considerable tax penalty. For him an attractive alternative would be to hedge his position by selling T bond futures.

An investor who uses T bond futures to hedge, like an investor who uses T bill futures to hedge, is shifting his risk from a speculation on rate levels to a speculation on spread variation. For the hedger of long instruments, knowledge of what spreads are, what causes them to change, and how they are likely to change is, if anything, more crucial than it is for the hedger of short-term instruments. The reason is that the hedger who uses T bond futures is likely to find that a deliverable long T bond differs considerably in current maturity, credit risk, or other characteristics from the bonds he is hedging or from the bonds he intends to buy when an anticipated cash inflow occurs. For the portfolio manager, this considerable imperfection in the hedge is offset by the enhanced opportunity offered to speculate profitably on spread variation.

Factors affecting spread

To evaluate the spread between the instrument being hedged and a deliverable T bond and to determine how that spread is likely to change, a portfolio manager must consider a number of factors. The first is a possible change in the instrument that is *cheapest* to deliver. This consideration does not arise for the hedger who uses T bill futures because the bills deliverable at the expiration of a bill contract are always homogeneous. In the T bond futures market, in contrast, several bonds that trade at different prices may be of deliverable grade at a given time. A change in the cheapest bond deliverable, such as occurred in early 1978 from the 7⅝s of 2002–07 to the 8¾s of 3003–08, will necessarily affect the spread at which T bond futures trade to other instruments.

A second important consideration is credit risk. When interest rates rise, yields on corporate bonds will typically rise faster than yields on governments, and yields on low-grade corporates will rise faster than yields on high-grade corporates.

A third important consideration is the current maturity of the instrument being hedged. Normally long-term instruments exhibit less yield volatility than short-term instruments. However, because the yield value of ¹/₃₂ decreases as current maturity lengthens, long-term instruments also typically exhibit more price volatility than short-term instruments. A bond's price volatility will, as noted in Chapter 6, also depend on whether it is selling at a discount or a premium. In a bear market discount bonds drop more rapidly in price than high-coupon bonds; they also rise more rapidly in price than high-coupon bonds in bull markets.

Finally, the hedger should take into account possible changes in supply and demand conditions in the markets for long Treasuries and for the instrument being hedged.

The hedge ratio

A careful study of these factors is likely to suggest that the portfolio manager should hedge on a ratio basis; that is, he should sell or buy a number of contracts such that the face value of his position in futures equals some ratio of the face value of the bonds or anticipated cash flow he is hedging. To illustrate, consider a portfolio manager who is hedging a position in corporate bonds against a rise in interest rates. Because of the additional credit risk to which corporates expose the investor, he anticipates that they will drop faster than long governments in the face of rising interest rates. Therefore to protect his position, he buys a number of futures contract equal to some ratio greater than 1 of the value of the bonds being hedged. To determine what ratio he should use, the hedger must consider all the factors we listed as affecting spread and, in particular, the current maturity of the instrument being hedged. In this respect, note that the arbitrage described in Chapter 9 involved essentially establishing a hedged position on a ratio basis in the cash market; the trade as such was a speculation on spread as opposed to price level variation.[5]

The hedger who uses the T bond futures market, like the hedger who uses the T bill futures market, retains through establishing his hedge the opportunity to speculate on spread variation and should consider such speculation as a potential source of profit. If, for example, the portfolio manager believes that any change in interest rates is likely to be upward, he should consider increasing the ratio of the contracts sold to the securities hedged so that if interest rates do rise, this not only will not subject his portfolio to a capital loss but also will yield a gain for the portfolio.

For anyone who uses the T bond futures market, other useful instruments are the actively traded Government National Mortgage Association (GNMA) futures contracts, which are for an essentially credit-risk-free instrument that has approximately half the current maturity of the longest Treasury bonds traded for future delivery. We have not discussed in this book either the cash or the futures market for GNMA pass-throughs because to do so would have led to a long discussion of bond market calculations, a subject on which a whole book could easily be written.

---

[5] See pages 128–33.

Foreign paper

part V

12

Covered interest arbitrage

As any investor in international markets will quickly observe, significant differences exist among the short-term rates offered by similar instruments denominated in different currencies, for example, between a Euro time deposit denominated in dollars and one denominated in Deutsche marks (DM), between U.S. and U.K. Treasury bills, between top-grade U.S. and Canadian commercial paper.

If an investor who is holding dollars sought only to obtain the highest short-term interest rates available, he would rarely invest in dollar-denominated paper. By buying paper denominated in a foreign currency, however, he would incur a considerable *foreign exchange risk,* that is, a risk that the exchange value of the currency in which he had invested might fall relative to the dollar. Most investors are not willing to incur a foreign exchange risk in investing short-term money. Thus, a portfolio manager who invests dollar balances in an instrument denominated in a foreign currency will typically *hedge* his resulting *long* position in that currency by doing a *swap;* that is, at the time he buys foreign currency in the *spot* market (foreign exchange market for cash delivery) to purchase an instrument denominated in a foreign currency, he will simultaneously sell that foreign currency *forward,* thereby eliminating his long position in foreign exchange and with it his exposure to a foreign exchange risk. By doing a swap, the investor locks in a fixed rate of return on his investment.

ESTIMATING THE SWAP COST

When a portfolio manager invests dollars in an instrument denominated in a foreign currency on a hedged basis, he is engaging in what is called *covered interest arbitrage.* The return he earns on this arbitrage will equal a *net* rate—the yield on the instrument minus (plus) a second rate, the cost of (yield on) the swap. Thus, to determine whether a domestic instrument or a similar foreign instrument purchased on a hedged basis would yield more, he must calculate the second rate.

An investor who swaps dollars into a foreign currency is in effect buying the foreign currency and then selling it. This suggests that the rate of return on the swap should be calculated as follows:

$$\text{Rate of return on swap (decimal)} = \left(\frac{\text{Selling rate} - \text{Buying rate}}{\text{Buying rate}}\right)\frac{360}{t}$$

where

$$t = \text{days transaction is outstanding}$$

We can restate this succinctly in symbols. Let

S = spot rate quoted on *U.S. direct terms, i.e., dollars per unit of foreign corrency*

F = *outright* forward rate in U.S. direct terms

then on a swap out of dollars into a foreign currency:

$$\text{Rate of return on swap} = \left(\frac{F - S}{S}\right)\frac{360}{t}$$

$$= \left(\frac{F}{S} - 1\right)\frac{360}{t}$$

Using this formula for the return on the swap, the investor who holds dollars can determine what rate he would earn by investing in an instrument denominated in a foreign currency on a hedged basis. Let

i_{fx} = rate offered by an instrument denominated in a foreign currency

i'_{fx} = *net* rate offered by this instrument, i.e., i_{fx} plus the rate of return on the swap

then

$$i'_{fx} = i_{fx} + \left(\frac{F}{S} - 1\right)\frac{360}{t}$$

COVERED INTEREST ARBITRAGE

Let

$i_\$$ = rate of return on a dollar-denominated instrument similar to a foreign instrument paying i_{fx}

Whenever i'_{fx} exceeds $i_\$$, that is, whenever a foreign instrument offers a greater return on a hedged basis than an instrument of the same maturity and quality (i.e., credit risk) in the domestic market, investors who hold dollars have an incentive to invest those dollars abroad in the foreign instrument. Such *arbitrage* will in turn tend to reduce the profitability of the transaction by raising the spot rate on the foreign currency and depressing the forward rate.

Thus, in markets where arbitrage is active because it is not prevented by exchange control or other factors, one would expect the net return offered on a hedged basis by an instrument denominated in a foreign currency to equal the rate offered by a similar instrument denominated in dollars. In symbols, this can be stated more succintly as follows: Where arbitrage is active, it should be that

$$i_\$ = i'_{fx}$$

$$= i_{fx} + \left(\frac{F}{S} - 1\right)\frac{360}{t}$$

This in turn implies that the difference between the foreign and domestic rates, which we call *the rate differential, should equal minus the rate of return on the swap; that is,*

$$i_{fx} - i_\$ = \left(1 - \frac{F}{S}\right)\frac{360}{t}$$

In markets, such as that for Eurocurrency time deposits, which are heavily arbitraged, the above relationship does in fact often prevail. An investor will consequently find that on a net basis the rate he can earn by investing dollars in a time deposit will be the same whether he makes a straight deposit of dollars or a foreign-currency-denominated deposit on a hedged basis.

In markets that are less heavily arbitraged, investing in a foreign instrument on a hedged basis may offer the investor who is holding dollars a greater return than that offered by a similar dollar-denominated instrument. Thus the investor whose horizons extend beyond the domestic market will need a new type of break-even number, namely, the rate differential, $i_{fx} - i_\$$, that must prevail between a given pair of markets in order that a hedged foreign instrument yields the same rate as a similar domestic instrument.

As noted, such break-even rate differentials are usually calculated as follows:

$$\left(1 - \frac{F}{S}\right)\frac{360}{t}$$

which equals

$$\left(\frac{S - F}{S}\right)\frac{360}{t}$$

The street, however, does not usually phrase the calculation this way. The reason is that in the foreign exchange market forward rates are not quoted on an *outright* basis, but rather as the *difference* between the spot and forward rates. This difference, $S - F$, is known as the *swap rate;* and in street descriptions of hedging foreign investments, the formula for calculating the break-even rate differential is written as follows:

$$\left(\frac{\text{Swap rate}}{\text{Spot rate}}\right)\frac{360}{t}$$

CALCULATING THE TRUE BREAK-EVEN RATE DIFFERENTIAL

The preceding formula for calculating the break-even rate differential on a hedged foreign investment is, like many street calculations, an approximation. In particular, it fails to take into account hedging of the foreign exchange earned in the form of interest on the foreign instrument. When interest rates are low, the discrepancy between the approximate return on a swap and the true rate is small, but when rates are high, it can rise to 50 basis points or more on a long transaction. The formula for calculating the *true* break-even rate differential is not appreciably more difficult than the one given earlier, and it is therefore the one that should be used.

To derive the precise formula for the break-even rate differential on a hedged foreign investment, consider an investor who has \$1 to invest. If he invests this \$1 for t days in a domestic instrument yielding $i_\$$, he will have at maturity a sum of dollars equal to

$$1 + i_\$ \frac{t}{360}$$

If, alternatively, he invests his \$1 in an instrument that is denominated in a foreign currency and that yields i_{fx}, the units of foreign currency he invests will be $1/S$, and the units of foreign currency he will hold t days hence will be

$$\frac{1}{S}\left(1 + i_{fx}\frac{t}{360}\right)$$

If he sells this sum of foreign currency forward, the amount of *dollars* he will have at the end of the investment period will be

$$\frac{F}{S}\left(1 + i_{fx}\frac{t}{360}\right)$$

Assume that investing in the dollar-denominated instrument and investing in the foreign instrument on a hedged basis both yield the portfolio manager the *same* sum of dollars, i.e.,

$$1 + i_{\$}\frac{t}{360} = \frac{F}{S}\left(1 - i_{fx}\frac{t}{360}\right)$$

By manipulating this equation, it is easy to show that

$$(i_{fx} - i_{\$})^* = true \text{ break-even rate differential}$$

is given by the following expression:

$$(i_{fx} - i_{\$})^* = \left(\frac{S}{F} - 1\right)\left(\frac{360}{t} + i_{\$}\right)$$

WEAK AND STRONG CURRENCIES

If a foreign currency is *strong*, i.e., is expected to *appreciate* in value relative to the dollar, then the forward rate will exceed the spot rate, and the left-hand side of the preceding equation will be negative. This tells us that the investor who swaps dollars into a strong currency will *gain* on the swap and that, in order that a hedged investment in an instrument denominated in that currency will yield him the same rate as a similar dollar-denominated instrument, i_{fx} must be *less than* $i_{\$}$.

If, alternatively, the foreign currency is *weak*, i.e., is expected to *depreciate* in value relative to the dollar, the spot rate will exceed the forward rate, and the left-hand side of the equation will be positive. For a hedged investment in an instrument denominated in such a currency to yield more on a *net* basis than $i_{\$}$, i_{fx} must *exceed* $i_{\$}$ by more than the percentage loss on the swap.

The general rule

Bearing the above in mind, we can state the following general rule:

The hedged foreign instrument is preferable to the domestic instrument whenever the interest rate differential existing in the market exceeds the true break-even rate differential, that is, whenever

$$i_{fx} - i_{\$} > \left(\frac{S}{F} - 1\right)\left(\frac{360}{t} + i_{\$}\right)$$

The only confusing thing about this rule is that $i_{fx} - i_{\$}$ may, as noted, be positive or negative. If it is negative—for example, $i_{fx} - i_{\$} = -3$ percent—then the foreign instrument will be preferable if the amount

$$\left(\frac{S}{F} - 1\right)\left(\frac{360}{t} + i_{\$}\right)$$

is either a smaller negative number (e.g., -2.5 percent) or any positive number. If, alternatively, $i_{fx} - i_{\$}$ is positive, the interpretation of "greater than" is clear; it means any larger positive number. To illustrate we give two examples below.

Calculating the break-even interest rate differential on a hedged investment in an instrument denominated in a foreign currency

Let

$i_{f.r}$ = rate on a 360-day-year basis offered by an instrument denominated in a foreign currency

$i_\$$ = rate on a 360-day-year basis offered on a dollar-denominated instrument similar to the foreign instrument paying $i_{f.r}$

t = days the transaction is outstanding

$(i_{fx} - i_\$)^*$ = *true* break-even rate differential between an investment in the dollar-denominated instrument and a hedged investment in the foreign instrument

Case I: The foreign exchange quotes are in U.S. *direct terms,* that is:

S = spot rate quoted as dollars per unit of foreign exchange

F = *outright* forward rate quoted as dollars per unit of foreign exchange

Then

$$(i_{f.r} - i_\$)^* = \left(\frac{S}{F} - 1\right)\left(\frac{360}{t} + i_\$\right)$$

Case II: The foreign exchange quotes are in *European terms,* that is:

S' = spot rate quoted as units of foreign exchange per dollar

F' = *outright* forward rate quoted as units of foreign exchange per dollar

Then

$$(i_{f.r} - i_\$)^* = \left(\frac{F'}{S'} - 1\right)\left(\frac{360}{t} + i_\$\right)$$

Case III: If $i_\$$ and $i_{f.r}$ are quoted on a 365-day-year basis, change 360 in the above equations to 365.

The break-even formula when quotes are in European terms

So far in our discussion, we have assumed that exchange rates are quoted in U.S. direct terms. If exchange rates are quoted in *European terms,* i.e., as units of foreign exchange per dollar, the formula for the true break-even rate differential must be adjusted accordingly. Let

S' = spot rate quoted in *European terms*, i.e., in units of foreign
exchange per dollar
F' = *outright* forward rate in European terms

Obviously,

$$S = \frac{1}{S'}$$

$$F = \frac{1}{F'}$$

From this it follows that

$$(i_{f.r} - i_\$)^* = \left(\frac{F'}{S'} - 1\right)\left(\frac{360}{t} + i_\$\right)$$

Example I: The foreign currency is strong. Consider an investor who held
dollars on 12/17/79 that he wanted to invest for 3 months. He could have invested
in a straight Eurodollar time deposit or he could have invested on a hedged basis
in a 3-month Euro DM deposit. On 12/17/79 rates were as follows:

$$S' = 1.732000 \text{ DM per dollar}$$
$$F' = 1.707473 \text{ DM per dollar}$$
$$i_\$ = 14\tfrac{7}{8}\%$$
$$i_{\text{DM}} = 9\%$$

Plugging the first three of these numbers into our break-even equation, we find that

$$(i_{\text{DM}} - i_\$)^* = \left(\frac{1.707473}{1.732000} - 1\right)\left(\frac{360}{90} + 0.14875\right)$$
$$= -5\tfrac{7}{8}\%$$

that is, a hedged investment in a Euro DM deposit would have yielded the same
return as a straight Eurodollar time deposit if the rate on the Euro DM deposit had
been $5\tfrac{7}{8}$ percentage points less than $i_\$$. It was, due to arbitrage, so a hedged Euro
DM time deposit offered our investor no advantage over a Eurodollar deposit.

Example II: The foreign currency is weak. Consider now a portfolio manager
who on 12/17/79 chose between a 3-month Eurodollar time deposit and a hedged 3-
month investment in Eurosterling (£). On that day rates were

$$S = \$2.200 \text{ per £}$$
$$F = \$2.1895 \text{ per £}$$
$$i_\$ = 14\tfrac{7}{8}\%$$
$$i_£ = 16\tfrac{7}{8}\%$$

Inserting the first three of these numbers into our equation, we find that[1]

$$(i_£ - i_\$)^* = \left(\frac{2.2000}{2.1895} - 1\right)\left(\frac{365}{90} + 0.14875\right)$$
$$= 2\%$$

---

[1] Note that Eurosterling rates, unlike other Eurodeposit rates, are quoted on a 365-day basis. An
accurate estimate of the break-even rate differential, $(i_£ - i_\$)^*$, can be obtained by substituting 365 for
360 in the break-even calculation, as we did.

Because sterling (£) is a weak currency, our investor would have had to earn 2 percentage points more on a Eurosterling deposit than on a Eurodollar deposit in order to break even on a hedged investment in a Eurosterling deposit. On 12/17/79 rates were such that this investment offered no advantage over a straight Eurodollar deposit. Again arbitrage was at work.

Shopping

We have suggested that, in markets where arbitrage is not prevented by exchange control or other government regulations, it will tend to equalize the return offered by hedged investments in similar instruments. Our Eurocurrency deposit examples, which were constructed from a bank quote board, support this contention.

These examples should not, however, be taken to imply that it is not worthwhile for a corporate account that wants to invest in size to shop around to determine whether a hedged investment would be more profitable than a straight dollar-denominated investment. Major banks that deal in foreign exchange tend to view large corporate accounts as holders of *cold* money (as opposed to *warm* money, which is loyal to one or more banks); and for that reason they give such accounts quotes based on what fits their own dealing positions at the moment. A large corporate account may, therefore, especially in active markets, get quite different quotes from different banks; moreover, it may be able to put together a hedged investment in an instrument denominated in a foreign currency that pays more than a similar dollar-denominated instrument. In such a situation, a corporation is likely to find itself doing different legs of the arbitrage with different banks.

This observation suggests a final comment. Euro Deutsche mark CDs have been issued by banks outside of London. A major drawback of such CDs is that they lack liquidity because no active secondary market exists for them. Since a Euro DM CD is nothing but a Eurodollar CD with a forward (or swap, if the investor holds DM) transaction tagged on, a large investor who is considering such an instrument should determine whether he could create, by buying a Eurodollar CD and selling the proceeds forward for DM, a synthetic Euro DM CD that is higher yielding and more liquid than a Euro DM CD offered by an issuing bank. Note the investor who creates a synthetic Euro DM CD retains liquidity because Eurodollar CDs are readily marketable and a forward transaction can be offset.

Glossary

Common money market and bond market terms

Accretion (of a discount): In portfolio accounting, a straight-line accumulation of capital gains on discount bonds in anticipation of receipt of par at maturity.

Accrued interest: Interest due from issue or from the last coupon date to the present on an interest-bearing security. The buyer of the security pays the quoted dollar price plus accrued interest.

Active: A market in which there is much trading.

After-tax real rate of return: Money after-tax rate of return minus the inflation rate.

Agencies: Federal agency securities.

Agency bank: A form of organization commonly used by foreign banks to enter the U.S. market. An agency bank cannot accept deposits or extend loans in its own name; it acts as an agent for the parent bank.

Agent: A firm that executes orders for or otherwise acts on behalf of another (the principal) and is subject to its control and authority. The agent may receive a fee or commission.

All-in cost: Total costs, explicit and other. Example: The all-in cost to a bank of CD money is the explicit rate of interest it pays on that deposit *plus* the FDIC premium it must pay on the deposit *plus* the hidden cost it incurs because it must hold some portion of that deposit in a non-interest-bearing reserve account at the Fed.

All or none (AON): Requirement that none of an order be executed unless all of it can be executed at the specified price.

Amortize: In portfolio accounting, periodic charges made against interest income on premium bonds in anticipation of receipt of the call price at call or of par value at maturity.

Arbitrage: Strictly defined, buying something where it is cheap and selling it where it is dear; e.g., a bank buys 3-month CD money in the U.S. market and sells 3-month money at a higher rate in the Eurodollar market. In the money market, often refers: (1) to a situation in which a trader buys one security and sells a similar security in the expectation that the spread in yields between the two instruments will narrow or widen to his profit, (2) to a swap between two similar issues based on an anticipated change in yield spreads, and (3) to situations where a higher return (or lower cost) can be achieved in the money market for one currency by utilizing another currency and swapping it on a fully hedged basis through the foreign exchange market.

Asked: The price at which securities are offered.

Away: A trade, quote, or market that does not originate with the dealer in question, e.g., "the bid is 98–10 away (from me)."

Back up: (1) When yields rise and prices fall, the market is said to back up. (2) When an investor swaps out of one security into another of shorter current maturity (e.g., out of a 2-year note into an 18-month note), he is said to back up.

Bank discount rate: Yield basis on which short-term, non-interest-bearing money market securities are quoted. A rate quoted on a discount basis understates bond equivalent yield. That must be calculated when comparing return against coupon securities.

Bank line: Line of credit granted by a bank to a customer.

Bank wire: A computer message system linking major banks. It is used not for effecting payments, but as a mechanism to advise the receiving bank of some action that has occurred, e.g., the payment by a customer of funds into that bank's account.

Bankers' acceptance (BA): A draft or bill of exchange accepted by a bank or trust company. The accepting institution guarantees payment on the bill.

BANs: Bond anticipation notes are issued by states and municipalities to obtain interim financing for projects that will eventually be funded long term through the sale of a bond issue.

Basis: (1) Number of days in the coupon period. (2) In *commodities* jargon, basis is the spread between a futures price and some other price. A money market participant would talk about *spread* rather than basis.

Basis point: $1/100$ of 1 percent.

Basis price: Price expressed in terms of yield to maturity or annual rate of return.

Bear market: A declining market or a period of pessimism when declines in the market are anticipated. (A way to remember: "Bear down.")

Bearer security: A security whose owner is not registered on the books of the issuer. A bearer security is payable to the holder.

Best-efforts basis: Securities dealers do not underwrite a new issue, but sell it on the basis of what can be sold. In the money market, usually refers to a firm order to buy or sell a given amount of securities or currency at whatever best price can be found over a given period of time; can also refer to a flexible amount (up to a limit) at a given rate.

Bid: The price offered for securities.

Block: A large amount of securities, normally much more than what constitutes a round lot in the market in question.

Book: A banker, especially a Euro banker, will refer to his bank's assets and liabilities as its "book." If the average maturity of the liabilities is less than that of the assets, the bank is running a **short** or **open** book.

Book-entry securities: The Treasury and the federal agencies are moving to a book-entry system in which securities are not represented by engraved pieces of paper but are maintained in computerized records at the Fed in the names of member banks, which in turn keep records of the securities they own as well as those they are holding for customers. In the case of other securities where a book-entry system has developed, engraved securities do exist somewhere in quite a few cases. These securities do not move from holder to holder but are usually kept in a central clearinghouse or by another agent.

Book value: The value at which a debt security is shown on the holder's balance sheet. Book value is often acquisition cost ± amortization/accretion, which may differ markedly from market value. It can be further defined as "tax book," "accreted book," or "amortized book" value.

Bridge financing: Interim financing of one sort or another.

British clearers: The large clearing banks that dominate deposit taking and short-term lending in the domestic sterling market in Great Britain.

Broker: A broker brings buyers and sellers together for a commission paid by the initiator of the transaction or by both sides; he does not position. In the money market, brokers are active in markets in which banks buy and sell money and in interdealer markets.

Bull market: A period of optimism when increases in market prices are anticipated. (A way to remember: "Bull ahead.")

Bullet loan: A bank term loan that calls for no amortization. The term is commonly used in the Euromarket.

Buy-back: Another term for a repurchase agreement.

Calendar: List of new bond issues scheduled to come to market shortly.

Call money: Interest-bearing bank deposits that can be withdrawn on 24-hours notice. Many Euro deposits take the form of call money.

Callable bond: A bond that the issuer has the right to redeem prior to maturity by paying some specified call price.

Canadian agencies: Agency banks established by Canadian banks in the United States.

Carry: The interest cost of financing securities held. (See also **Negative carry** and **Positive carry**.)

Cash management bill: Very short-maturity bills that the Treasury occasionally sells because its cash balances are down and it needs money for a few days.

Cash market: Traditionally this term has been used to denote the market in which commodities were traded against cash for immediate delivery. Since the inception of futures markets for T bills and other debt securities, a distinction has been made between the cash markets in which these securities trade for immediate delivery and the futures markets in which they trade for future delivery.

Cash settlement: In the money market a transaction is said to be made for cash settlement if the securities purchased are delivered against payment in Fed funds on the same day the trade is made.

Certificate of deposit (CD): A time deposit with a specific maturity evidenced by a certificate. Large-denomination CDs are typically negotiable.

CHIPS: The New York Clearing House's computerized Clearing House Interbank Payments System. Most Euro transactions are cleared and settled through CHIPS rather than over the Fed wire.

Circle: Underwriters, actual or potential as the case may be, often seek out and "circle" retail interest in a new issue before final pricing. The customer circled has basically made a commitment to purchase the note or bond *or* to purchase it if it comes at an agreed-upon price. In the latter case, if the price is other than that stipulated, the customer supposedly has first offer at the actual price.

Clear: A trade is carried out by the seller delivering securities and the buyer delivering funds in proper form. A trade that does not clear is said to **fail**.

Clearinghouse funds: Payments made through the New York Clearing House's computerized Clearing House Interbank Payments System. Clearinghouse debits and credits are settled in Fed funds on the first business day after clearing.

Commercial paper: An unsecured promissory note with a fixed maturity of no more than 270 days. Commercial paper is normally sold at a discount from face value.

Competitive bid: (1) Bid tendered in a Treasury auction by an investor for a specific amount of securities at a specific yield or price. (2) Issuers, municipal and public utilities, often sell new issues by asking for competitive bids from one or more syndicates.

Confirmation: A memorandum to the other side of a trade detailing all relevant data.

Consortium banks: A merchant banking subsidiary set up by several banks that may or may not be of the same nationality. Consortium banks are common in the Euromarket and are active in loan syndication.

Convertible bond: A bond containing a provision that permits conversion between the issuer's bonds and common stock at some fixed exchange ratio.

Corporate bond equivalent: See **Equivalent bond yield.**

Corporate taxable equivalent: Rate of return required on a par bond to produce the same after-tax yield to maturity that the premium or discount bond quoted would.

Country risk: See **Sovereign risk.**

Coupon: (1) The annual rate of interest that a bond's issuer promises to pay the bondholder on the bond's face value. (2) A certificate attached to a bond evidencing interest due on a payment date.

Cover: To eliminate a short position by buying the securities shorted.

Covered interest arbitrage: A portfolio manager invests dollars in an instrument denominated in a foreign currency and hedges his resulting foreign exchange risk by selling the proceeds of the investment forward for dollars.

Credit risk: The risk that an issuer of debt securities or a borrower may default on his obligations, or that payment may not be made on sale of a negotiable instrument. (See **Overnight delivery risk.**)

Cross hedge: Hedging a risk in a cash market security by buying or selling a futures contract for a different but similar instrument.

CRTs: Abbreviation for the cathode-ray tubes used to display market quotes.

Current coupon: A bond selling at or close to par, that is, a bond with a coupon close to the yields currently offered on new bonds of similar maturity and credit risk.

Current issue: In Treasury bills and notes, the most recently auctioned issue. Trading is more active in current issues than in off-the-run issues.

Current maturity: Current time to maturity on an outstanding note, bond, or other money market instrument; for example, a 5-year note 1 year after issue has a current maturity of 4 years.

Current yield: Coupon payments on a security as a percentage of the security's market price. In many instances the price should be *gross* of accrued interest, particularly on instruments where no coupon is left to be paid until maturity.

Cushion bonds: High-coupon bonds that sell at only a moderate premium because they are callable at a price below that at which a comparable noncallable bond would sell. Cushion bonds offer considerable downside protection in a falling market.

Day trading: Intraday trading in securities for profit as opposed to investing for profit.

Dealer: A dealer, as opposed to a broker, acts as a principal in all transactions, buying and selling for his own account.

Dealer loan: Overnight, collateralized loan made to a dealer financing his position by borrowing from a money market bank.

Debenture: A bond secured only by the general credit of the issuer.

Debt leverage: The amplification in the return earned on equity funds when an investment is financed partly with borrowed money.

Debt securities: IOUs created through loan-type transactions—commercial paper, bank CDs, bills, bonds, and other instruments.

Default: Failure to make timely payment of interest or principal on a debt security or to otherwise comply with the provisions of a bond indenture.

Demand line of credit: A bank line of credit that enables a customer to borrow on a daily or on-demand basis.

Direct paper: Commercial paper sold directly by the issuer to investors.

Direct placement: Selling a new issue not by offering it for sale publicly, but by placing it with one or several institutional investors.

Discount basis: See **Bank discount rate.**

Discount bond: A bond selling below par.

Discount house: British institution that uses call and overnight money obtained from banks to invest in and trade money market instruments.

Discount paper: See Discount securities.

Discount rate: The rate of interest charged by the Fed to member banks that borrow at the discount window. The discount rate is an add-on rate.

Discount securities: Non-interest-bearing money market instruments that are issued at a discount and redeemed at maturity for full face value, e.g., U.S. Treasury bills.

Discount window: Facility provided by the Fed enabling member banks to borrow reserves against collateral in the form of governments or other acceptable paper.

Disintermediation: The investing of funds that would normally have been placed with a bank or other financial intermediary directly into debt securities issued by ultimate borrowers, e.g., into bills or bonds.

Distributed: After a Treasury auction, there will be many new issues in dealers' hands. As those securities are sold to retail, the issue is said to be distributed.

Diversification: Dividing investment funds among a variety of securities offering independent returns.

DM: Deutsche (German) marks.

Documented discount notes: Commercial paper backed by normal bank lines plus a letter of credit from a bank stating that it will pay off the paper at maturity if the borrower does not. Such paper is also referred to as **LOC** (letter of credit) **paper.**

Dollar bonds: Municipal revenue bonds for which quotes are given in dollar prices. Not to be confused with "U.S. Dollar" bonds, a common term of reference in the Eurobond market.

Dollar price of a bond: Percentage of face value at which a bond is quoted.

Don't know (DK, DKed): "Don't know the trade"—a street expression used whenever one party lacks knowledge of a trade or receives conflicting instructions from the other party (for example, with respect to payment).

Due bill: An instrument evidencing the obligation of a seller to deliver securities sold to the buyer. Occasionally used in the bill market.

Dutch auction: Auction in which the lowest price necessary to sell the entire offering becomes the price at which all securities offered are sold. This technique has been used in Treasury auctions.

Edge Act corporation: A subsidiary of a U.S. bank set up to carry out international banking business. Most such subs are located within the United States.

Either/or facility: An agreement permitting a bank customer to borrow either domestic dollars from the bank's head office or Eurodollars from one of its foreign branches.

Either-way market: In the interbank Eurodollar deposit market, an either-way market is one in which the bid and asked rates are identical.

Eligible bankers' acceptances: In the BA market an acceptance may be referred to as eligible because it is acceptable by the Fed as collateral at the discount window and/or because the accepting bank can sell it without incurring a reserve requirement.

Equivalent bond yield: Annual yield on a short-term, non–interest-bearing security calculated so as to be comparable to yields quoted on coupon securities.

Equivalent taxable yield: The yield on a taxable security that would leave the investor with the same after-tax return he would earn by holding a tax-exempt municipal; for example, for an investor taxed at a 50 percent marginal rate, equivalent taxable yield on a muni note issued at 3 percent would be 6 percent.

Euro CDs: CDs issued by a U.S. bank branch or foreign bank located outside the United States. Almost all Euro CDs are issued in London.

Euro lines: Lines of credit granted by banks (foreign or foreign branches of U.S. banks) for Eurocurrencies.

Eurobonds: Bonds issued in Europe outside the confines of any national capital market. A Eurobond may or may not be denominated in the currency of the issuer.

Eurocurrency deposits: Deposits made in a bank or bank branch that is not located in the country in whose currency the deposit is denominated. Dollars deposited in a London bank are Eurodollars; German marks deposited there are Euromarks.

Eurodollars: U.S. dollars deposited in a U.S. bank branch or a foreign bank located outside the United States.

Excess reserves: Balances held by a bank at the Fed in excess of those required.

Exchange rate: The price at which one currency trades for another.

Exempt securities: Instruments exempt from the registration requirements of the Securities Act of 1933 or the margin requirements of the Securities and Exchange Act of 1934. Such securities include governments, agencies, municipal securities, commercial paper, and private placements.

Extension swap: Extending maturity through a swap, e.g., selling a 2-year note and buying one with a slightly longer current maturity.

Fail: A trade is said to fail if on settlement date either the seller fails to deliver securities in proper form or the buyer fails to deliver funds in proper form.

Fed funds: See **Federal funds.**

Fed wire: A computer system linking member banks to the Fed, used for making interbank payments of Fed funds and for making deliveries of and payments for Treasury and agency securities.

Federal credit agencies: Agencies of the federal government set up to supply credit to various classes of institutions and individuals, e.g., S&Ls, small business firms, students, farmers, farm cooperatives, and exporters.

Federal Deposit Insurance Corporation (FDIC): A federal institution that insures bank deposits, currently up to $40,000 per deposit.

Federal Financing Bank: A federal institution that lends to a wide array of federal credit agencies funds it obtains by borrowing from the U.S. Treasury.

Federal funds: (1) Non-interest-bearing deposits held by member banks at the Federal Reserve. (2) Used to denote "immediately available" funds in the clearing sense.

Federal funds rate: The rate of interest at which Fed funds are traded. This rate is currently pegged by the Federal Reserve through open-market operations.

Federal Home Loan Banks (FHLB): The institutions that regulate and lend to savings and loan associations. The Federal Home Loan Banks play a role analogous to that played by the Federal Reserve Banks vis-à-vis member commercial banks.

Figuring the tail: Calculating the yield at which a future money market instrument (one available some period hence) is purchased when that future security is created by buying an existing instrument and financing the initial portion of its life with a term RP.

Firm: Refers to an order to buy or sell that can be executed without confirmation for some fixed period.

Fixed dates: In the Euromarket the standard periods for which Euros are traded (1 month out to a year) are referred to as the fixed dates.

Fixed-dollar security: A nonnegotiable debt security that can be redeemed at some fixed price or according to some schedule of fixed values (e.g., bank deposits and government savings bonds).

Fixed-rate loan: A loan on which the rate paid by the borrower is fixed for the life of the loan.

Flat trades: (1) A bond in default trades flat; that is, the price quoted covers both principal and unpaid, accrued interest. (2) Any security that trades without accrued interest or at a price that includes accrued interest is said to trade flat.

Float: The difference between the credits given by the Fed to banks' reserve accounts on checks being cleared through the Fed and the debits made to banks' reserve accounts on these same checks. Float is always positive, because in the clearing of a check, the credit sometimes precedes the debit. Float adds to the money supply.

Floating-rate note: A note that pays an interest rate tied to current money market rates. The holder may have the right to demand redemption at par on specified dates.

Floating supply: The amount of securities believed to be available for immediate purchase, that is, in the hands of dealers and investors wanting to sell.

Flower bonds: Government bonds that are acceptable at par in payment of federal estate taxes when owned by the decedent at the time of death.

Foreign bond: A bond issued by a nondomestic borrower in the domestic capital market.

Foreign exchange rate: The price at which one currency trades for another.

Foreign exchange risk: The risk that a long or short position in a foreign currency might, due to an adverse movement in the relevant exchange rate, have to be closed out at a loss. The long or short position may arise out of a financial or commercial transaction.

Forward Fed funds: Fed funds traded for future delivery.

Forward forward contract: In Eurocurrencies, a contract under which a deposit of fixed maturity is agreed to at a fixed price for future delivery.

Forward market: A market in which participants agree to trade some commodity, security, or foreign exchange at a fixed price at some future date.

Forward rate: The rate at which forward transactions in some specific maturity are being made, e.g., the dollar price at which DM can be bought for delivery 3 months hence.

Free reserves: Excess reserves minus member bank borrowings at the Fed.

Full-coupon bond: A bond with a coupon equal to the going market rate and consequently selling at or near par.

Futures market: A market in which contracts for future delivery of a commodity or a security are bought and sold.

General obligation bonds: Municipal securities secured by the issuer's pledge of its full faith, credit, and taxing power.

Give up: The loss in yield that occurs when a block of bonds is swapped for another block of lower-coupon bonds. Can also be referred to as "after-tax give up" when the implications of the profit (loss) on taxes are considered.

Glass-Steagall Act: A 1933 act in which Congress forbade commercial banks to own, underwrite, or deal in corporate stock and corporate bonds.

Go-around: When the Fed offers to buy securities, to sell securities, to do repo, or to do reverses, it solicits competitive bids or offers, as the case may be, from all primary dealers. This procedure is known as a go-around.

Good delivery: A delivery in which everything—endorsement, any necessary attached legal papers, etc.—is in order.

Governments: Negotiable U.S. Treasury securities.

Gross spread: The difference between the price that the issuer receives for its securities and the price that investors pay for them. This spread equals the selling concession plus the management and underwriting fees.

Haircut: Margin in an RP transaction, that is, the difference between the actual market value measured at the bid side of the market and the value used in an RP agreement.

Handle: The whole-dollar price of a bid or offer is referred to as the *handle*. For example, if a security is quoted 101–10 bid and 101–11 offered, 101 is the handle. Traders are assumed to know the handle, so a trader would quote that market to another by saying he was at 10–11. (The 10 and 11 refer to 32nds.)

Hedge: To reduce risk, (1) by taking a position in futures equal and opposite to an existing or anticipated cash position, or (2) by shorting a security similar to one in which a long position has been established.

Hit: A dealer who agrees to sell at the bid price quoted by another dealer is said to *hit* that bid.

In the box: This means that a dealer has a wire receipt for securities indicating that effective delivery on them has been made. This jargon is a holdover from the time when Treasuries took the form of physical securities and were stored in a rack.

Indenture of a bond: A legal statement spelling out the obligations of the bond issuer and the rights of the bondholder.

Investment banker: A firm that engages in the origination, underwriting, and distribution of new issues.

Joint account: An agreement between two or more firms to share risk and financing responsibility in purchasing or underwriting securities.

Junk bonds: High-risk bonds that have low credit ratings or are in default.

Leverage: See **Debt leverage.**

Leveraged lease: The lessor provides only a minor portion of the cost of the leased equipment, borrowing the rest from another lender.

LIBOR: The London Interbank Offered Rate on Eurodollar deposits traded between banks. There is a different LIBOR rate for each deposit maturity. Different banks may quote slightly different LIBOR rates because they use different reference banks.

Lifting a leg: Closing out one side of a long-short arbitrage before the other is closed.

Line of credit: An arrangement by which a bank agrees to lend to the line holder during some specified period any amount up to the full amount of the line.

Liquidity: A liquid asset is one that can be converted easily and rapidly into cash without a substantial loss of value. In the money market, a security is said to be liquid if the spread between bid and asked prices is narrow and reasonable size can be done at those quotes.

Liquidity diversification: Investing in a variety of maturities to reduce the price risk to which holding long bonds exposes the investor.

Liquidity risk: In banking, risk that monies needed to fund assets may not be available in sufficient quantities at some future date. Implies an imbalance in committed maturities of assets and liabilities.

Lock-up CDs: CDs that are issued with the tacit understanding that the buyer will not trade the certificate. Quite often the issuing bank will insist that the certificate be safekept by it to ensure that the understanding is honored by the buyer.

Locked market: A market is said to be locked if the bid price equals the asked price. This can occur, for example, if the market is brokered and brokerage is paid by one side only, the initiator of the transaction.

Long: (1) Owning a debt security, stock, or other asset. (2) Owning more than one has contracted to deliver.

Long bonds: Bonds with a long current maturity.

Long coupons: (1) Bonds or notes with a long current maturity. (2) A bond on which one of the coupon periods, usually the first, is longer than the others or than standard.

Long hedge: *Purchase* of a *futures* contract to lock in the yield at which an anticipated cash inflow can be invested.

Make a market: A dealer is said to make a market when he quotes bid and offered prices at which he stands ready to buy and sell.

Margin: In an RP or a reverse repurchase transaction, the amount by which the market value of the securities collateralizing the transaction exceeds the amount lent.

Marginal tax rate: The tax rate that would have to be paid on any additional dollars of taxable income earned.

Market value: The price at which a security is trading and could presumably be purchased or sold.

Marketability: A negotiable security is said to have good marketability if there is an active secondary market in which it can easily be resold.

Match fund: A bank is said to match fund a loan or other asset when it does so by buying (taking) a deposit of the same maturity. The term is commonly used in the Euromarket.

Matched book: If the distribution of the maturities of a bank's liabilities equals that of its assets, it is said to be running a *matched book*. The term is commonly used in the Euromarket.

Merchant bank: A British term for a bank that specializes not in lending out its own funds, but in providing various financial services such as accepting bills arising out of trade, underwriting new issues, and providing advice on acquisitions, mergers, foreign exchange, portfolio management, etc.

Money market: The market in which short-term debt instruments (bills, commercial paper, bankers' acceptances, etc.) are issued and traded.

Money market (center) bank: A bank that is one of the nation's largest and consequently plays an active and important role in every sector of the money market.

Money market fund: Mutual fund that invests solely in money market instruments.

Money rate of return: Annual money return as a percentage of asset value.

Money supply definitions currently used by the Fed:
M1–A: Currency plus demand deposits.
M1–B: M1–A plus other checkable deposits.
M2:   M1–B plus overnight RPs and money market funds and savings and small (less than $100,000) time deposits.
M3:   M–2 plus large time deposits and term RPs.
L: M–3 plus other liquid assets.

Mortgage bond: Bond secured by a lien on property, equipment, or other real assets.

Multicurrency clause: Such a clause on a Euro loan permits the borrower to switch from one currency to another on a rollover date.

Municipal (muni) notes: Short-term notes issued by municipalities in anticipation of tax receipts, proceeds from a bond issue, or other revenues.

Municipals: Securities issued by state and local governments and their agencies.

Naked position: A long or short position that is not hedged.

Negative carry: The net cost incurred when the cost of carry exceeds the yield on the securities being financed.

Negotiable certificate of deposit: A large-denomination (generally $1 million) CD that can be sold but cannot be cashed in before maturity.

Negotiated sale: Situation in which the terms of an offering are determined by negotiation between the issuer and the underwriter rather than through competitive bidding by underwriting groups.

Neutral period: In the Euromarket, a period over which Eurodollars are sold is said to be *neutral* if it does not start or end on either a Friday or the day before a holiday.

New-issues market: The market in which a new issue of securities is first sold to investors.

New money: In a Treasury refunding, the amount by which the par value of the securities offered exceeds that of those maturing.

Noncompetitive bid: In a Treasury auction, bidding for a specific amount of securities at the price, whatever it may turn out to be, equal to the average price of the accepted competitive bids.

Note: Coupon issues with a relatively short original maturity are often called *notes*. Muni notes, however, have maturities ranging from a month to a year and pay interest only at maturity. Treasury notes are coupon securities that have an original maturity of up to 10 years.

Odd lot: Less than a round lot.

Off-the-run issue: In Treasuries and agencies, an issue that is not included in dealer or broker runs. In bills and notes normally only current issues are quoted.

Offer: Price asked by a seller of securities.

One-man picture: The picture quoted by a broker is said to be a one-man picture if both the bid and the asked prices come from the same source.

One-sided (one-way) market: A market in which only one side, the bid or the asked, is quoted or firm.

Open book: See **Unmatched book.**

Open repo: A repo with no definite term. The agreement is made on a day-to-day basis and either the borrower or the lender may choose to terminate. The rate paid is higher than on overnight repo and is subject to adjustment if rates move.

Opportunity cost: The cost of pursuing one course of action measured in terms of the forgone return offered by the most attractive alternative.

Option: (1) **Call option:** A contract sold for a price that gives the holder the right to buy from the writer of the option over a specified period a specified amount of securities at a specified price. (2) **Put option:** A contract sold for a price that gives the holder the right to sell to the writer of the contract over a period a specified amount of securities at a specified price.

Original maturity: Maturity at issue. For example, a 5-year note has an original maturity at issue of 5 years; one year later it has a current maturity of 4 years.

Over-the-counter (OTC) market: Market created by dealer trading as opposed to the auction market prevailing on organized exchanges.

Overnight delivery risk: A risk brought about because differences in time zones between settlement centers require that payment or delivery on one side of a transaction be made without knowing until the next day whether funds have been received in account on the other side. Particularly apparent where delivery takes place in Europe for payment in dollars in New York.

Paper: Money market instruments, commercial paper and other.

Paper gain (loss): Unrealized capital gain (loss) on securities held in portfolio, based on a comparison of current market price to original cost.

Par: (1) Price of 100 percent. (2) The principal amount at which the issuer of a debt security contracts to redeem that security at maturity, *face value.*

Par bond: A bond selling at par.

Pass-through: A mortgage-backed security on which payments of interest and principal on the underlying mortgages are passed through by an agent to the security holder.

Paydown: In a Treasury refunding, the amount by which the par value of the securities maturing exceeds that of those sold.

Pay-up: (1) The loss of cash resulting from a swap into higher-price bonds. (2) The need (or willingness) of a bank or other borrower to pay a higher rate in order to get funds.

Pickup: The gain in yield that occurs when a block of bonds is swapped for another block of higher-coupon bonds.

Picture: The bid and asked prices quoted by a broker for a given security.

Placement: A bank depositing Eurodollars with (selling Eurodollars to) another bank is often said to be making a placement.

Plus: Dealers in governments normally quote bids and offers in 32nds. To quote a bid or offer in 64ths, they use pluses; for example, a dealer who bids 4+ is bidding the handle plus $4/32 + 1/64$, which equals the handle plus $9/64$.

PNs: Project notes are issued by municipalities to finance federally sponsored programs in urban renewal and housing. They are guaranteed by the U.S. Department of Housing and Urban Development.

Point: (1) 100 basis points = 1 percent. (2) One percent of the face value of a note or bond. (3) In the foreign exchange market, the lowest level at which the currency is priced. Example: "One point" is the difference between sterling prices of $1.8080 and $1.8081.

Portfolio: Collection of securities held by an investor.

Position: (1) To go long or short in a security. (2) The amount of securities owned (long position) or owed (short position).

Positive carry: The net gain earned when the cost of carry is less than the yield on the securities being financed.

Premium: (1) The amount by which the price at which an issue is trading exceeds the issue's par value. (2) The amount that must be paid in excess of par to call or refund an issue before maturity. (3) In money market parlance, the fact that a particular bank's CDs trade at a rate higher than others of its class, or that a bank has to pay up to acquire funds.

Premium bond: Bond selling above par.

Prepayment: A payment made ahead of the scheduled payment date.

Presold issue: An issue that is sold out before the coupon announcement.

Price risk: The risk that a debt security's price may change due to a rise or fall in the going level of interest rates.

Prime rate: The rate at which banks lend to their best (prime) customers. The all-in cost of a bank loan to a prime credit equals the prime rate plus the cost of holding compensating balances.

Principal: (1) The face amount or par value of a debt security. (2) One who acts as a dealer buying and selling for his own account.

Private placement: An issue that is offered to a single or a few investors as opposed to being publicly offered. Private placements do not have to be registered with the SEC.

Prospectus: A detailed statement prepared by an issuer and filed with the SEC prior to the sale of a new issue. The prospectus gives detailed information on the issue and on the issuer's condition and prospects.

Put: See **Option.**

RANs: Revenue anticipation notes are issued by states and municipalities to finance current expenditures in anticipation of the future receipt of nontax revenues.

Rate risk: In banking, the risk that profits may decline or losses occur because a rise in interest rates forces up the cost of funding fixed-rate loans or other fixed-rate assets.

Ratings: An evaluation given by Moody's, Standard & Poor's, Fitch, or other rating services of a security's creditworthiness.

Real market: The bid and offer prices at which a dealer could do size. Quotes in the brokers market may reflect not the real market, but pictures painted by dealers playing trading games.

Red herring: A preliminary prospectus containing all the information required by the Securities and Exchange Commission except the offering price and coupon of a new issue.

Refunding: Redemption of securities with funds raised through the sale of a new issue.

Registered bond: A bond whose owner is registered with the issuer.

Regular way settlement: In the money and bond markets, the regular basis on which some security trades are settled is that delivery of the securities purchased is made against payment in Fed funds on the day following the transaction.

Regulation D: Fed regulation currently that required member banks to hold reserves against their net borrowings from foreign offices of other banks over a 28-day averaging period. Reg D has been merged with Reg M.

Regulation M: Fed regulation currently requiring member banks to hold reserves against their net borrowings from their foreign branches over a 28-day averaging period. Reg M has also required member banks to hold reserves against Eurodollars lent by their foreign branches to domestic corporations for domestic purposes.

Regulation Q: Fed regulation imposing lids on the rates that banks may pay on savings and time deposits. Currently time deposits with a denomination of $100,000 or more are exempt from Reg Q.

Reinvestment rate: (1) The rate at which an investor assumes interest payments made on a debt security can be reinvested over the life of that security. (2) Also, the rate at which funds from a maturity or sale of a security can be reinvested. Often used in comparison to "give up" yield.

Relative value: The attractiveness—measured in terms of risk, liquidity, and return—of one instrument relative to another, or for a given instrument, of one maturity relative to another.

Reopen an issue: The Treasury, when it wants to sell additional securities, will occasionally sell more of an existing issue (reopen it) rather than offer a new issue.

Repo: See **Repurchase agreement.**

Repurchase agreement (RP or repo): A holder of securities sells these securities to an investor with an agreement to repurchase them at a fixed price on a fixed date. The security "buyer" in effect lends the "seller" money for the period of the agreement, and the terms of the agreement are structured to compensate him for this. Dealers use RP extensively to finance their positions. Exception: When the Fed is said to be doing RP, it is lending money, that is, increasing bank reserves.

Reserve requirements: The percentages of different types of deposits that member banks are required to hold on deposit at the Fed.

Retail: Individual and institutional customers as opposed to dealers and brokers.

Revenue bond: A municipal bond secured by revenue from tolls, user charges, or rents derived from the facility financed.

Reverse: See **Reverse repurchase agreement.**

Reverse repurchase agreement: Most typically a repurchase agreement initiated by the lender of funds. Reverses are used by dealers to borrow securities they have shorted. Exception: When the Fed is said to be doing reverses, it is borrowing money, that is, absorbing reserves.

Revolver: See **Revolving line of credit.**

Revolving line of credit: A bank line of credit on which the customer pays a commitment fee and can take down and repay funds according to his needs. Normally the line involves a firm commitment from the bank for a period of several years.

Risk: Degree of uncertainty of return on an asset.

Roll over: Reinvest funds received from a maturing security in a new issue of the same or a similar security.

Rollover: Most term loans in the Euromarket are made on a rollover basis, which means that the loan is periodically repriced at an agreed spread over the appropriate, currently prevailing LIBOR rate.

Round lot: In the money market, round lot refers to the minimum amount for which dealers' quotes are good. This may range from $100,000 to $5 million, depending on the size and liquidity of the issue traded.

RP: See **Repurchase agreement.**

Run: A run consists of a series of bid and asked quotes for different securities or maturities. Dealers give to and ask for runs from each other.

S&L: See **Savings and loan association.**

Safekeep: For a fee banks will safekeep (i.e., hold in their vault, clip coupons on, and present for payment at maturity) bonds and money market instruments.

Sale repurchase agreement: See **Repurchase agreement.**

Savings and loan association: National- or state-chartered institution that accepts savings deposits and invests the bulk of the funds thus received in mortgages.

Savings deposit: Interest-bearing deposit at a savings institution that has no specific maturity.

Scale: A bank that offers to pay different rates of interest on CDs of varying maturities is said to "post a scale." Commercial paper issuers also post scales.

Seasoned issue: An issue that has been well distributed and trades well in the secondary market.

Secondary market: The market in which previously issued securities are traded.

Sector: Refers to a group of securities that are similar with respect to maturity, type, rating, and/or coupon.

Securities and Exchange Commission (SEC): Agency created by Congress to protect investors in securities transactions by administering various securities acts.

Serial bonds: A bond issue in which maturities are staggered over a number of years.

Settle: See **Clear**.

Settlement date: The date on which a trade is cleared by delivery of securities against funds. The settlement data may be the trade date or a later date.

Shop: In street jargon, a money market or bond dealership.

Shopping: Seeking to obtain the best bid or offer available by calling a number of dealers and/or brokers.

Short: A market participant assumes a short position by selling a security he does not own. The seller makes delivery by borrowing the security sold or reversing it in.

Short bonds: Bonds with a short current maturity.

Short book: See **Unmatched book**.

Short coupons: Bonds or notes with a short current maturity.

Short hedge: *Sale* of a *futures* contract to hedge, for example, a position in cash securities or an anticipated borrowing need.

Short sale: The sale of securities not owned by the seller in the expectation that the price of these securities will fall or as part of an arbitrage. A short sale must eventually be covered by a purchase of the securities sold.

Sinking fund: Indentures on corporate issues often require that the issuer make annual payments to a sinking fund, the proceeds of which are used to retire randomly selected bonds in the issue.

Size: Large in size, as in "size offering" or "in there for size." What constitutes size varies with the sector of the market.

Skip-day settlement: The trade is settled one business day beyond what is normal.

Sovereign risk: The special risks, if any, that attach to a security (or deposit or loan) because the borrower's country of residence differs from that of the investor's. Also referred to as **country risk**.

Specific issues market: The market in which dealers reverse in securities they want to short.

Spectail: A dealer that does business with retail but concentrates more on acquiring and financing its own speculative position.

Spot market: Market for immediate as opposed to future delivery. In the spot market for foreign exchange, settlement is two business days ahead.

Spot rate: The price prevailing in the spot market.

Spread: (1) Difference between bid and asked prices on a security. (2) Difference between yields on or prices of two securities of differing sorts or differing maturities. (3) In underwriting, difference between price realized by the issuer and price paid by the investor. (4) Difference between two prices or two rates. What a commodities trader would refer to as the *basis*.

Spreading: In the futures market, buying one futures contract and selling a nearby one to profit from an anticipated narrowing or widening of the spread over time.

Stop-out price: The lowest price (highest yield) accepted by the Treasury in an auction of a new issue.

Street: Brokers, dealers, and other knowledgeable members of the financial community; from Wall Street financial community.

Subject: Refers to a bid or offer that cannot be executed without confirmation from the customer.

Subordinated debenture: The claims of holders of this issue rank after those of holders of various other unsecured debts incurred by the issuer.

Swap: (1) In securities, selling one issue and buying another. (2) In foreign exchange, buying a currency spot and simultaneously selling it forward.

Swap rate: In the foreign exchange market, the difference between the spot and forward rates at which a currency is traded.

Swing line: See **Demand line of credit.**

Swissy: Market jargon for Swiss francs.

Switch: British English for a swap, that is, buying a currency spot and selling it forward.

TABs (tax anticipation bills): Special bills that the Treasury occasionally issues. They mature on corporate quarterly income tax dates and can be used at face value by corporations to pay their tax liabilities.

Tail: (1) The difference between the average price in Treasury auctions and the stopout price. (2) A *future* money market instrument (one available some period hence) created by buying an existing instrument and financing the initial portion of its life with term RP.

Take: (1) A dealer or customer who agrees to buy at another dealer's offered price is said to take that offer. (2) Euro bankers speak of taking deposits rather than buying money.

Take-out: (1) A cash surplus generated by the sale of one block of securities and the purchase of another, e.g., selling a block of bonds at 99 and buying another block at 95. (2) A bid made to a seller of a security that is designed (and generally agreed) to take him out of the market.

Taking a view: A London expression for forming an opinion as to where interest rates are going and acting on it.

TANs: Tax anticipation notes issued by states or municipalities to finance current operations in anticipation of future tax receipts.

Technical condition of a market: Demand and supply factors affecting price, in particular the net position—long or short—of dealers.

Tenor: Maturity.

Term bonds: A bond issue in which all bonds mature at the same time.

Term Fed funds: Fed funds sold for a period of time longer than overnight.

Term loan: Loan extended by a bank for more than the normal 90-day period. A term loan might run 5 years or more.

Term RP (repo): RP borrowings for a period longer than overnight, may be 30, 60, or even 90 days.

Thin market: A market in which trading volume is low and in which consequently bid and asked quotes are wide and the liquidity of the instrument traded is low.

Tight market: A tight market, as opposed to a thin market, is one in which volume is large, trading is active and highly competitive, and spreads between bid and ask prices are narrow.

Time deposit: Interest-bearing deposit at a savings institution that has a specific maturity.

Tom next: In the interbank market in Eurodollar deposits and the foreign exchange market, the value (delivery) date on a Tom next transaction is the next business day. (Refers to "tomorrow next.")

Trade date: The date on which a transaction is initiated. The settlement date may be the trade date or a later date.

Trade on top of: Trade at a narrow or no spread in basis points to some other instrument.

Trading paper: CDs purchased by accounts that are likely to resell them. The term is commonly used in the Euromarket.

Treasurer's check: A check issued by a bank to make a payment. Treasurer's checks outstanding are counted as part of a bank's reservable deposits and as part of the money supply.

Treasury bill: A non-interest-bearing discount security issued by the U.S. Treasury to finance the national debt. Most bills are issued to mature in 3 months, 6 months, or 1 year.

TT&L account: Treasury tax and loan account at a bank.

Turnaround: Securities bought and sold for settlement on the same day.

Turnaround time: The time available or needed to effect a turnaround.

Two-sided market: A market in which both bid and asked prices, good for the standard unit of trading, are quoted.

Two-way market: Market in which both a bid and an asked price are quoted.

Underwriter: A dealer who purchases new issues from the issuer and distributes them to investors. Underwriting is one function of an investment banker.

Unmatched book: If the average maturity of a bank's liabilities is less than that of its assets, it is said to be running an unmatched book. The term is commonly used in the Euromarket. Equivalent expressions are **open book** and **short book.**

Value date: In the market for Eurodollar deposits and foreign exchange, value date refers to the delivery date of funds traded. Normally it is on spot transactions two days after a transaction is agreed upon and the future date in the case of a forward foreign exchange trade.

Variable-price security: A security, such as stocks or bonds, that sells at a fluctuating, market-determined price.

Variable-rate CDs: Short-term CDs that pay interest periodically on *roll* dates; on each roll date the coupon on the CD is adjusted to reflect current market rates.

Variable-rate loan: Loan made at an interest rate that fluctuates with the prime.

Visible supply: New muni bond issues scheduled to come to market within the next 30 days.

When-issued trades: Typically there is a lag between the time a new bond is announced and sold and the time it is actually issued. During this interval, the security trades **wi,** "when, as, and if issued."

Wi: When, as, and if issued. See **When-issued trades.**

Wi wi: T bills trade on a wi basis between the day they are auctioned and the day settlement is made. Bills traded before they are auctioned are said to be traded wi wi.

Without: If 70 were bid in the market and there was no offer, the quote would be "70 bid without." The expression *without* indicates a one-way market.

Yankee bond: A foreign bond issued in the U.S. market, payable in dollars, and registered with the SEC.

Yankee CD: A CD issued in the domestic market (typically in New York) by a branch of a foreign bank.

Yield curve: A graph showing, for securities that all expose the investor to the same credit risk, the relationship at a given point in time between yield and current maturity. Yield curves are typically drawn using yields on governments of various maturities.

Yield to maturity: The rate of return yielded by a debt security held to maturity when both interest payments and the investor's capital gain or loss on the security are taken into account.

Index

G–H

Governments; *see* U.S. Treasury notes and bonds
Haircut, 46, 117–19
Hedging in foreign exchange; *see* Foreign exchange
Hedging using futures; *see* Futures markets
Holding period yield
 CDs, 77–80
 discount securities, 53
 short agencies, 89–92, 95–96
 short governments, 89–92, 95–96

I

Implied repo rate, 158–66
Interest-bearing securities, 61–138; *see also* Certificates of deposit; Federal agency notes and bonds; Repurchase agreements; *and* U.S. Treasury notes and bonds
Interest rate formulas
 average daily yield, 142–48
 bill formulas; *see* Discount securities
 bill futures; *see* Futures markets
 bond formulas; *see* Federal agency notes and bonds, *and* U. S. Treasury
 break-even formulas; *see* Break-even analysis
 CD formulas; *see* Certificates of deposit
 compound interest rate, 17, 23–24
  on coupons, 64–67, 80
  over a period of less than one year, 37–40
  variable-rate CDs, 84
 converting a discount rate to a simple interest rate, 18–20, 31–35, 45
 converting from a 360-day to a 365-day basis and vice versa, 20
 discount security formulas; *see* Discount securities
 future value, 114–17
 holding period yield
  bills, 53
  CDs, 77–80
  short agencies, 89–92, 95–96
  short governments, 89–92, 95–96
 implied forward rate (bills), 54–57, 158–66
 implied repo rate, 161–66
 present value, 63–66, 107–11
 simple interest rate, 15–16, 20
 strip yield curve, 158–66

tails, 41–45, 47–51, 74–77, 161–66
value of an 01, 30–31
yield value of 1/32, 69–70
Interest rates (measures of), 15–24
 annualizing a rate, 16, 144–45
  with compounding, 23–24, 36–40, 45–46
 average daily yield, 142–48
 bill parity; *see* implied forward rate (bills) *below*
 CD yields, primary and secondary; *see* Certificates of deposit
 Compound interest, 16–18; *see also* Reinvestment of interest
  on coupons, 64–67, 80
  daily RP, 45–46, 76
  derivation of formula for, 23–24, 37–40
  interpretation of, 39–40
  over less than one year, 37–40
  variable-rate CDs, 84
 Converting from 360-day to 365-day basis and vice versa, 18–20, 45, 73
 equivalent bond yield on a discount security, 31–35, 45, 67
 future value, 114–17
 holding period yield
  bills, 53
  CDs, 77–80
  short agencies, 101–3
  short governments, 89–92, 95–96
 implied forward rate (bills), 54–57, 158–66
 notation, 20–22
 present value, 63–66, 107–11
 simple interest rate, 15–16, 20
 reinvestment rate; *see also* Reinvestment of interest
  externally specified, 114–17
  reinvestment rate, 39–40, 113–17
 taxable coupon equivalent, 123–26
 value of an 01, 30–31
 yield to maturity, 33, 39, 62–63
  interpretation of, 66–67
 yield after tax, 121–23
 yield value of 1/32, 69–70

L–M

Leap year, 19, 106 n
Leverage, 141, 147–48; *see also* Repurchase agreements
Marking a portfolio to market, 141–42

Municipal bonds; *for calculation of price, accrued interest and yield, see* Federal agency notes and bonds
 dual tax exempts, 126–28
 method of accruing interest, 99–101
 true yield in last coupon period, 103–4
Municipal notes, 14
 accruing interest, 99–101
 dual tax exempts, 126–28
 repoing, 104
 tax considerations, 14, 123–24
 true yield, 103–4

N

Negative carry, 45
 on a short, 49
Newton's method for calculating yield on a long bond, 136–38
Notation, 20–22
 parentheses and brackets, 23
 subscripts, 21

P–Q

Par (face value), 61, 67
Performance measures, 139–48
 average daily yield, 142–49
  annualizing, 143–44
  discount securities, 143–44
  interest-bearing securities, 144–45
  to measure performance, 145–48
 book value, 140–41
 leverage, 141, 147–48
 marking to market, 141–42
 weighted averages of yields, 139–40
Positive carry, 44; *see also* Reverse to Maturity *and* Tails
Premium bond, 64, 68
Present value, 63–64, 107–11
 in pricing intermediate-term CDs, 84–86
Price risk, 70, 132
Project notes, 14

Quote sheets, 30, 62–63, 100, 122
 tax-calculations used on, 121–25
Quotes:
 BAs, 61
 bills, 30, 61
 CDs, 61
 coupons, 61–63, 99–100
 foreign exchange, 174–175, 177–78

R

Ratings of credit risk 11, 14
Regulation Q, 9